GOTHIC GROTESQUES

Borgo Press Books by BRIAN STABLEFORD

GOTHIC GROTESQUES

ESSAYS ON FANTASTIC LITERATURE

by

Brian Stableford

THE BORGO PRESS

An Imprint of Wildside Press LLC

MMIX

*I.O. Evans Studies in the Philosophy
and Criticism of Literature*
ISSN 0271-9061

Number Forty-Five

www.wildsidepress.com

FIRST EDITION

CONTENTS

INTRODUCTION

This collection mingles articles on horror fiction and Gothic rock music with articles on fantasy and science fiction. Although its title is perhaps more appropriate to the first and second categories than the third and fourth, much of what it has to say about science fiction emphasizes the grotesquerie of the genre, while fantasy was once identified by Nathan Drake as the "sportive" aspect of Gothic fiction, so there is nothing in it that strays too far from the dominant rubric.

The collection also mingles articles written for fanzines with articles of a supposedly more respectable stripe, which appeared in collections of academic articles and surveys of SF issued by academic publishers, but I have never credited books of the latter sort with any superior respectability; they mostly belong to a curious subgenre of "academic pulp", which exists to provide academics with the publication opportunities that are the currency of their career advancement. I have never been a career academic, although I have occasionally toiled within the groves of the qualifications industry in order to make money—academics are ludicrously well-paid by comparison with professional writers—so I have always felt free to indulge in a little genuine scholarship in writing such essays. (Scholarship is nowadays as conspicuous by its absence from most academic writing as it is from most fanzine writing, most editors in both fields being conspicuously hostile to it, but I sneak in what I can where I can.)

The first two articles appeared in fanzines; the first was written in response to a request from the editor, but the fact that the other was published reflects the extent of my moral credit with the editor of the magazines in which it appeared, who would not have given a home to such eccentric material had he not felt that he owed me a little scope for self-indulgence. "Horror in Science Fiction" first appeared under the slightly more cumbersome title "Horror in Science Fiction Novels Through 1960" in *Scream Factory* 13 (Spring 1994).

The second essay appeared as "Discotheque for the Devil's Party: Black Metal, Pagan Rock and the Tradition of Literary Satanism" in two parts in *The New York Review of Science Fiction* 86 & 87 (October/November 1995).

The third article, which appeared under the more pretentious title "*Sang* for Supper: Notes on the Metaphorical Use of Vampires in *The Empire of Fear* and *Young Blood*" in *Blood Read: The Vampire as Metaphor in Contemporary Culture* edited by Joan Gordon & Veronica Hollinger, published by the University of Pennsylvania Press in 1997, was written at the invitation of the editors, who suggested that I might care to look at some of my own work in the vampire genre. I saw no harm in attempting to distance myself from the work in order to look at it more objectively (or at least to pretend) but some readers thought the device of writing about my own work in the third person was rather silly.

In spite of the lukewarm response to "*Sang* for Supper", the same editors invited me to do something similar for another anthology they were editing, for which they proposed to use the punning title *Going Postal*, linking the common use of the phrase (referring to an incident in which a disgruntled employee of the US Post Office took a gun to work and massacred his colleagues) to such voguish terms as "postmodernism" and "posthumanism". In keeping with the intended title of the volume I produced the eighth essay in the present collection, under the elaborately ingenious title "Dead Letters and Their Inheritors: Ecospasmic Crashes and the Postmortal Condition in Brian Stableford's Histories of the Future", but the anthology eventually appeared as *Edging into the Future: Science Fiction and Contemporary Cultural Transformation* (University of Pennsylvania Press, 2002), so the effect of the tortuous wordplay was utterly lost. The reaction to the essay was even more hostile than the response to my first such experiment, so I am unlikely to try anything similar again.

The New York Review of Science Fiction 115 (March 1998) offered a home to "Last and First Man: Tomorrow's Adam and Eternity's Eve" (issue 126, February 1999) when it was rudely expelled from a volume of essays edited by David Seed after I refused to sign a letter of release provided by the volume's publisher, Macmillan, which required me to surrender all rights in the piece in perpetuity, without any compensation whatsoever. I am well used to working for nothing, but it seemed to me extremely unreasonable for a publisher who was getting the work for free to rob me of the right to use my own work elsewhere should the opportunity ever arise (as it does here). I have made some slight revisions to the essay to take aboard additional information kindly—and freely—provided by contributors to the *NYRSF*'s letter column, for which I am very grateful.

"The Art of the Ghost Story" appears here in English for the first time; it was commissioned for a special issue of the excellent French magazine *Ténèbres* by the editors, Daniel Conrad and Benoît Domis, and appeared there as "L'Art de la Ghost Story" in issue 14 (Août, 2001). "Re-Enchantment in the Aftermath of War" is similarly making its debut in English, having been commissioned for a German language anthology by its Czech editor, Jacek Rzeszotnik; it first appeared as "Wiederverzauberung als Folge des Krieges: Fantasy-Novellen von Britischen Schriftstellerinnen (1919-1928)" ["Re-enchantment in the Aftermath of War: Fantasy novels by British Female Writers, 1919-28"] in *Zwischen Flucht und Herrschaft: Phantastische Frauenliteratur*, published by EDFC in 2002. "The Gothic Lifestyle from Byron to Buffy" is unpublished in any form; it was written to be read at a research seminar at King Alfred's College Winchester, where I was doing some part-time teaching, on 28 February 2001. That initial audience numbered approximately five, but I hope that sales of this volume might eventually double, or even treble, that number.

The final two articles were both commissioned for use in guidebooks to the SF genre produced by prestigious academic publishers in the UK—the topic was assigned in each case, the second editor being understandably determined to avoid any duplication of material with the earlier volume. "Science Fiction Before the Genre" was in *The Cambridge Companion to Science Fiction* edited by Edward James and Farah Mendlesohn, published by Cambridge University Press in 2003; "Science Fiction and Ecology" was in *The Blackwell Companion to Science Fiction* edited by David Seed (I am a forgiving soul), published by Blackwell in 2005. I received the princely payment of a hundred pounds for each essay, which works out as a fraction over £14 per thousand words, not counting the bibliographies, which were rather extensive. The prevalence of such rates of pay helps to explain why most "professional writers" in the UK earn considerably less than the national minimum age of £5.05 per hour. The ultimate wages of scholarship, like that of sin, is death, but I am told that sin generally pays much better in the interim. Alas, I am now too old to change my virtuous ways, so I shall never have the opportunity to find out.

—Brian Stableford, August 2006

GOTHIC GROTESQUES, BY BRIAN STABLEFORD

HORROR IN SCIENCE FICTION

Horror is sometimes thought of as an emotion closely akin to but subtly different from terror. This is not wrong—one can certainly speak of feeling horror, perhaps to the extent of being horror-stricken or overcome by horror—but it may not be the most convenient avenue of definition. Horror is also, and perhaps more essentially, a form of aesthetic response. Whereas terror is a reaction to a perceived threat to oneself, horror is usually the response of an observer contemplating the potential or actual outcome of such a threat affecting others as well as, or instead of, him/her. It is partly because readers adopt the situation of intimate voyeurs relative to the characters in stories that fiction dealing with terrifying matters is usually referred to as "horror fiction".

We find it convenient to demarcate a genre of horror fiction because there are some stories whose subject matter is intrinsically and quintessentially disturbing. The genre is made up, on the one hand, of stories of the supernatural, which deal with the decay and rupture of the order of the world that confronts the reasoning mind, and, on the other hand of stories of psychological aberration, which deal with the corruption and breakdown of the reasoning mind itself. There are, however, horrific motifs to be found in all literary genres, as there are in all kinds of non-fictional reportage, from yellow journalism and advertisements to medical textbooks and academic discourse.

Most fictional genres, like most areas of reportage, tend to favor a particular repertoire of horrors. Thrillers, like yellow journalism, are profoundly fond of rape and serial murder; romances, like advertisements, trade heavily on fear of embarrassment and feelings of inadequacy; grittily realistic novels, like medical textbooks, are strong on discomfiting symptoms and surgical mutilations; *contes philosophiques*, like authentic philosophical discourse, are haunted by the dread of the unknowable, the unnamable and the unprovable. Of all literary genres, however, none—not even the horror genre itself—is more prolific in the matter of manufacturing and deploying horrors than science fiction, which is capable of dealing with extrapolations and exaggerations of all the above-mentioned kinds of horror, and many more besides.

Science fiction has never represented itself as an essentially horrific genre, at least so far as written SF is concerned (the fact that cinematic SF was, until fairly recently, regarded as a mere subspecies of the horror film has been the cause of some chagrin in the SF community). The half-dozen American editors who played a key role in shaping the SF genre following the invention of the label were mostly resolute in declaring—sometimes insistently—that science fiction ought to be an upbeat genre, whose main function is to celebrate the future triumphs of human endeavor and evolution. This manifesto did not, however, prevent any of them from exploiting the aesthetic force of horrific motifs; John W. Campbell Jr.—who played St. Paul to Hugo Gernsback's Christ within the great tradition of missionary SF—wrote one of the classics of pulp horror-SF, "Who Goes There?" (1938).

Lacking any such positively-inclined manifesto, science fiction *avant la lettre* and science fiction produced in Europe tended to have a somewhat darker edge than the swashbuckling futuristic costume drama that quickly became the staple diet of the pulp SF magazines. Although the fictional handmaiden of social philosophy, the twice-misnamed "Utopian novel", was one of the literary ancestors of science fiction, the vast majority of nineteenth century literary texts that can be retrospectively claimed for the genre are severely skeptical of the idea that technological sophistication automatically works to the betterment of mankind. Perhaps this skepticism was unjustified—the evidence of all previous history surely supported the notion that technological progress facilitated moral progress—but it was nevertheless commonplace; for this reason, the history of what the Clute/Nicholls *Encyclopedia of Science Fiction* calls "proto-science fiction" is deeply steeped in horrific imagery. Arguments over the most appropriate work with which to begin a history of SF are, of course, incapable of reaching any firm conclusion but the most widely-cited starting-point, Mary Shelley's *Frankenstein* (1818), is also commonly regarded as a key work in the Gothic tradition from which modern horror fiction evolved, and Robert Louis Stevenson's split personality story *The Strange Case of Dr Jekyll and Mr. Hyde* (1886) is of similar cardinal significance in both traditions.

It is hardly surprising that early works contemplating a dramatic expansion of technical practicality should have been attracted to threats rather than promises. An awareness that the world is changing, and that new possibilities are constantly emerging, is bound to generate fear and horror as well as hope and wonder. It is the fear that usually comes first to mind, and the horrific that usually makes the more immediate impression on the fecund imagination. Life becomes dramatic when death threatens, and any literary examination of *War and Peace* worth its salt would be bound to place war at centre-stage while implying that peace is somewhere in the wings: a distant, and possibly unattainable, refuge. Mary Shelley's husband was a declared atheist and enthusiastic champion of progress, who thought Prometheus utterly undeserving of the savage fate visited upon him by the jealous gods, but it is understandable nevertheless that her pioneering tale of a modern Prometheus should be so startled by and steeped in horrific imagery as to have become a symbol for all those mentally-impoverished imbeciles who came to see scientific knowledge as a dire thing that man was "not meant to know".

* * * * * * *

Mary Shelley's second proto-SF novel, *The Last Man* (1826), also makes extravagant use of horrific imagery, while inviting the reader to contemplate the demolition of civilization, the depopulation of the world and the awfulness of finding oneself alone when everything one loved and valued has perished. This too is understandable. Catastrophe stories form a sub-genre located in a grey area where science fiction and the thriller genre overlap, and much of their narrative drive derives from the horror of contemplating the disintegration of the social order that insulates us (not very comfortably and not very securely) from the Hobbesian "war of all against all" that might otherwise hold sway.

The great plague that figures in *The Last Man,* like the analogues that feature in most of its successors, is a natural catastrophe, which punishes civilized men for believing themselves secure from the vicissitudes of chance, but catastrophe stories showed no sign of dying out as medical science advanced and human ingenuity increased the capacity of civilized folk to withstand the ravages of disease. It was, in fact, the other way around: the imagination was moved to the contemplation of even bigger, even nastier disasters, which no merely human power could possibly prevent. By the end of the nineteenth century cosmic catastrophes involving colliding worlds had become commonplace.

Even in those distant days, however, horror did not reign unchallenged over the contemplation of disaster; there was a minority who thought that the destruction of contemporary civilization was to be welcomed. Richard Jefferies' *After London* (1885) is emphatically *not* a horror story, and the kind of post-catastrophe romanticism developed in it was to ameliorate, at least to some degree, most of the disaster novels to be published in the following century. This is particularly true of British writers, who instituted a veritable tradition of "cozy catastrophe stories" that extends from Jefferies through S. Fowler Wright's *Deluge* (1928) and John Collier's *Tom's A-Cold* (1933) to the sequence John Wyndham began with *The Day of the Triffids* (1951) and the similar sequence begun by John Christopher's *The Death of Grass* (1956), but it also affected American writers and is particularly obvious in the pulp magazine disaster stories written in the wake of George Allan England's *Darkness and Dawn* (1914). Even writers firmly committed to the cause of civilization could usually find something heartening in the thought of its destruction, if only because wiping the slate clean would permit the job to be done properly the second time around. In this respect, the horrific element of proto-SF was damped down by comparison with the horror that flourished in tales of supernatural evil and mental disintegration (which are, of course, bad by definition).

Catastrophist fiction had broadened its range considerably by the end of the nineteenth century. Many people were becoming increasingly anxious about the fact that technological progress was a two-edged sword, because the science that increased our power to defend ourselves against catastrophe also—by the same token— increased our power to visit disasters upon one another, in the form of ever-more-violent wars and ever-more-efficient oppressions. By the end of the nineteenth century, it was possible to think of the march of technology itself as a kind of ongoing catastrophe, and this became a great stimulus to the proliferation of proto-SF.

The writers of nineteenth century "scientific romance" rarely conceived of themselves as prophets of doom. They were more often inclined to see themselves as harbingers of a new summer— because, after all, where fear and horror had led, hope and wonder had eventually followed—but it was the horror that usually stood out in their work at first glance, and stood unchallenged in the minds of those observers who were not inclined to take a second.

14

* * * * * * *

It is perhaps ironic that a fascination with horrific imagery is very prominent in the works of the founding father of British scientific romance, H. G. Wells, in spite of the fact that he was ambitious to be—and, indeed, proved to be—the last of the great Utopian dreamers. *The Time Machine* (1895) features the monstrous Morlocks who emerge from their Underworld by night to prey upon the gentle Eloi, and goes on to inform its readers that, in the fullness of time, the sum of human endeavor will come to nothing. *The Island of Dr Moreau* (1986) discovers such revulsion in its depiction of the hopeful Beast-Men who eventually revolt against their creator that the man who witnesses the tragedy is thereafter unable to see anything but self-deluding bestiality in the affairs of his fellow men. *The War of the Worlds* (1898) inspired a whole subgenre of horrific "alien menace" stories by presenting monstrous Martians driven by the exhaustion of their own resources to become ruthless invaders of Earth, competitors in a universal struggle for existence that humankind is ill-equipped to win. *The First Men in the Moon* (1901), though far less melodramatic, did little to counterbalance the earlier novel's equation of alien and evil and nothing at all to flatter human delusions of grandeur.

Wells struck this particularly rich vein of horrific imagery by virtue of taking prolific inspiration from biological science—an example followed by several later writers of scientific romance. William Hope Hodgson mined the same vein in those of his stories that are most readily considered as science fiction, and S. Fowler Wright was to take matters further in his Wells-inspired novel of far-future evolution *The World Below* (1929). Tales of alien life have, of course, continued to exploit the horrific potential intrinsic to biological speculation to the full, although this line of thought was taken up far more enthusiastically by the American pulp writers than by Wells' British followers. Invasions of Earth by repulsive aliens were a staple of the specialized pulps in the early days and interspecies warfare was a commonplace of the "space opera" developed by Edmond Hamilton, E. E. "Doc" Smith, Jack Williamson and John W. Campbell Jr. A horrific element is ever-present in such stories, at its most effective when there is some particular *intimacy* in the posed threat. Although the old cliché about monsters that take an obscene interest in the heroine lacks any kind of sociobiological logic, aliens always seemed that much nastier when they actually wanted to get *inside* people, or to lay their eggs inside them, or insidiously to suck the vital juices out of them.

To some extent, the fertility of biological speculation as a producer of horrors merely reflects the fact that the easiest way to construct monsters is to combine the features of creatures that most people find repulsive, and science fiction obligingly provides an ideative context in which such chimeras may be set; but there is more to the matter than that. As J. B. S. Haldane was to point out in his classic essay *Daedalus; or, Science and the Future* (1924), all biological innovations generate unease, because they seem at first sight to be violations of a "natural order". Later, they may be accommodated to our idea of the natural order, but when they are new, biotechnologies—however benign or advantageous they may be—always provoke a horrified reaction. What we think of as "nature" is, of course, very largely an artifact, and what we think of as "human nature" is entirely an artifact, but it remains the case that contemplation of any further change in "nature" or "human nature" is inclined to fill us with ominous foreboding. Insofar as speculative fiction draws inspiration from biology, therefore, it is apt to acquire a cutting edge of horror.

Paradoxical as it may seem, this generalization applies even to such biological possibilities as discovering new technological means to conquer disease and expand the human lifespan, thus defeating the fundamental horror (*angst*, in Martin Heidegger's terminology) that haunts all self-conscious existence: the horror of death. Perverse as it may seem, such works as Walter Besant's *The Inner House* (1888), Karel Čapek's *The Makropoulos Secret* (1925), David H. Keller's "Life Everlasting" (1934) and Aldous Huxley's *After Many a Summer* (1939) all contrive to discover horror in the idea of winning the war against disease and death. Given this, it is hardly surprising that less edifying notions—for instance, the idea that, in the natural course of affairs, *Homo sapiens* will one day be replaced by a more capable species—tend to provoke rather extreme reactions.

* * * * * * *

Where proto-SF dealt with strictly utilitarian machinery of a safely inorganic kind, its imagery did tend to be much brighter. Jules Verne's science fiction, which is preoccupied with *vehicles*—balloons, ships, submarines, space capsules, airships, etc.—is virtually devoid of horror, although even Verne found cause for alarm in the idea of more powerful weapons, and accepted (in *The Begum's*

Fortune, 1879) that machinery could be deployed in the cause of oppression as easily as the cause of liberation. The sinister aspect of functional machinery was, however, graphically displayed in tales of future dystopia and future war, and—more subtly—in tales of machines mimicking human form. This last category of anxiety-prone SF is particularly interesting, by virtue of an intrinsic ambivalence, more profound than that which turned some catastrophe stories into celebratory fantasies. Humanoid automata, like hypothetical members of the species *Homo superior*, generally got a bad press in proto-SF, but there were some writers who could not resist taking the opportunity of using such stories as vehicles for misanthropic sentiments, suggesting that "mechanical men" or more highly-evolved "supermen" might in some respects be preferable to the less-than-perfect real thing.

When the SF genre was firmly demarcated, this kind of ambivalence was quickly brought to the fore. Several pulp SF writers were quick to undertake the task of liberating robots from the kind of blind bigotry displayed to excess by men who were unthinkingly hostile to technology and progress. Isaac Asimov was not the first of these crusaders, but he eventually became the most ardent. He was in no doubt as to the strength of the feeling that he felt honor-bound to demolish (which he chose to call "the Frankenstein complex") but he was also in no doubt that it was a thoroughly bad thing. For this reason, he was enthusiastic to become not only a writer of non-horrific science fiction, but a writer of science fiction that consciously and conscientiously opposed horrific science fiction. In this way, Asimov—and the kind of science fiction he came to embody and represent in the minds of readers—brought to full fruition a long-term trend that constitutes a rather strange and interesting literary phenomenon: the evolution of the "anti-horror story".

Many other genres had featured tales of horrors overcome and horrors rendered harmless, but SF was the first genre to feature stories that set out with propagandistic fervor to persuade people that their reflexive reactions of horror might be misguided, and might stand in need of urgent reconstruction. The consequences of this development have been considerable. The emergence of SF as a genre created a literary space in which it was not merely possible, but virtually compulsory, to ask questions about what really is or ought to be horrific. Some SF writers were thus encouraged to set out in search of new and ultimate horrors, while others set out to rob certain tacitly-accepted horrific images of their power to appall.

* * * * * * *

Despite the exceptions provided by enthusiastic Vernian romance, the great majority of proto-SF stories, and very many stories in the early SF pulps, belong to the "no good will come of it all" school of thought, which holds that the best thing that could possibly happen to any new invention is that it should blow up before doing too much damage, and that its inventor and the formula of its manufacture should both be annihilated in the explosion. As the SF genre became recognizable, though—some little time before the label was coined and specialist pulp magazines were created to form its core—it inevitably became a medium that both displayed and questioned this kind of stick-in-the-mud conservatism.

The dynamics of science-fictional thought were such that, although its first narrative recourse was always to the anxious and the horrific, it could not stop there. Writers of SF might be drawn to the aesthetics of horror like moths to a flame, but only a few of them could be content with reaching story-climaxes where the horrors were averted or escaped. However convenient or ironically appropriate it might be for an inventor to perish along with his machine, that could never be a credible or satisfactory ending in a world where new discoveries were constantly being made, and even the writers who liked writing that kind of story were aware of it. In science fiction, a horror story could never be a terminus; it could only be a way-station *en route* to a fuller and more sober consideration of its central thesis.

For this reason, the role played by horror in genre SF is markedly different from the role that it plays in other genres. This is evident even in the crudest SF, and even in the SF that has no higher aspiration than to be a subspecies of horror. Had Mary Shelley written a sequel to *Frankenstein* it would doubtless have been far more adventurous than the many sequels to the 1931 film version, but even those carefully-repetitive and determinedly down-market products found themselves forced to look at the monster in a more careful and more even-handed way.

There is a sense in which SF stories, quite unlike the stories in any other genre, are incapable of really *ending*. They can stop, but they cannot become self-enclosed, because they can never leave the world unchanged, no matter how resolutely they eliminate their innovations. Once identified, the SF genre inevitably became a kind of ideological battleground, where Luddites and advocates of progress took up arms in order to fight their corners, and horror became a psychological weapon in that war. The rehabilitation of the robot is the most striking example of a swiftly-won battle, but SF writers also set to work on more problematic quests.

The rehabilitation of the alien was begun in the specialist magazines in such stories as Raymond Z. Gallun's "Old Faithful" (1934), and was carried forward dutifully, in spite of all the *War of the Worlds* remixes that continued to appear in dozens—Eric Frank Russell's *Sinister Barrier* (1939) being one of the more interesting of them. For every graphic tale of alien horror, there was a counterbalancing exercise in apologetics, sometimes explicitly framed as an ideological reply (as Gallun's story is to Wells'). Thus, even the most consummately nasty tales of alien invasion and inter-species warfare—Robert Heinlein's *The Puppet Masters* (1951) and *Starship Troopers* (1959) among them—were ultimately to be provided with conscientious rebuttals and careful reappraisals such as Ted White's *By Furies Possessed* (1970) and Joe Haldeman's *The Forever War* (1974), both of which belonged to a period in which the alien menace story had seemed in danger (perhaps belatedly) of becoming "politically incorrect". Although the 1950s was the heyday of the schlock-horror monster movie, the contemplation of alien nature in magazine SF had by then become much more sophisticated, and the element of horror was often handled with considerable subtlety, as in Philip Jose Farmer's carefully unmelodramatic *The Lovers* (1952; expanded 1961).

Horror SF and anti-horror SF necessarily exist in a state of dramatic tension. In more sophisticated stories, the elements work in dialectical opposition within the same text; thus, novels like J. D. Beresford's early superman story *The Hampdenshire Wonder* (1911) and his catastrophe story *Goslings* (1913) are scrupulous in weighing their horrific moments against more hopeful visions. Magazine SF was rarely as well-rounded, but did not have to be, precisely because the specialist magazines provided a context and an environment with whose contents writers and readers were familiar. Such anti-horror superman stories as A. E. Van Vogt's *Slan* (1940) and Jack Williamson's *Darker Than You Think* (1940) succeed as stories partly because they conscientiously set themselves against a kind of horror that is taken for granted in John Taine's *Seeds of Life* (1931) and John Russell Fearn's *The Intelligence Gigantic* (1933).

* * * * * * *

In respect of robots, aliens, supermen, and even natural catastrophes, the pattern of SF's evolution has resulted in a diminution of the "horrific reflex". The skepticism of SF has served to overcome, at least to a degree, the automatic repulsion that many people feel when confronted with something new and strange. In due course, the skepticism born of SF even began to flow back into the horror genre itself. It is at least arguable that the most spectacular modern product of anti-horrific thought is not the sickly sentimental cuteness of such aliens as *E.T.* and such robots as those that feature in *Star Wars* but rather the great array of stories that partly or wholly rehabilitate such supernatural figures as the vampire—to the extent that vampires can nowadays take tragic or heroic roles more easily than straightforwardly monstrous ones. The fact that the horror genre itself has, in recent years, become host to the *contes philosophiques* of "dark fantasy", which subject the aesthetics of horror to scrupulous investigation, owes much to the example set by those SF writers who have been disposed to challenge received wisdom in the name of progress.

There has, however, been a countercurrent that has carried some notions in the opposite direction, increasing rather than diminishing their horrific attributes. In nineteenth century proto-SF, future wars were often seen as something to be welcomed, or at worst as a necessary evil. There was a boom in enthusiastic future war stories in Britain after the publication of George Griffith's *The Angel of the Revolution* (1887), which helped to create the myth of a "war to end war" that was ultimately used to sell the war of 1914-18 to those who served as its cannon-fodder. The example of the actual war did far more to change attitudes than the inherent logic of futuristic fiction, but futuristic fiction was not slow to take up the thread of the argument. British future war fiction between the two world wars, from Edward Shanks's bitter *People of the Ruins* (1920) to Philip George Chadwick's luridly nasty-minded *The Death Guard* (1939), played a very different tune, which grew even more strident following the use of the atom-bomb to end the war against Japan. The nuclear war story became the ultimate in SF horror stories during the 1950s, in the US as well as the UK, the horror being all the more effective in quietly realistic stories like Judith Merril's *Shadow on the Hearth* (1950), which brought the possibility into the context of everyday domestic life.

Anxiety in respect of war is not the only anxiety to have intensified dramatically in the course of the twentieth century, and the fear of totalitarian oppression is similarly reflected in horrific literary images of the future. Here too there has been a noticeable movement away from lurid scenery towards the depiction of routines of everyday life that seem all the more horrible for being half-familiar and almost ordinary; thus Ignatius Donnelly's melodramatic *Caesar's Column* (1890) began a trend that led—via such extended fables as Yegevny Zamyatin's *We* (1924)—to George Orwell's *Nineteen Eighty-Four* (1949).

As regards both war and totalitarianism, actual world history has given us so much to think about that science fiction has been reduced to a passively reflective role, which contrasts somewhat with the more independent role the genre has played in investigating purely hypothetical figures like humanoid robots and alien beings. There is, however, one train of science-fictional thought that has discovered and amplified horror in an arena where real-world thought has steadfastly refused to look for it. Science fiction—particularly magazine SF—has always been slightly uneasy in dealing with the idea of God, but it has always been able to avoid treading on too many devout toes by enquiring instead as to the consequences that would ensue if there were, in fact, god-*like* beings that could do all the things the God of the Old Testament was said to have done.

Whether couched as cautionary fables like Wells' "The Man Who Could Work Miracles" (1898) and Jerome Bixby's "It's a *Good* Life" (1953), or as full-blown metaphysical fantasies like Olaf Stapledon's *Star-Maker* (1937) and Philip Jose Farmer's "Father" (1955), stories along these lines have delivered a virtually-unanimous verdict: the idea that there might actually be such things as gods, or that men might actually acquire literally godlike power, is utterly and unequivocally horrific. The most extreme and sustained extrapolation of this world-view is perhaps to be found in H. P. Lovecraft's later Cthulhu Mythos tales, which go to great pains to emphasize the horrific implications of the hypothetical discovery that human beings were created instead of having evolved; it is hardly surprising that these are the SF stories that have been most avidly conscripted into the great tradition of modern horror fiction.

In this respect, science fiction as a genre is implacably opposed to religious faith, in spite of the fact that it still plays host to a number of writers whose infection with the disease of faith has progressed to a pathological degree. There is more at stake than matters of mere dogma, however, for the bolder metaphysical fantasies in this vein reach far beyond the infantile idiocies of fundamentalist believers. The corrosive *angst* underlying stories of this kind is perfectly capable of dissolving much deeper layers of metaphysical conviction; the ultimate in science-fictional horror stories are those which take Cartesian doubt to quasi-solipsistic extremes. Robert A. Heinlein was a pioneer in this field, albeit a slightly cack-handed one, with such stories as "They" (1941) and "The Unpleasant Profession of Jonathan Hoag" (1942), but its peculiar art was brought much nearer to perfection by Philip K. Dick, in a long series of novels in which what we take to be "reality" proves to be an all-to-fragile delusion. *Eye in the Sky* (1957) was his first major exercise in this vein, but it was to be followed by many others.

* * * * * * *

Science-fictional horror stories partake of all the virtues that horror lends to other literary genres—shock value, the intensification of narrative suspense, and so on—but SF is particularly useful in playing host to stories where horror becomes a subject-matter rather than a mere instrument of effect. The pretence (it *is* a pretence) that SF mounts, of being intellectually responsible, and dealing only with actual possibilities, justifies the turnaround by virtue of which horrified characters can suddenly say: "Hold on! Exactly what is it we're scared of, and why? What's the rational way to approach this problem?"

From the point of view of connoisseurs of horror, this may not be a good thing; if what the reader enjoys is the *frisson* itself, the last thing a story needs is a backward step that subjects the *frisson* to methodical analysis. One result of such re-examination, however, is the discovery and refinement of new and sharper horrors, which extend and refurbish the range of *frisson*-generating imagery. It is hardly surprising that modern horror fiction has come to rely increasingly upon science-fictional imagery and upon logically-revised variants of its traditional apparatus. Now that "dark fantasy" is flourishing, and the boundaries between the various commercial genres of imaginative fiction are becoming increasingly unclear, science fiction is no longer the only genre in which there is a conspicuous conflict between horrific theses and anti-horrific antitheses, but it is still the genre where that dialectic is most fruitful in producing new syntheses.

It is to be hoped that SF will retain its status as the acid-bath in which the most ill-judged of our horrific reflexes might be eroded, and perhaps eventually obliterated. Science fiction has already played a role in teaching us to be less afraid of all that qualifies, in the broadest sense, as "the alien"; we ought fervently to desire that it might yet play a significant role in teaching us to be less afraid of biotechnology. It is not, as yet, easy to see what other things we ought to become less or more afraid of, but there is every reason to hope that the SF writers of the future will find an adequate supply.

DISCOTHEQUE FOR THE DEVIL'S PARTY

Nancy Springer's *Metal Angel* (1994) is the story of Volos, an angel who defects from the angelic choir, taking on frail flesh in order that he might dedicate himself to the production of the kind of music he really loves: rock music. He provides the voice, but the words he sings are supplied by the deeply frustrated daughter of a Fundamentalist preacher, whose own taste for "the devil's music" is ruthlessly repressed by those around her. It is not until she hears her lyrics being sung by the angel—having been unknowingly plundered by magical empathy—that she is able to break free from her stultifying cultural background. Her resentful pursuers inevitably take their revenge upon the incarnate angel, savagely hacking off the wings that are the main evidence of his true nature, and hence of his apostasy.

An interview in *Locus* reveals that *Metal Angel* was written three years before *Larque on the Wing*, Nancy Springer's other 1994 publication. "I sweated blood over *Metal Angel*," she says. "I wanted to do *the* book." *Metal Angel* carries forward certain themes and preoccupations from *Apocalypse* (1989), but makes them much more explicit; *Apocalypse* had been the first book the author produced after her husband abandoned his career as a Lutheran pastor—an event of which she says in the *Locus* interview: "One of the proudest and happiest feats of my life was to free him, literally liberate him, from the Lutheran ministry."

Volos is, of course, a recent recruit to a long literary tradition of heroic fallen angels, whose defection from the Divine Cause is seen as a brave rebellion against an unjust tyranny. It is a tradition whose origin can be traced to William Blake's ironic remark, made in 1793, that when John Milton wrote *Paradise Lost* he had been "of the devil's party without knowing it"—a judgment that was considerably expanded by Percy Shelley in his *Defence of Poetry* (written 1821; published 1840):

"Milton's poem contains within itself a philosophical refutation of that system, of which, by a strange and natural antithesis, it has been a chief popular support. Nothing can exceed the energy and magnificence of the character of Satan as expressed in *Paradise Lost*. Milton's Devil as a moral being is as far superior to his God as one who perseveres in some purpose, which he has conceived to be excellent, in spite of adversity and torture, is to one who in the cold security of undoubted triumph inflicts the most horrible revenge upon his enemy...with the alleged design of exasperating him to new torments."

Blake and Shelley were, of course, prepared to practice what they preached. Blake's "prophetic books" developed his own alternative mythology in which Orc, the son of Los and Enitharmon, bursts the bonds that enchain him to become a heroic rebel against Urizen, the tyrannical deviser of moral codes. Shelley's *Prometheus Unbound* (1820) offers a similar account of revolution and redemption, in which the tyrant Jupiter is vanquished and a new era of liberty and harmony ensues. Both writers found it convenient, for diplomatic reasons among others, to substitute other figures for the Satan of the Christian Mythos, but they nevertheless stand at the head of a rich tradition of "literary Satanism", which expressed strident challenges to the moral and political authority of Church and State by proposing that a certain precious fraction of what Church and State were allied in hating and despising was actually admirable. Such literary Satanists set out to re-draw the Establishment's map of good and evil, according to their own more generous sensibilities.

Although Charles Baudelaire was willing to address Satan directly, in a litany included in *Les Fleurs du mal* (1857), most literary Satanists continued to use evasive tactics. In Britain, Oscar Wilde's hymn to the "goat-foot god of Arcady" in "Pan" (1881) set a precedent that other writers associated with the short-lived English Decadent Movement followed. Nor was the influence of these exemplars confined to literary fantasy; Baudelaire's litany became a significant inspiration of Jules Michelet's scholarly fantasy *La Sorcière* (1862), which represented the victims of Medieval witch-hunts as heroic rebels against the ideological tyranny of the Church and provided them with an (entirely imaginary) set of rituals for their "communion of revolt". Wilde's Pan was quickly appropriated as an object of ritual by the flamboyant lifestyle fantasist Aleister Crowley, perhaps under the influence of Edgar Jepson's heretical fantasy *The Horned Shepherd* (1904).

The first fallen angel to figure in a work of guarded literary Satanism produced in Britain was the one featured in H. G. Wells' *The Wonderful Visit* (1895), who was carefully deemed to have fallen from the Land of Dreams rather than the Christian Heaven, and who functioned as an innocent observer unable to comprehend the iniquities of Victorian society. Such punctilious restraint was unnecessary on the other side of *la Manche*, where Anatole France imported a sympathetic Satan into the novella "La Tragédie humaine" (in *Le Puits de Sainte Claire*, 1895) and then went on to produce the great classic of Literary Satanism in *La Révolte des anges* (1914). This tells the story of the renegade guardian angel Arcade, whose readings in philosophy and science reveal to him that his Creator is merely a local tyrant whose claims to legitimate moral dictatorship are spurious. Arcade finds many other fallen angels living quietly among humankind, working as teachers or musicians, and attempts to form an army of rebellion, but Satan—who is now a humble gardener—explains to him that the violent overthrow of tyrants merely leads to their replacement, and that the real battle is for the hearts and minds of men.

There is something of Wells' angel in Springer's Volos, who is similarly possessed of an extraordinary innocence, but there is rather more of Arcade in his outrage against the tyranny of God—an outrage that is more than amply justified by the oppressive fervor of God's self-appointed representatives on Earth. Unlike the angel in Helen Beauclerk's *The Love of the Foolish Angel* (1929), who fell by accident, Volos has jumped; he is, in essence, a heavenly dropout whose gravitation towards the American counter-culture is entirely natural. Whereas the musically-inclined fallen angels of Anatole France's novel had little alternative but to associate the spirit of musical rebellion with such relatively staid figures as Wagner, Volos can easily identify "devil's music" of a much more subversive kind—and he knows that there is a legion of alienated teenagers desperate to hear his siren song.

Volos is by no means the only supernatural being in recent literary fantasy to be drawn to rock music in this way. Supernatural stories about rock musicians have become commonplace; *In Dreams* (1992), edited by Paul J. McAuley and Kim Newman, is an anthology of them. Poppy Z. Brite's work regularly features the band Lost Souls, fronted by the psychically-gifted Ghost. *Metal Angel*'s publisher, Roc, also issued Nancy Collins' *Wild Blood* in 1994, which features a rock band whose members are werewolves; in 1992 Roc had published Gael Baudino's *Gossamer Ax*, in which a disenchanted fairy harpist enjoys a magical renewal by courtesy of rock music.

A significant watershed in the history of this peculiar subgenre had been reached in 1985, in the conclusion of Anne Rice's *The Vampire Lestat*, when the eponymous fantasy-figure—then still on the threshold of worldwide celebrity—discovered that the one role in the contemporary world to which his distinctively-alienated personality and exotic needs were perfectly adapted was front-man for a rock band. He was, of course, following a precedent already established in S. P. Somtow's conscientiously-Wagnerian *Vampire Junction* (1984) but Lestat was the character who took the idea to a mass audience and established himself as an important icon in a "Gothic" subculture that employed musical allegiance as one of its key identifiers. Somtow eventually produced a sequel to his pioneering work in *Valentine* (1992), not long before Rice's Lestat became the narrator of the most elaborate and most sustained of all recent exercises in literary Satanism, *Memnoch the Devil* (1994)—whose substance I shall discuss more fully in due course.

The existence of these other works makes it slightly remarkable that Nancy Springer found it so difficult to sell *Metal Angel*, but she was taking this process of literary evolution a significant step further into dangerous territory, by substituting an angel for less explicitly anti-Christian figures. "Unfortunately," she remarks in the *Locus* interview, "the Establishment was not ready for a bisexual angel." The Establishment never has been, and probably never will be, but we live in a world where there is a host of dissenters opposed to the Establishment, and it is to the members of this host that the tradition of Literary Satanism speaks—and to which, increasingly, it is beginning to sing.

* * * * * * *

There is, of course, nothing new in the notion that rock music is an instrument of the devil, and no cause for astonishment in the fact that some rock musicians have responded by making a prideful display of their opposition to the kind of people who make such charges. Like most literary Satanists, most rock musicians have found it politic to be evasive in their "Satanism", but some have not. In particular, the subculture associated with heavy metal music has always been avid to appropriate symbols of stark opposition to any and all middle-class shibboleths, and it was only to be expected that this particular subgenre should give rise to self-proclaimed Satanist bands.

Since the pioneering days of Black Sabbath and Black Widow in the late 1960s numerous practitioners of heavy metal have drawn upon Satanist imagery of various easily-portable kinds. (It is no co-incidence that the genre's devotees modelled their dress code on the Hell's Angels of California.) It is hardly surprising that such tactics of opposition eventually attracted tokenistic witch-hunts from those they were designed to affront. Nor is it surprising that the attacks in question rapidly plumbed bathetic depths of absurdity, as when the members of Judas Priest were hauled into court to face a charge of having implanted subliminal exhortations to suicide in one of their albums.

A significant landmark in the evolution of Satanist heavy metal music was the release in 1981 of *Welcome to Hell*, the debut album of the band Venom, who continued their career with *Black Metal* and *At War with Satan*. Venom was a trio based in North-East England, whose members adopted the pseudonyms Cronos, Mantas and Abaddon in order to represent themselves as Satanists; the band had been born (appropriately enough) when two of their number met at a Judas Priest gig. The title track of their first album followed the similarly-inclined "Son of Satan", but it was the later track "In League With Satan" (which the band also released as a single) that expressed Venom's supposed allegiance most explicitly. They even took the trouble of running the singer's voice backwards in the incantatory passages. The lyrics of the remaining tracks on *Welcome to Hell* run the usual gamut of contemporary deadly sins.

Venom's Satanism always remained conscientiously tongue-in-cheek, although their scripts naturally required a scowling manner of delivery that went way beyond the straight-faced. The extremism of their pose attracted various imitators, the most successful of whom have been the American band Deicide. Deicide began life as Amon before securing a record contract on the basis of their second demo tape, *Sacrificial* (1989), which kicked off with "Lunatic of God's Creation" and included "Crucifixation" and "Carnage in the Temple of the Damned"; all these tracks were eventually re-recorded for their debut album, *Deicide* (1990).

Deicide's particular brand of heavy metal is usually referred to as "death metal", but the title of Venom's second album was borrowed as a generic description for a cluster of bands that emerged in the early 1990s in Norway. Other significant influences on which these "black metal" bands drew included the Swedish band Bathory, whose career extends from the mid-1980s to the present, and the Swiss band Hellhammer.

The main originator of Norwegian black metal was Øysten Aarseth, *alias* Euronymous, of the band Mayhem. Mayhem were of some significance as a musical exemplar but Aarseth was able to play a more influential role by virtue of the fact that he ran his own shop, called Helvete (i.e., Hell), and his own record label, Deathlike Silence. These enterprises became the rallying-point for a group of black metal enthusiasts who called themselves the Inner Circle. By virtue of offering peer-group support, the existence of the Inner Circle allowed the "Satanist" activities of its members to be extrapolated from stage performances and lyric-writing into full-scale lifestyle fantasies.

This Inner Circle consisted of approximately a dozen young men, most, if not all, of them teenagers, but the fact that they were divided into several rival bands—Darkthrone, Emperor and Burzum among them—introduced a competitive element that resulted in an unfortunate escalation of their collective lifestyle fantasy. Their attempts to outdo one another in the Satanist cause quickly got out of hand. Rumors of their involvement with arson attacks on churches and the desecration of graveyards gained explosive impetus in August 1993 when Varg Vikernes, *alias* Count Grishnackh—by then the only member of Burzum—stabbed and killed Aarseth/Euronymous. Vikernes was subsequently sentenced to twenty-one years imprisonment, and his conviction was followed by others. Bard Eithun of Emperor was sentenced to fourteen years for the murder of a homosexual who had propositioned him, and various other members of the Inner Circle were convicted of arson.

The publicity generated by this affair in 1994 was, of course, double-edged. On the one hand, it set off yet another moral panic about the evil effects of heavy metal music. This was aggravated in Britain by the conviction at Maidstone Crown Court of 18-year-old Paul Timms, who claimed leadership of a British black metal band called Necropolis, for criminal damage against seven churches and a graveyard in and around Tunbridge Wells. On the other hand, it boosted the sales of black metal music to levels it could never otherwise have achieved, resulting in a rapid proliferation of new bands throughout Europe; the black metal compilation album *Blackend* (1995), released by Plastic Head, features nineteen such bands.

His conviction conferred a strange kind of stardom on Varg Vikernes. "Count Grishnackh" (who borrowed both his pseudonym and the name of his band from J. R. R. Tolkien's *Lord of the Rings*) continues to give regular interviews from his cell and has promised to continue his now-booming career by taking full advantage of the two weeks' annual leave granted to Norwegian long-term prisoners. Thanks to these interviews, and similar interviews with members of Darkthrone and Emperor, the ideology of Norwegian black metal has been subjected to close scrutiny and interrogation—a process that has probably been the most significant factor in its evolution. The inevitable result of this pressure was that Vikernes was enthusiastic to reinterpret his own Satanism in a more flattering light, and eventually found it politic to forsake the label altogether.

The explicit but essentially non-serious Satanism of Venom and Deicide tends to extol the power of Satan as a force in the world—which is, of course, exactly what the godly are worried about. The tendency is for their lyrics to celebrate an imminent "Satanic apocalypse" that will sweep away the old moral order, without taking the trouble to specify what will replace it. An example notable for the clarity of its delivery (a rare commodity in death metal) is Pentagram's album *Day of Reckoning* (1993), the theme of its title track echoing again and again in such tracks as "When the Screams Come" and "Wartime". "Burning Saviour" carefully revises the Christian notion of redemption along Satanist lines, gleefully suggesting that it is the self-righteous who are scheduled to burn in eternal flames.

This kind of Satanism has to take the Christian Satan pretty much as given, because the pose would otherwise lose its shock value. The whole point of literary Satanism, by contrast, is to proclaim that Satan is in some sense misunderstood: that the "evil" that he was invented to personify has at least some good in it, while the "good" that condemns his followers to eternal torment is much less virtuous than it claims. Many literary Satanists, as we have observed, deploy alternative icons of opposition to orthodoxy (Prometheus, Pan, witches or other fallen angels) with the intention of demonstrating that the accusations of implicit evil leveled at them are mistaken and false. As soon as they were called upon to justify their Satanist stance, Varg Vikernes and other members of the Inner Circle elected to follow this escape-route. Count Grishnackh proclaimed in an interview given to the fanzine *Ultrakill!* that he was a worshipper of Odin rather than the Christian Satan, and a follower of "the Viking way" that would hopefully lead him to eternal life in Valhalla (a warriors' paradise that could hardly quibble about the membership-qualifications of homicidal berserkers).

By this means, the ideology of Norwegian black metal has been transmuted into a lament for a lost pagan heritage once associated with Viking glory, whose eclipse by Christianity allegedly reduced Norway from the status of Dark Age superpower to contemporary EC marginality. The dark Millenarianism typical of death metal groups, already fused with the imagery of Götterdämmerung, is thus interpreted as an anticipation of a triumphant return of paganism and of a quasi-barbaric but ultra-virile way of life. This move was not without precedent; Hellhammer had earlier undergone a transmutation into the slightly more refined Celtic Frost, some of whose lyrics were adapted from the works of that great popularizer of barbaric virility, Robert E. Howard.

Count Grishnackh's interviewers were not noticeably appeased by this self-redefinition, which seemed to most of them to reek of Nazi mythology and thus to add Fascist sympathies to the list of his sins. Much Norwegian black metal does exhibit a strident nationalist fervor based in some notion of a Scandinavian *volksgeist*, although it does not seem to embrace or advocate any particular political program. This notion lends itself to considerable elaboration, as evidenced by a long article signed "Kadmon" in the Austrian fanzine *Aorta*, which offers a detailed account of Teutonic folklore relating to the Oskorei, the Norwegian version of the Wild Hunt, and then evaluates black metal as "Oskorei Romantikk" and as "pagans' noise", characterizing it as "powerful, violent, dark and grim" and calling attention to "the eternal recurrence of certain Leitmotivs, the dark ablaze atmosphere, the dark and viscid sound landscape". For Kadmon, black metal is "a pagan avant-garde, a Nordic occulture reconciling myth and modern world".

It is, of course, highly probable that none of this was in the minds of the unfortunate Euronymous and his Inner Circle when they first took up the Satanist cause of black metal, but it is typical of the way in which lifestyle fantasies become elaborated when they are subjected to criticism or invited to expand. The history of black metal is still unfolding in this respect, and probably has some way yet to go.

* * * * * * *

One problem with heavy metal music as an expressive medium is that it is very noisy, not merely in the literal sense but in the technical sense defined by Simon Reynolds in his book *Blissed Out* (1990):

If music is like a language, if it communicates some kind of emotional or spiritual message, then noise is best defined as interference, something which blocks transmission, jams the code, prevents sense being made. The subliminal message of most music is that the universe is essentially benign, that if there is sadness or tragedy, this is resolved at the level of some higher harmony. Noise troubles this worldview. That is why noise groups invariably deal with subject-matter that is anti-humanist—extremes of abjection, obsession, trauma, atrocity, possession—all of which undermine humanism's confidence that...we can become the subjects of our lives, and work together for the general progress of the commonwealth.

Given this, it is only to be expected that the oppositional strategies of heavy metal should be abrupt and straightforward. The heavy metal scene is, therefore, an expectable modern location for explicit Satanism of an apocalyptic stripe. Not all Satanist rock music is heavy metal music, however; several examples of a very different species are to be found on the far side of the Atlantic, where they fit readily enough into an alternative cultural context.

The Satanist churches founded in America by lifestyle fantasists—most famously the one founded in California by Anton LaVey—have always been set solidly in the theatrical and libertine tradition of the eighteenth century Hellfire clubs, whose primary emphasis (and sole *raison d'être*) was on the uninhibited enjoyment of wild partying. Set firmly and wholeheartedly within this ideological milieu, *Burn, Baby, Burn!* (1993) by The Electric Hellfire Club deploys the technology and techniques of disco music to produce music designed for dancing rather than headbanging. The album begins with a ritual "Invocation", but the "Age of Fire" celebrated in the opening dance-track is as much a contemporary happening as a forthcoming apocalypse. Although it takes time out to celebrate the exploits of the most active contemporary folk-demon in the serial-killer song "Mr 44" the album's primary intent is to rescue and revamp the old hippie ethos, whose ideals are celebrated in "Psychedelic Sacrifice", "The Electric Hellfire Acid Test" and "The Black Bus". This is lightly seasoned with a sprinkling of modish S&M in the whiplash-laden "Where Violence is Golden", but that too is very much according to tradition.

The noisy, mock-sinister and quasi-apocalyptic sensationalism of Deicide exists in parallel, therefore, with a good deal of material that is more overtly playful and much more upbeat. Voice of Destruction's maxi-single *Black are the Souls of the Damned* (1992) only gives a part of its space over to the pure disco of the "digital-dance-mix" of "Caught in the Act" but it has closer links to The Electric Hellfire Club than to death metal. Even the first version of its title track is equipped with rather more imaginative sound-effects, and the second goes overboard in making prolific use of samples plundered from old horror movies. Such samples are also deployed, more frugally but with telling effect, on *Burn, Baby, Burn!*, and this method of creating an ideative link between songs and movies is one of the key features of a more complex musical rhetoric that often invokes supernatural figures and thus lends itself readily to the evasive tactics of the more diplomatic literary Satanists.

Horror films first laid down the imaginative bridges that permitted such figures as the vampire to move away from being mere emblems of evil. They did so not by embracing the calculated literary Satanism of Anne Rice *et al* (although they paved the way for its acceptance) but simply by revealing the hitherto-covert sexuality of such figures in glorious Technicolor, vividly eroticizing the most significant monster/victim encounters. Such films always used background music in order to heighten audience sensation, thus helping to develop and refine a rich lexicon of "meaningful chords"; bands like The Electric Hellfire Club and Voice of Destruction take advantage of a reversal of this process, using snippets of "background dialogue" to link their audiences to a ready-made set of subliminal associations.

Disco music is much less noisy than heavy metal music, both in the literal sense and in Reynolds' sense of the term, but because its primary function is to facilitate dancing it is fundamentally repetitive. Most rock music is, of course, employed as dance-music, but disco music is by definition obsessive in this cause; its primary function is to assist in an ecstatic submersion of linear consciousness (often, in practice, with the assistance of similarly-inclined psychotropic drugs like MDMA, *alias* ecstasy). Like heavy metal, therefore, disco music has a certain ready-made affinity with the straightforwardness of explicit Satanism.

Snippets of background dialogue are not the only things that can be sampled from movies in order to borrow the emotional resonances that films ingrain in their habitual watchers; the lexicon of meaningful chords is available too. To make fruitful use of this lexicon, however, it is necessary to produce songs that are rather more complex than disco music can readily entertain. It is, therefore, a different sector of the rock spectrum that has developed a space in which more subtle symbols of rebellion and dissent are deployed and developed: a sector that is usually defined in Britain as "Goth", although some German record labels also employ the term "Dark Wave".

* * * * * * *

The Goth subculture, which first emerged in the punk era of the late 1970s, is most obviously demarcated by its striking dress code. This involves all-black attire, occasionally ameliorated by a dash of red velvet and lavishly augmented with heavy imitation-silver jewelry. Dyed-black hair, often wildly splayed, is customary and make-up tends to the garish, particularly about the eyes. The principal models for this look were Siouxsie Sioux of Siouxsie and the Banshees and Robert Smith of The Cure, but as those bands evolved away from their punk origins they adopted styles rather different from the one that became definitive of Goth music.

Mick Mercer's first handbook of the genre, *Gothic Rock* (1994) shrewdly linked the essence of Gothic lifestyle fantasy to the description given by Edgar Allan Poe of the lifestyle of C. Auguste Dupin in "The Murders in the Rue Morgue", but the long and winding line of descent that carried that image forward to its end-users arrived *via* cheap horror movies, renewed and reinforced by cinematic images of sinister but sexy vampires.

After an early phase in which London-based bands like Alien Sex Fiend and Sex Gang Children were prominent, the heartland of the British Goth subculture was established in the north; the definitive British Goth band became the Leeds-based The Sisters of Mercy, whose front-man, Andrew Eldritch, defined both the mood of the music and its characteristic style of presentation during the late 1980s. The black-clad band played in semi-darkness, further obscured by the liberal outpourings of a smoke-machine, while Eldritch intoned his lyrics in a deep and conspicuously raw baritone voice. The other significant Goth bands of the late 1980s were The Mission and Fields of the Nephilim. German Gothic rock evolved in parallel, with early exemplars like X-mal Deutschland and Calling Dead Red Roses establishing a distinct base, but was subsequently very heavily influenced by the leading British bands; as it became commonplace for German bands to sing in English, many of their vocalists modelled their style and their material on the British exemplars.

Andrew Eldritch's lyrics never exhibited any interest in religious or fantastic imagery, but the songs written by his main rivals, Wayne Hussey of The Mission and Carl McCoy of Fields of the Nephilim, became increasingly infused with occult and mystical imagery. A straightforwardly anti-religious input into the subculture was contrived by the American band Christian Death, which somehow became affiliated to the Goth canon in spite of retaining a rather chaotic punkish style. When Christian Death's original founder, Rozz Williams, had abandoned the band to the care of the pseudonymous Valor, it began to make even more of its anti-religious stance, displaying it extravagantly in such tracks as "This is Heresy", "Four Horsemen" and "Church of No Return", all of which are included on an album recorded live at London's Marquee Club, *The Heretic's Alive* (1989).

Christian Death do not warrant description as literary Satanists—where the name of Satan is mentioned in their lyrics, as in "Born in a Womb, Died in a Tomb" in the Hate section of *All the Love, All the Hate* (1989), it has entirely negative connotations—but their strident catalogues of complaint employ a more expansive framework than is typical of post-punk exercises in nihilistic angst. When Goths do make use of Satanist motifs—as, for instance, when the recently-founded Goth label Grave News gave their first compilation CD, *Dreams in the Witch House* (1995) the index Fetish 666, and inserted into the small print a note that it was produced "By Appointment to his Satanic Majesty"—they tend to do so far more slyly and more wittily than the exponents of death metal.

The decisive period in the history of British Goth, so far as the subject-matter of the present article is concerned, arrived when Fields of the Nephilim enjoyed a brief period of chart success at the end of the 1980s. In the interviews that Carl McCoy gave, in consequence of this success, he became increasingly vociferous about his strong interest in the occult and his devout paganism. These ideas came increasingly to the fore in the songs he wrote, culminating in an ambitious and highly original concept album called *Elizium* (1990). Although McCoy split from his backing musicians not long afterwards, this success drew many other vociferously pagan bands into the Gothic scene, some of which worked in the same musical style and some of which merely embraced a similar ideology. The most important of these new bands, in terms of their productivity and the complexity of their imagery, are the British band Incubus Succubus (who recently renamed themselves Inkubus Sukkubus) and the German band The Garden of Delight.

Paganism is, of course, not at all the same kind of dissent from Christian orthodoxy as explicit Satanism, although Varg Vikernes' reinterpretation of his own standpoint as Odin-worship demonstrates the ease with which one might segue into the other. It is, however, worth noting that, whether its exponents know it or not, modern paganism owes the greater part of its inspiration to an explicitly Satanist work: Jules Michelet's *La Sorcière* (translated into English as *Satanism and Witchcraft*, 1939). If we are to understand the extraordinarily convoluted history of modern paganism—and, in particular, the fascinating manner in which it entwines literary fantasies, scholarly fantasies and lifestyle fantasies into a complex tapestry of poses and pretences, it is vital to understand the curious origins and the astonishingly widespread influence of that remarkable book.

* * * * * * *

Jules Michelet was a French historian whose reputation as a conscientiously-biased chronicler of French political affairs remains unsullied, although none of his academic admirers would admit *La Sorcière* to a list of his reputable publications. Michelet was also an influential philosopher of history, and his views on the essential nature of the historian's enterprise were ancestral to those of such writers as R. C. Collingwood.

What philosophers of this stripe argue is that the historian's "understanding" of his subject-matter is not at all like the "understanding" that natural scientists seek to obtain. Although natural scientists can understand phenomena by relating them to invariable physical laws and chemical transactions, the historian finds such generalizations hard to come by, and useless in practice. A historian can only understand what happened in history by means of an act of imaginative identification, by which he places himself "in the shoes" of the people of the past and attempts to grasp the rationale underlying their actions. (In my novel *The Werewolves of London*, published in 1991, Sir Edward Tallentyre puts forward this argument in order to sustain his claim that "all history is to some extent fantasy".

Although the text does not say so he—or, rather, I—had *La Sorcière* very much in mind.)

Michelet's application of this method of identificatory understanding to the substance of French political history reaped considerable rewards. The method does, however, involve a certain hazard, which is that, when a nineteenth-century intellectual, with certain powerfully-held moral and political beliefs, places himself in the shoes of a historical actor about whose beliefs and opinions almost nothing is known, he can hardly help importing his own views and prejudices to fill the void. If and when this happens, the historian cannot and will not produce an accurate account of the phenomena as they really were, but will instead transfigure them into a curious moral allegory, in which the intellect of the present contemplates the iniquities of the past from a viewpoint ironically akin to that of a demonic possessor.

When Michelet wrote *La Sorcière,* he knew full well that this was what he was doing, and that what he was producing was a kind of scholarly fantasy; the sixth of his brief appendices is an effective confession of this fact. The text makes constant reference to fairy tales and their metaphorical significance; its first chapter relates, as an emblematic exemplar, the anecdotal tale of the Bride of Corinth found in Philostratus' life of Apollonius of Tyana, which—thanks to Goethe's recomplication of it, which Michelet took care to deplore—became the ancestor of all modern vampire stories. Michelet doubtless felt, however, that the moral lesson that he was attempting to put across—put crudely, that we should all rejoice in the decline of the Catholic Church and pray for its extinction—amply justified the distortion of actual history.

Prior to the publication of *La Sorcière*, all reputable historians had accepted that the witches hunted by Medieval inquisitors had been innocent, and that the entire mythology of Sabbats and pacts with the devil had been cooked up by the witch-hunters as an instrument of persecution, according to a recipe that had been used to slander and demonize heretics for centuries. When Michelet placed himself in the shoes of accused witches, however, he found it convenient to see things very differently.

Was it not possible, and appropriate, Michelet reasoned, that people unjustly accused of being Satanists might have responded by *becoming* Satanists? Was it not possible, and understandable, that the kinds of people unjustly singled out for persecution in this way—most of whom would have been midwives and practitioners of folk-medicine—might have responded to the accusation that their "magic" was Satanic by saying, bravely and defiantly, that, if that were so, then they were proud to be Satan's followers? Was it not possible, and justified, that such people might have banded together to celebrate a "communion of revolt" that hailed Satan as a Promethean angel of light, exactly as he had been hailed in more recent and more enlightened times by Shelley and Baudelaire?

Michelet decided that, whether it was possible or not, such a rebellion would certainly have been entirely appropriate, understandable and justified. Thus, the archetypal figure of the Sorceress, whose avatars the Medieval witches allegedly were, becomes, in his extended parable, the proudly defiant and indefatigable heroine of the fight against the Tyrant Church. (The occasional male sorcerer is included in the account, but Michelet insists throughout that his is essentially a tale of women's struggles against Church-maintained patriarchy.)

The book was, of course, a great popular success. The scholarly fantasy it contained was soon elaborated by others; Charles Godfrey Leland's deft literary hoax *Aradia: The Gospel of the Witches* (1899) and Edgar Jepson's earnest anti-Christian allegory *The Horned Shepherd* elaborated the thesis that the accused witches had actually been following ancient pagan rites that the Church was anxious to extirpate. This idea was enthusiastically taken up by the most successful of all modern scholarly fantasists, Margaret Murray. Murray's reformulation of the witches' communion of revolt in the image of fertility cults lifted from James Frazer's *Golden Bough* in *The Witch-Cult in Western Europe* (1921) was adopted, lock, stock and barrel, by a generation of lifestyle fantasists avid to become unjustly-persecuted but defiantly proud witches and careful custodians of ancient wisdom. Murray, in her turn, became the chief inspiration of another conscious but very influential scholarly fantasist, Robert Graves, whose mock-anthropological account of *The White Goddess* (1947), admittedly concocted by means of the poetic imagination rather than by reference to actual data, provided another oppositional icon to supplement (and largely to displace) Satan and Pan. Like Michelet and Leland (but, perhaps curiously, unlike Murray), Graves was an extravagant feminist, gifting his Sorceresses with an object of worship that symbolized not merely the virtue but also the power of the female sex.

Meanwhile, Michelet's revamped and equally prideful image of the male "black magician" had been taken up by a whole generation of lifestyle fantasists equally avid to revive the traditions of Renaissance magic in a more stylish and grandiose fashion. The mercurial

Éliphas Lévi made such poses so fashionable that *fin-de-siècle* Paris was awash with mages and mystics, whose activities were afforded exactly the right kind of publicity by Joris-Karl Huysmans' documentary novel *Là-Bas* (1891), in which an ardent disciple of Jules Michelet (Durtal introduces his project in exactly that fashion) employs his historical method to put himself in the shoes of Gilles de Rais, the Marshal of France and associate of Joan of Arc who became the subject of a famous fifteenth-century sorcery trial.

Huysmans' hero also conducts an investigation of the contemporary Satanists who, he is assured, are the direct intellectual descendants of Gilles de Rais. Huysmans must have known that his Gilles was a phantom of the speculative imagination; he probably accepted, as is almost certainly the case, that Gilles was framed by his enemy the Duke of Brittany—inspired by the example of the English churchmen who had used a charge of witchcraft to fit up the Maid of Orléans—and signed his sensational confession purely in order to avoid torture. (It is, of course, invariably the case that the libels leveled at men always outlast them far better than their good deeds.) Huysmans also recognized, however, that Gilles de Rais would be a very useful figure to deploy in a complex morality play lamenting the iniquities of the modern world and the impuissance of modern religious faith.

The substance of Michelet's book started a snowball rolling, which soon became so vast that all awareness of its origins was lost, but the method that Michelet pioneered was as widely influential in its own right. Modern historians placing themselves imaginatively in the shoes of ancient astrologers, alchemists and all manner of other mystics had no difficulty at all in reconfiguring those "magical arts" and "occult sciences" in such a way as to make them more appealing, and more seemingly significant, to a twentieth-century audience. It did not matter in the least how little historical evidence there was on which to base these great leaps of the imagination; indeed, the less there was on which to build, the more scope there was for architectural ingenuity. Nor did it matter in the least whether the documents that comprised the histories were genuine or not; the fakes tended to be much more useful than the real thing, because they had usually been faked with the ends of scholarly fantasy and/or lifestyle fantasy very much in mind.

* * * * * * *

At least insofar as his public pose is concerned, Carl McCoy—the driving force of Fields of the Nephilim—is solidly if rather peripherally set in the earnest and relatively profound tradition of lifestyle fantasy that descends from Michelet. The music that the band played towards the end of their brief career was very much an extrapolation and instrument of the particular occult fantasy that he developed.

In an interview in *Melody Maker* McCoy commented on the *Elizium* album and its longest individual sequence, "Sumerland (What Dreams May Come)", in the following terms:

> I'm exploring my own mind, my own heaven and hell, achieving higher levels of consciousness. There are ways of doing this, based on a couple of rituals. They're all feints at death, getting to a point just like when you pass out. What you get are glimpses of death. It's a completely different state of mind, a perception, and people have used it for all sorts of purposes.
>
> Elyzium [sic] is a Greek word for the place where the soul descends after departing from life. It's like an eternal life, and it's final... [Sumerland is] a place where souls lie sleeping, waiting for their reincarnation...a belief of the Sumerians, who were the first known civilization.... I'm interested in the Sumerian magic, which every magical system is based on. Sumerian people were really in touch with the natural sources. That's where the Nephilim came from. They were a superior race of beings from another planet in the solar system who came down to earth and created the human being. There are areas of genetic engineering, here.
>
> The Nephilim were the deity of the Sumerians, the gods.

The word *nephilim* is Hebrew; it occurs twice in the Old Testament—in *Genesis* 6:4 and *Numbers* 13:33—and is translated as "giants" in the Authorized Version. In various items of Old Testament apocrypha and pseudoepigraphia, notably the Book of Enoch, the *nephilim* are associated with the mythology of the War in Heaven, after which many rebel angels were exiled to the earth. (Anatole France drew upon this mythology in formulating his own account of the rebel angels in *La Révolte des anges,* and the Book of Enoch is the primary source quoted in Anne Rice's account of *Memnoch the Devil.*) If the word is interpreted in this way, *Genesis* 6:4 provides an explicit claim that the rebel angels fathered children on human women. How all this might relate to the inscriptions to be found on Sumerian stone tablets—whose survival into the present establishes Sumer as the first civilization known to history—and to the whole matter of Sumerian influences on Hebrew mythology, effected during the period of the Babylonian captivity, is somewhat controversial (which means, of course, that it is open to many interpretations).

The particular reformulation of these materials to be found in the lyrics of the Fields of the Nephilim has been subjected to intense and admirably meticulous scrutiny by Paula O'Keefe in a series of articles in the fanzine *Kia*. O'Keefe observes that McCoy's fascination with Sumerian imagery is syncretically combined with—and seemingly grew out of—a fascination with the literary work of H. P. Lovecraft, particularly with the Cthulhu Mythos. The second of the three Fields of the Nephilim albums, *The Nephilim* (1988), includes "The Watchman" and "Last Exit for the Lost", both of which invoke the name of Cthulhu.

The link between the Cthulhu Mythos and Sumerian mythology is forged by identifying Cthulhu with the Sumerian Tiamat, a symbol of Chaos. This linkage is peripherally made in a volume of supposed commentaries on Lovecraft's imaginary *Necronomicon*, which was compiled as a literary hoax by George Hay, Colin Wilson and David Langford in 1978, but it is much more elaborately laid out (almost certainly by coincidence, as the books were produced independently) in a 1977 book signed "Simon", which purported to be a translation of the *Necronomicon* itself. This process of syncretization is "justified" (and was presumably inspired) by the fact that both the Book of Enoch and the Cthulhu Mythos make reference to "Watchers" (the Arkham House collection of August Derleth's Lovecraftian pastiches—from which a good deal of the Cthulhu Mythos apparatus is actually derived—is called *The Watchers out of Time*.)

This syncresis is further complicated by virtue of the attempts made by the occultist Kenneth Grant to construe the Cthulhu Mythos as a version of the metaphysical system described and extrapolated by Aleister Crowley; Carl McCoy has also cited as an influence the artist and occultist Austin Osman Spare, who was closely associated with Crowley's various exercises in cultish lifestyle fantasy. Fields of the Nephilim's most successful single release was

"Moonchild" (1988), named after Crowley's 1929 novel. If this were not enough, McCoy's friendship with Storm Constantine has resulted in a degree of mutual influence that has already affected some of her novels and will be much more elaborately displayed in her trilogy about the Enochian Watchers and their descendants, begun with *Stalking Tender Prey* (1995).

Lovecraftian imagery is banished from the lyrics featured on *Elizium*, save for a few faint echoes, which none but the cognoscenti would be likely to pick up—for instance, the instrumental introduction is titled "Dead but Dreaming"—but the evolution of the music that they accompany is relatively seamless. The music in question is multi-layered, blending the booming guitars that were the hallmark of the band's early work into a much richer orchestral tapestry woven by clever use of a synthesizer. It is, of course, difficult to describe music in print, but Paula O'Keefe boldly tackles the implicitly impressionistic task in a suitably expansive manner, speaking of the album's "fathomless serenity and power" and making copious references to its supposed capacity to introduce a state of "trance".

The forty-five minute suite (which is not broken up into individual "songs", although the album is provided with a track-listing identifying different sequences) is certainly hypnotic in spite of its insistent drumbeat, and it is also beautiful. Although McCoy's singing voice is very raw indeed and there is a good deal of plaintive mournfulness in the ambience of the music, the final effect is uplifting, as one would expect from a piece that symbolically tracks the journey of a disincarnate soul through "Sumerland" and the "Wail of Sumer" to the paradisal summation of "And There Will Your Heart Be Also".

Had the original Fields of the Nephilim not broken up, this evolution would undoubtedly have been taken further by now. The break-up was, however, a mere matter of delay; McCoy's new band—simply called Nefilim [*sic*]—has been promising the imminent release of its first material for some time. The temporary hiatus has, however, been filled by four albums released by The Garden of Delight.

* * * * * * *

The founder and front-man of The Garden of Delight is Artaud Franzmann, who is identified on later albums simply as Artaud; his backing line-up has undergone several changes in the course of the band's career. Whereas the focus of McCoy's interests progressed from the Cthulhu Mythos to Sumerian mythology, Artaud's went in the other direction. The first Garden of Delight album, *Enki's Temple* (1992), features seven tracks—some of them avant-gardist instrumentals—all referring to that mythology. Where there are lyrics, significant mention is made of the Watchmen, especially in the song addressed to Innana.

Innana is the earliest name associated with a Mother Goddess; she was eventually merged into the much more famous Babylonian goddess Ishtar, the Astarté of the Syrians. It is through her name that the substance of Sumerian mythology can be linked to the fanciful material in Graves' *The White Goddess*, which syncretically amalgamates all mother goddesses into a single entity, who was supposedly a universal object of worship before the takeover of patriarchal all-fathers like Zeus and Jehovah. The Garden of Delight's second album, *Epitaph* (1992), includes a track entitled "The White Goddess" as well as the stylish anti-Christian "Christendom", whose chorus begins "We don't need this Christ-and-doom/We don't need this kind of love".

The incorporation of Irishmen Terry O'Connell and Adrian Hates into The Garden of Delight's line-up moved their musical style decisively in the direction of Fields of the Nephilim's and may also have been partly responsible for the importation of Lovecraftian imagery into *Sargonid Seal* (1993). Here the usual Sumerian mythology is supplemented by "Shared Creation", whose sleeve-note claims that it was inspired by "The Trail of Cthulhu" by "J. Wison". Only the final track of this album—which does not feature O'Connell and Hates—retains the impressionistic ambient avant-gardism more widely featured on the earlier albums.

The fourth Garden of Delight album, *Necromanteion IV* (1994), features Lovecraftian material much more extravagantly, although the title track claims Rosicrucian significance. "Spirit Invocation" and "Watchers out of Time" are both addressed to Cthulhu; "Downwards to a Sea" is expanded from a phrase of Lovecraft's and "The Relation of Light to Shadow" is allegedly inspired by the Comte d'Erlette's *Cultes des Goules*. (The Comte d'Erlette was Lovecraft's fanciful nickname for August Derleth, attached to one of the many other imaginary books devised in imitation of the *Necronomicon*.)

Necromanteion IV's sleeve notes are decorated with quotes taken from J. V. Andreae (the author of at least two of the three pamphlets that provided the foundation-stones of Rosicrucian lifestyle fantasy), Éliphas Lévi, Jules Bois (a French occultist who transmuted the substance of Huysmans' *Là-Bas* into scholarly fantasy), Aleister Crowley and the Rituals of the Golden Dawn as well as one from Lovecraft and one allegedly taken from Clark Ashton Smith's contribution to the Lovecraft circle's list of *livres maudits*, the Book of Eibon.

Although the lyrics still suffer somewhat from Artaud's rather tentative grasp of the English language (not greatly enhanced, it appears, by his English-speaking henchmen) the music featured on *Necromanteion IV* is a remarkable sophistication of that featured on the earlier albums; it is rich, sonorous, and defiantly robust in spite the conscientious mournfulness of the last four tracks. Although it has obvious affinities with the style of *Elizium* it is by no means straightforwardly imitative. The forcefully strident guitar-sounds that the Fields of the Nephilim retained from early singles "Power" (1986) and "Preacher Man" (1987) have their very different counterpart in the legacy of Artaud's earlier avant-gardism, whose most conspicuous elements include tinkling bells and the sounds of running water. (Sound samples of running water are very popular with bands of this general stripe.) Whereas Fields of the Nephilim retained more rock than Gothicism in their hybrid formulation, even at the end, The Garden of Delight still have more Gothicism than rock in theirs.

Just as heavy metal purists often claim that Burzum is not a heavy metal band at all, so Gothic purists might question the entitlement of The Garden of Delight to be considered as practitioners of Gothic rock (they have no entry in Mick Mercer's book, although that was completed before material from their record label, Dion Fortune, became easily obtainable in Britain), but they have certainly found their British audience within the Gothic subculture, as have two other bands that make considerable use of the same inspirational materials: Endura and The Whores of Babylon.

Endura's *Dreams of Dark Waters* (1994) mostly consists of avant-gardist ambient music with little or no use of voices, but the one word that stands out very clearly in the muttered "lyric" of the title-track is "Cthulhu" and another track is entitled "R'lyeh Awakens"—or would be had not the proofreader for the (German) record label failed to pick up a typographical error. Although there is unlikely to have been any direct influence, Endura's musical style is not dissimilar to early Garden of Delight, but it captures and extrapolates a much more sinister mood; it is subtly disturbing in a manner that recalls the careful understatement of the more psychologically-inclined Gothic novels. The band had planned to release a second album, *The Great God Pan*, which would apparently have extended their range of references and influences considerably, but the material from it will now be distributed over two as-yet-untitled albums.

The Whores of Babylon's debut album *Metropolis* (1994) is far more grandiose and elaborate than anything The Garden of Delight have done, but contrives to be somewhat less earnest in spite of its imperiousness. Its use of Babylonian references, although copious, is markedly different from that of Fields of the Nephilim or The Garden of Delight, concentrating with quasi-academic scrupulousness on matters of historical record rather than syncretized mythological icons. "The Fall of Agade" refers to the conquest of the central city of the kingdom of Akkad by the Sumerians, which first consolidated the Babylonian empire, while "Empire of the Jackal" refers to pre-dynastic Egypt.

The Whores of Babylon are perhaps the most sophisticated lyricists working in the entire Goth field and the choice of Pieter Bruegel's painting of the Tower of Babel to illustrate their record sleeve testifies to an intellectualism that they are not loath to parade. The anti-Christian lyrics of "Stigmata" are cleverly combined with music that carries forward the fabulous bombast of "Oblivion" and leads naturally enough to the celebratory exoticism of "Babylon". The Whores of Babylon's use of running water makes an intriguing contrast with Endura's, reflecting the bounty of a desert spring rather than the sullenness of mist-shrouded tarns. Their range extends all the way to a disco remix of "Carnal Desires" (credited to fellow Bristolians Portishead, whose Beth Gibbons provides backing vocals for "Stigmata") and thus makes tentative contact with the extraordinarily vivid dance-music of another band whose lyrics possess an uncommon eloquence: Incubus Succubus.

* * * * * * *

Whether or not Tony and Candia McKormack, the husband and wife team who constitute the core of Incubus Succubus, have ever read Michelet's *La Sorcière,* they are certainly his direct literary descendants, elaborating in their songs virtually every aspect of his work. The only significant point on which they diverge from his world-view is that they (naturally) make more of native British folklore than of the French *contes des fées* that provide his metaphorical reference-points. They also tend to make much more use of erotic motifs than Michelet, but they do so within a framework more-or-less defined by the tale of the Bride of Corinth, save only for the fact that songs written by Candia tend to employ a supernatural male in place of Philostratus' bride of the grave.

Michelet's scathing treatment of the tyranny and violence of the Christian Church is echoed in such Incubus Succubus songs as "Burning Times", "Church of Madness", "All the Devil's Men" and "Conquistadors". His (somewhat understated) socialist sympathies are given voice in "The Leveller" although a more typical note of social protest is sounded in "The Rape of Maude Bowen". Incubus Succubus' straightforward dance numbers include "Old Hornie"—whose choral injunction is to "sing to Herne tonight/And join his dance of life"—and "Goblin Jig", but others in a similar vein are strategically interrupted by choruses that take the form of anthem-like chants. Both of their CD albums (their first album, *Beltaine*, 1992, was only released on tape, and six more songs were given interim release on the *Corn King* tape in 1995) are titled for such anthems: *Belladonna and Aconite* (1993) and *Wytches* (1994). The latter addresses a syncretically-conceived female deity by a whole series of her names: "Isis, Astarté, Hecate, Diana/Anahita, Kali, Innana!" in a manner that provides a remarkable parallel to the chants credited to the revivified Goddess's contemporary followers in Elizabeth Hand's *Waking the Moon* (1995). The former involves hallucinogenic plants credited with giving witches the "gift of flight"; both are rousingly effective despite the necessity in the second case of rhyming "belladonna" with "mandragora". One of Michelet's accounts of a male sorcerer—the case of Urbain Grandier, subsequently made even more famous by Aldous Huxley and Ken Russell—is recapitulated in "Devils".

Several of Incubus Succubus' more contemplative songs refer to Mother Goddess figures in various guises, notably "Dark Mother", "Queen of the May", "Trinity" and the haunting "Samhain". Other addressees of mock hymns feature in "Beltaine", "Corn King" and "Song to Pan", while "Underworld" extends the range of mythological references to Egypt. Pan is not the only nature-spirit embraced by this extraordinarily generous syncretism; "Midnight Queen" offers another. The entire enterprise is summed up in the vibrant "Pagan Born" although such conscientiously exultant numbers have their subtler counterpoint in a series of erotic ballads, which range from the seductively insistent "I Am the One", "Song of the Siren" and "Call out my Name" to the delicately effective "Gypsy Lament", "Vlad" and "Prince of Shadows".

This imagery provides a very full catalogue of the imaginative apparatus of modern "paganism"—a term that presently seems to be crowding out such previously-fashionable equivalents as "witch-craft" or "wicca", although it refers to much the same mix of ideas. Incubus Succubus were a natural choice as special guests (alongside Terry Pratchett!) for Britain's first Pagan Convention, BroomCon, held at the University of Essex in July 1995. The band's members enter into their lifestyle fantasy as wholeheartedly as anyone—although they are in no danger whatsoever of being carried to such hazardous extremes as the leading exponents of black metal—and the principal thrust of their endeavor is to enliven that kind of fantasy in every way possible.

In stark contrast to many of the bands mentioned above, whose enterprises are often studio-bound, Incubus Succubus are highly competent performers, who do an excellent job of rousing audiences to a state of cheerful excitement. (Although Fields of the Nephilim were also a very fine live band, capable of transferring all the complexities of *Elizium* into their stage shows, it might be stretching a point to describe the excitement they communicated as "cheerful".) There is nothing in the least tentative about the "Satanism" of Incubus Succubus, however evasive it might be in selecting its motifs, but the band is in no way confined by the limitations that afflict the endeavors of black metal bands. They may play loudly but they do not play *noisily*; their music is not as complicated or as richly-layered as the quasi-symphonic compositions of Fields of the Nephilim or The Whores of Babylon, but it is equally effective in its own way.

* * * * * * *

An examination of the interrelationships between literary fantasies, scholarly fantasies and lifestyle fantasies need not involve itself in passing judgment on the intrinsic merits of the three activities, but it might be worth making some comment, lest all three be taken as inherently pejorative terms.

Literary fantasy is, of course, a thoroughly worthwhile activity. The recent fashionability of the idea that realistic fiction is somehow innately superior to fantastic fiction is an absurdity. Private fantasizing is a vitally necessary activity, and literary fantasy plays an invaluable educative role as well as providing scope for useful thought-experiments in moral philosophy. The arguments set out in such celebrated essays as Oscar Wilde's "The Decay of Lying"

(1889) and J. R. R. Tolkien's "On Fairy Tales" (1947) are perfectly adequate to establish this conclusion beyond the shadow of a doubt.

As for lifestyle fantasy, it is first necessary to observe that a "lifestyle" *is* a kind of fantasy that one attempts to act out; it is an intrinsic part of the process by which we seek to define and establish the "social selves" that we display to the world. It is true that many individuals construct their lifestyles according to models handed down by tradition or advertised (both overtly and covertly) in the mass media, but the stubborn conformity of such individuals is a deliberate refusal to exercise the imagination that is in no way admirable. In the same way that there is no particular virtue in literary realism, there is no particular virtue in those kinds of conformity that make strenuous efforts to cultivate a relentless dullness; they represent a determined aspiration towards the lowest common denominator of social achievement that is both feeble and pusillanimous.

Many people who cultivate more fanciful lifestyles do so by conforming to alternative stereotypes, and the fact that such lifestyles sometimes require the dogmatic assertion of "facts" that are demonstrably false opens the way to suspicions of stupidity, but they do offer scope for bold self-expression that would otherwise be very difficult to find or support, and true originality in the business of self-creation inevitably goes hand-in-hand with extravagant exercises in lifestyle fantasy.

Scholarly fantasies are, of course, deemed evil and dangerous by those whose sole commitment is to the truth. Natural scientists and historians often react with naked loathing to scholarly fantasies that attempt to reduce established knowledge to the status of arbitrary orthodoxy, and it is entirely understandable that they should. When people commit their belief to scholarly fantasies (whether they are the creators of those fantasies or merely their consumers) real dangers can emerge; no one objectively contemplating the catalogue of horrors inflicted by men of faith on those they deem to be heretics could possibly avoid the conclusion that the hijacking of moral philosophy by devotees of the scriptures has been the worst disaster ever to afflict mankind.

Even bearing this in mind, though, we ought to remember that most scholarly fantasies are fairly harmless, and the harm done by the few must be weighed against the usefulness of the many. If the only useful product of scholarship were, in fact, the truth, we would have figured out long ago exactly where the limits of empirically-licensed belief are. The ironic truth is that products of scholarship that have nothing to do with matters of truth vastly outnumber the others and are useful in all kinds of ways. To attack them simply on the grounds of their absurdity is to miss the point. The importance of *La Sorcière* as a scholarly fantasy does not arise from the fact that it was the product of a serious historian using a method that he otherwise employed to serious effect, but the fact that it laid out an ideology of opposition that many people who thought themselves disadvantaged by the *status quo* found useful as a fountainhead of skepticism, indignation and hope.

There are, of course, many people who would consider the syncretic amalgamation of Sumerian mythology, Crowleyesque occultism and the Cthulhu Mythos to be an abomination whose nefandous quality is made all the more obvious by recognition of its borrowings from such tainted sources as the Book of Enoch, *The White Goddess* and the fake *Necronomicons*. Purist fans of H. P. Lovecraft deplore this development, stigmatizing it as "Lovecraftianity" and taking care to remind us that the so-called Cthulhu Mythos was in any case an invention of August Derleth's apocrypha that has no substantial warrant in the authentic canon. My purpose in calling attention to this matter, however, is not to raise the question of whether these notions are true (which could hardly occupy our minds for a moment) but to raise the question of why they are appealing to the people who have become interested in them. In particular, I want to address the issue of how and why these notions are making themselves *felt* in the great arena of "the devil's music".

* * * * * * *

Musical taste is, of course, a significant aspect of lifestyle—and not merely for the young, or for those whose musical allegiances are associated with particular dress codes. Although there is no necessary connection between the subject-matter of a musical genre and the affectations of its followers, some convergence of interest is highly likely to take place, especially in relatively esoteric genres like black metal and Goth, which recruit new performers from the ranks of their fans rather than having them manufactured by the marketing departments of big record companies.

The importation of themes from modern Gothic fantasy into the lyrics of second-generation Gothic bands was inevitable. Given that so many of those attracted to the Gothic lifestyle found significant inspiration in the imagery of horror films, and then found role models and imaginary soul mates among the sexy vampires featured in books by Anne Rice *et al*, it is only to be expected that vampire iconography will exert an increasing influence upon the poses adopted by Goth musicians and the lyrics they perform. There is, however, more at issue here than mere matters of coincidence and conformity; how much more may easily be demonstrated by examination of two of the recent exercises in conspicuous literary Satanism to which I called attention in the introduction to this essay: *Metal Angel* and *Memnoch the Devil*.

Memnoch the Devil is, at first glance, an unlikely enterprise for its author to undertake. Earlier volumes featuring the Vampire Lestat seemed to assume a universe that is thoroughly secularized, though not de-supernaturalized. In *The Vampire Lestat* the superstitious vampires of eighteenth-century Paris would not enter the cathedral of Notre Dame lest they be struck down by the wrath of God, but when Lestat put their fear to the test nothing happened; his subsequent researches into his origins and nature revealed no evidence at all of the existence of God or the Devil. On the other hand, the very fact that the question kept coming up suggested that it was an itch that would not be quieted.

It is, therefore, not entirely surprising that in *Memnoch the Devil* Lestat finds out that God and the Devil *do* exist, and that the Devil—who does not like to be called Satan—wants to recruit him as a star player for the diabolical team. By way of persuading his chosen appointee to accept his offer, Memnoch takes Lestat to Heaven to meet God, relates his entire life story (with full explanations of his conduct), whips him back in time to witness the crucifixion, and then takes him to Hell so that the purpose of that peculiar enterprise can be made clear.

This is unusual territory for bestselling writers; Marie Corelli's *The Sorrows of Satan* (1895) is the only previous venture of this kind by an author possessed of an audience as broad and as numerous as Anne Rice's, and Rice grasps the nettle much more firmly than Marie Corelli did. Indeed, it is arguable that Rice grasps the nettle more firmly than anyone has ever done before.

Like Anatole France and Carl McCoy, Rice derives her account of the War in Heaven—which here becomes a Philosophical Disagreement in Heaven—from selected passages of the apocryphal Book of Enoch, making the archetypal fallen angel into a Watcher who becomes too intimately involved with those he watches. This allows Memnoch to play the Promethean role celebrated by virtually all previous literary Satanists, but Rice adds a cunning twist that allows him to retain both his status as overlord of Hell and the honest respect of his great adversary, God. By this means, Rice cleverly interweaves her modified Enochian history into modern conceptions of the history of the Earth and the evolution of human societies. Her loyal readers might come to the conclusion that she has done a far better job of negotiating a marriage between the interests of Heaven and Hell than William Blake ever contrived.

Memnoch the Devil takes a much more lenient view of God than *Metal Angel* (though not quite as lenient as *The Sorrows of Satan*), but that makes it all the more interesting that Anne Rice and Nancy Springer agree on one highly significant point: the nature of Heaven. Most Christian fantasists have found it politic to shirk the job of telling readers what Heaven is like, preferring to concentrate—in the interests of psychological terrorism as well as those of competent melodrama—on lurid descriptions of Hell. The most commonly-recruited imagery makes Heaven a kind of rural paradise—an Arcadia or a new Eden—but Rice and Springer both go for the second-best bet: that the paradisal quality of Heaven is somehow contained in its music.

This is a clever narrative move, in that it excuses the fact that the grandeur of Heaven cannot be communicated in mere words, save in a vaguely impressionistic manner, but there is more than a trivial matter of convenience at stake. One suspects that for Anne Rice, as for Nancy Springer, her exercise in literary Satanism is in some sense *the* book: the one that cuts deepest into the heart of all matters. Their attempts to portray Heaven in terms of its music is an honest reflection of the fact that there is indeed something in the experience of music that speaks to us of Heaven.

"The subliminal message of most music," Simon Reynolds claims, "is that the universe is essentially benign, that if there is sadness or tragedy, this is resolved at the level of some higher harmony." Rice and Springer both accept this judgment; where they differ is in judging the worth of that "higher harmony". Anne Rice thinks that it justifies everything, including God's indifference to the populations of Earth and Hell; Nancy Springer thinks that it justifies nothing, especially that.

The readers of these two texts have no way of arbitrating between Volos' claim that the music of Heaven is ineffably boring, because it consists of infinite repetitions of stereotyped paeans of praise (of which he has become heartily sick), and Lestat's claim that the music of Heaven really is divine, and really does deliver the soul to the reverberant thrill of eternal ecstasy; it is, at the end of the day, a matter of taste.

Readers of *Memnoch the Devil* will have to make up their own minds as to whether Lestat is right in deciding that Heaven really is Heaven, and that God is not the cruel, unfeeling despot that Volos makes Him out to be. It is important to realize, however, that the matter is by no means a straightforward choice. The contrast between God's blissed-out music, which communicates His particular "spiritual message", and the Devil's discotheque, is not as simple as that between harmony and "noise". Nancy Springer assures us that what Simon Reynolds identifies as the task of "becom[ing] the subjects of our lives, and work[ing] together for the general progress of the commonwealth" may require us to perceive the falsity of old harmonies and to discover new ones—or at least to explore the possibility that this can be done.

According to tradition, the heavenly Music of the Spheres is a purified music, in which chords exist in isolation, but we know full well that real music is not like that; we know that earthly music is full of tunes and melodies, and that the words that accompany it can sing of anything at all, without any given necessity to attain perfect pitch. The wisdom of lore and legend has always assured us that, even though God owns the harmonies, the Devil has all the best tunes. If we accept this, it becomes obvious that literary Satanism will generate echoes in modern music, and that those echoes will grow in volume and sophistication to signify—in the self-sufficient fashion in which music does contrive to signify ideas—the full range of literary Satanist ideas and literary Satanist methods. It is good that it should, because those readers who find Anne Rice's vision of Heaven so morally indefensible as to be appalling—as I do—may need all the help they can get in reaching out into other imaginative spaces, where they might find very different kinds of solace, enlivenment and fascination.

Music certainly can help in this endeavor—and, if Anne Rice and Nancy Springer are right to decide that analogies with music represent our best hope of envisioning Heaven, it may well be invaluable in any such quest.

* * * * * * *

Like most works in which dubious history is reformulated as rousing allegory, Michelet's *La Sorcière* closes with a look towards the future. He concludes, sadly, that the Sorceress *per se* has perished forever, but that one of her many aspects has survived, and will never die. The aspect that has survived, he thinks, and will persist in the task of leading us towards enlightenment (an enlightenment he conceives of as Nature in rebellion against the forces of Anti-Nature, thus establishing himself as a pioneer of modern ecological mysticism) is that symbolized by the fairy: the wholly illusory but nevertheless useful product of the humble but hopeful imagination. In this claim Michelet was correct; that kind of fantasy has gone from strength to strength, overspilling its folkloristic origins into literary fantasy, lifestyle fantasy and scholarly fantasy, and cementing an alliance between them that whirls all their materials around in ever-tighter circles, as if in some mad cavorting dance.

In *The Werewolves of London* Sir Edward Tallentyre went on to observe that if all history is to some extent fantasy, then all fantasy must be to some extent history. He—or rather I—meant what he said. Historians are not the only enquiring minds who must place themselves imaginatively in the shoes of others; such a move is the very essence of the act of hearing or reading stories. Hearers and readers have always known, even if true historians really ought to ignore the fact, that it is usually easier to put oneself in wholly imaginary shoes than in real ones. They adapt far more comfortably to the idiosyncratic form of the wearer, and they have the abundant scope of seven-league boots; they provide us with places to stand from which we can look back at ourselves, and see ourselves for the strange creatures we are.

Oddly enough, one of the few places imaginary shoes cannot take us is Heaven; we always seem to get lost on the way, although we find it all too easy to locate and tramp across the wastelands of Hell. Music acts upon our minds in a different way, which has more to do with sensations and emotions than with intellect and reason. Whether a desirable Heaven might be made of music or not, the voice of music encourages us to think that it might. Insofar as we need the skeptical voice of literary Satanism to help us resist the oppressions of intolerant authority—and I think that we do need it— we also need the Devil's discotheque to remind us that the human imagination is a far more prolific synthesizer than the most carefully-trained church choir.

SANG FOR SUPPER

In Rémy de Gourmont's brief Decadent fantasy "Le Magnolia" (in *Histoires magiques*, 1894) a young woman named Arabelle is about to be married to a dying man, in order to satisfy his final wish. She finds a symbolic parallel of her situation in the last remaining blossoms on a magnolia tree. One is already withered, but the other is still beautiful. The symbolism of the magnolia flower—a corolla of white petals surrounding a splash of vivid red—is explicitly stated: "la vie était signifiée dans la neige des corolles charnues par une goutte de sang". Arabelle laments the fate of her husband-to-be, saying: "Il va mourir avec les secondes fleurs du magnolia, celui qui devait aviver d'une goutte de sang la fleur que je suis."

Gourmont's second use of the phrase "goutte de sang" is, of course, euphemistic; the veiled reference is to semen rather than to blood. A translator attempting to render the story into English, having no parallel wordplay to exploit, would be forced to preserve the double meaning by recruiting some weak-kneed phrase like "vital fluid". This is a pity, because it adds an extra layer of confusion to what is already a curious pattern of equivalence. One consequence of this is that the French are better-equipped than the English to understand the kind of vampire story in which the symbolism of blood and semen is inextricably entwined, so that the nourishment of blood becomes a partly-reversed mirror of sexual intercourse.

In the climax of "Le Magnolia", of course, the husband achieves after death the defloration that he was unable to accomplish in life, although the result certainly does not warrant the use of a verb like "aviver". Arabelle is supernaturally drawn to the magnolia, where a shadow awaits her, and when she goes to meet it "l'ombre étendit les bras, des bras fluides et serpentins, puis less laissa tomber, telles deux vipères d'enfer, sur les épaules, où elles se tordirent en sifflant". In accordance with the iron law of narrative propriety, Arabelle is found—drained of her vital fluids by those "hellish vipers"—with a withered magnolia flower clutched in her dead hand.

* * * * * * *

In another fairly characteristic product of the French Decadent Movement "Le Verre de sang" (in *Buveurs d'âmes*, 1893) by Jean Lorrain the reader discovers a woman waiting patiently in a hotel lobby, confronted by a symbolic display of flowers in a vase of Venetian glass. These flowers, unlike Gourmont's effetely effeminate magnolia, are possessed of "une dureté cruelle et suggestive"; the irises seem like "fers de hallebarde" and the narcissi like shooting-stars "tombées d'un ciel de nuit d'hiver".

Lorrain gradually and teasingly unfolds the explanation of why the actress is there. She has been a famous actress, renowned for her Nordic good looks and her immunity to romance, but she gave up her career in order to marry an Italian diplomat—not because she loved *him,* but because she loved his young daughter. Having given up everything for her loved one, though, the unfortunate actress found that her inamorata slowly began to fade away. The doctors she has consulted agree that the "tuberculosis" that is killing the little girl was brought on by the actress's overabundant love for her, and that the only possible cure is for her to take a daily draught of fresh blood in the local abattoir. The actress, who finds the odor of the abattoir unbearable, always waits in the hotel while the girl takes her medicine—but when her loved one returns and kisses her on the lips her instinctive revulsion to the taste of blood is miraculously transformed into its opposite.

Given that "La Verre du sang" is one of the very few tales of lesbian pedophilia ever penned it is perhaps unsurprising that it proceeds in an unexpected and rather implausible direction, but it is worth noting that the doctors of *fin de siècle* Paris did have rather eccentric ideas about the causes of disease; Pasteur's theories had not yet driven out their rivals. Jean Lorrain was himself both homosexual and consumptive, and probably suspected—if he did not actually believe—that the two might be causally connected. The daily dose of fresh blood did indeed figure among the prescriptions he tried out (as did drinking ether, which didn't work either, but whose hallucinatory effects inspired many of his most vivid horror stories). "Le Verre de sang" thus qualifies as one of the few stories of non-supernatural vampirism based on actual experience, and there is no doubt that its complex network of metaphors was constructed with genuine feeling.

* * * * * * *

These two stories present interesting interminglings of the notions of vampirism and sexual perversity. (A marriage between a
dying man and a young girl may not fall into any familiar category
of "perversity", but it is a discomfiting notion nevertheless). The
former is more conventional, transmuting perversity into horror according to a familiar moral alchemy, but it should be noted that, at
the time he wrote "Le Magnolia," Gourmont had not yet fallen victim to the disfiguring disease that wrecked his life as surely as tuberculosis wrecked Lorrain's. The disease in question was then
known as "tubercular lupus" and the quacks who compounded
Lorrain's misery with their lousy advice presumably viewed Gourmont's case in much the same light; it is hardly surprising that
Gourmont's later fiction became increasingly obsessed with and
ironically sympathetic to offbeat lust of various kinds. Lorrain's
story, like all his work, is determinedly suspicious of the kind of
moral judgment that Gourmont's takes for granted; it is a horror
story of sorts, but it also poses a calculated moral challenge: an invitation to the reader to examine his (or her) own idiosyncrasies, fantasies and fascinations.

The symbolism of both these stories is entirely conscious and
explicit, and they provide useful paradigm cases that allow us to perceive similar—although less conscious and less explicit—patterns of
symbolism in other works. It is no coincidence that the era that produced "Le Magnolia" and "La Verre du sang" also saw the publication of Richard Krafft-Ebing's *Psychopathia Sexualis* (1886). This
was the work that helped to popularize the notion of real-world
vampirism *as* a form of sexual perversion, but the idea was hardly
new, and the reductive "explanation" of vampirism as a peculiar
form of fetishism did less justice to the complexity of human fascination with the idea of vampires than the exploratory work done by
earlier *littérateurs* had done. John Polidori's graphic representation
of avid sexual appetite as vampiric lust in The Vampyre (1819) was
undoubtedly based in hysterical spite against his one-time employer
Lord Byron, but what it produced in the figure of Lord Ruthven was
a peculiarly charismatic figure who retained a good deal of the sex-
appeal that made Byron—in the words of the luckless Lady Caroline
Lamb—so "dangerous to know".

The extraordinary power of unorthodox lust is admitted, if not
exactly celebrated, by most of the nineteenth century classics of
vampire fiction. Théophile Gautier's nouvelle "La Morte amour-

euse" is an exquisitely lurid account of a young priest's lust for a wicked and very beautiful parishioner, whose seduction of him cannot reach its climax until she is dead. He is saved from death by his superior, but Gautier raises the awkward question—which also crops up in the similar nouvelle "Arria Marcella"—of whether real life can possibly have anything to offer that is anywhere near as intensely intoxicating as the love of a sexy vampire. Outside France—which, being a Catholic country, was fertile ground for the nurture of Romantic and sentimental Satanists of all kinds—sympathy for vampires was inevitably more muted, but never entirely obliterated by the conscientious horror of its contemplation. An oft-reprinted story ostensibly translated from the German *circa* 1820 and falsely attributed to Ludwig Tieck, variously called "The Bride of the Grave" and "Wake not the Dead!" takes a much dimmer view of the propriety of female vampirism, as does J. Sheridan Le Fanu's remarkable lesbian fantasy "Carmilla" (1872), but both stories are still vividly erotic.

Polidori's fascinated loathing is reproduced in numerous English stories of a similar kind, but becomes much more problematic in some. John Keats, in "Lamia" (1820), and Vernon Lee, in "Amour Dure" (1890) and "Prince Alberic and the Snake-Lady" (1896), were both able to perceive a measure of ironically life-enhancing potential in vampiric romance. This was presumably not unconnected with the facts that Keats was dying of tuberculosis (perhaps further complicated by hopeless passion) while Vernon Lee was a homosexual-in-exile, but this in no way diminishes the stature of their work. Bram Stoker—who, according to some critics, might have been showing the earlier symptoms of syphilis at the time—was far too horror-stricken to take a sympathetic view of *Dracula* (1897), but Fred Saberhagen, reinterpreting the events of that novel in the light of sympathetic reason in *The Dracula Tape* (1975), might arguably be said to have revealed the remarkable extent to which Stoker belonged to the devil's party without knowing it.

* * * * * * *

It was not, of course, absolutely necessary to be the victim of a socially-stigmatized disease before one could become interested in vampires, even in the nineteenth century; nor was it a firm requirement that one should be uneasily aware of a certain unorthodoxy in one's sexual tastes or fantasies—but such circumstances obviously helped. Nowadays, of course, the significance of such predispositions has declined very markedly; we live in more enlightened times.

Modern ideas about disease are very different from those which burdened Jean Lorrain and Rémy de Gourmont. Even the vilest of the multitudinous quacks who nowadays pose as exponents of "alternative medicine" is unlikely to suggest that tuberculosis is the result of sexual perversion, or that it might be cured by drinking daily doses of fresh blood. Not all of our neighbors have yet become virtuous liberals, content to say that any and all routes to sexual fulfillment are unexceptionable, provided only that they do not involve coercion, but they are getting there. The war that will end war by securing a final victory for understanding and tolerance is still going on, and there are many battles still to be fought against racism, sexism and the hordes of Islam (to name but a few of our enemies), but the good guys are definitely winning.

One of the more eccentric of the very many ways in which this unfolding victory has been celebrated is the production of numerous modern stories in which good liberals display their tolerance by extending it, with retrospective apologies, to the real and imaginary scapegoats of past eras. The monstrousness of such figures is revealed by re-examination to have been the product of ignorance and folly, and our relative enlightenment is celebrated by a new willingness to look for the pathetic and the heroic in yesterday's demons. We all feel sorry for the many innocents who were tortured and burned (or hanged) by our forefathers as heretics and/or witches, and we take some pride in saying so. In much the same way, at least some of us are prepared to entertain the notion that Lord Ruthven, like his human model, might after all have been worthy of love—or, at least, sufficiently thrilling, while on the job, to make mere matters of worthiness irrelevant.

Modern vampires, like Count Kotor's family in Pierre Kast's *Les Vampires de l'Alfama* (1975), can function as heroic symbols of philosophical enlightenment, scientific progress and sexual liberation, while those who hunt them down can be portrayed as bigoted psychopaths. A child of the free-and-easy 1960s who met a vampire, as the one in Jane Gaskell's *The Shiny Narrow Grin* (1964) did, would have been far more likely to think "Groovy!" than "Aaaargh!" Unfortunate immortals who have internalized and long carried with them the awful burden of generations of hatred, like the heroes of Anne Rice's *Interview with the Vampire* (1976) and its sequels, are ripe for psychoanalytic redemption, and any right-on shrink of today who happens to run into a vampire, as the one in

Suzy McKee Charnas's *The Vampire Tapestry* does, will naturally do her level best to help him feel good about himself (although, as Charnas scrupulously points out, it will not necessarily be to a vampire's advantage to find out that there is a lot of authentic heart-wringing humanity lurking in his predatory psyche). And when today's novelist looks back on the various phases of a vampire's career, as Chelsea Quinn Yarbro does in *Hôtel Transylvania* (1978) and its sequels, she has the delicious option of being able to portray him as an infinitely superior version of Lord Byron: sane, good and a pleasure to be laid by—a veritable lamb in rake's clothing!

* * * * * * *

It bears repeating that is not necessary, in order to write works like the abovementioned modern vampire stories, to be a literal social outsider in the way that Jean Lorrain always was and Rémy de Gourmont unfortunately became. Modern writers of vampire stories are, for the most part, amiable and well-adjusted people. One of the benefits of living in a chaotically pluralistic society, however, is that almost everyone with an atom of imagination can very easily see himself (or herself) as an outsider of some sort.

Many of the words that we have coined in order to describe this state of outsiderhood are vaguely pejorative—those old sociological favorites "alienation" and "anomie" are cardinal examples—but we still can, and should, think of the capacity to imagine oneself as an outsider as a *benefit*. Those unfortunate people who long for reconnection to some kind of quasi-organic social whole, whether it be on the scale of the nuclear family or the socialist Utopia, are suffering from a delusive disorder closely akin to other saccharine sicknesses like nostalgia and romantic infatuation. It is true that feeling like an alien is conducive to a certain paranoid unease, but it is surely time to recognize and admit that anyone in today's world who does not feel at least slightly paranoid is as mad as a hatter.

Given all this, it is not at all surprising that modern fictions whose purpose is the elaborate and fascinated study of the hypothetical existential predicament of the vampire should be popular.

Not all exercises in vampire fiction are consciously and elaborately based in a deep-seated sense of the author's own alien-ness, and one would naturally be wary of drawing such a conclusion in respect of an author who had never put such a conviction on the public record. In the case of Brian Stableford, however, there is no need to draw upon privileged information in order to establish that this is the case. Readers interested in the particular evolution and precise form of this sensibility can find a tediously elaborate account of it in the autobiographical essay that Stableford wrote for the "Profession of Science Fiction" series in the journal *Foundation*, which makes it obvious that a profoundly awkward sense of alien-ness colored Stableford's literary taste long before he was capable of analyzing it, and later became an important aspect of his various critical analyses of the history of the literary vampire (most notably the essay "Eroticism in Supernatural Literature" in *The Survey of Modern Fantasy Literature*, 1983). His two vampire novels, *The Empire of Fear* (1988) and *Young Blood* (1992), must be viewed as a kind of spin-off from this interested critical analysis.

* * * * * * *

The Empire of Fear (1988) grew out of a short story, "The Man Who Loved the Vampire Lady" (written in 1986 but not published until 1988). The story develops a science-fictional version of vampirism, which roots the powers and predilections of its blood-dependent species in their physiology. These vampires are not fugitive predators forever in hiding; their peculiar superhumanity has given them the means to become an aristocracy ruling over the mass of "common men" throughout Europe and Asia.

The traditional image of the vampire must of necessity be altered if vampirism is to be made a matter of biology rather than being frankly supernatural. Those trappings that seem purely superstitious and logically incoherent—fear of crosses; the absence of reflections in mirrors; a necessity to sleep in coffins lined with native soil—have to be discarded. Stableford goes further than this in one vital respect; his vampires can walk abroad in daylight. The three indispensable characteristics of the vampire that he retains are: (a) the necessity to feed on human blood; (b) longevity and relative invulnerability to injury; and (c) extraordinary sexual attractiveness. The first of these attributes is, of course, definitive; the second is merely traditional; the third lies at the heart of the purely literary functions of the motif.

The reconstruction of vampires as living beings rather than undead ones inevitably requires some rethinking in respect of the mechanism by which vampires make more vampires. Even writers working with more traditional vampires have been forced to make modifications of this kind by the logical problems implicit in the population explosion effect described by Stephen King in *'Salem's*

Lot (1975). Mindful of the claims made by certain critics that *Dracula* can be read as an allegory of syphilis, Stableford decided to make the biological vampirism of "The Man Who Loved the Vampire Lady" a form of sexually-transmitted disease; the real world had obligingly provided a topical exemplar. In the world of "The Man Who Loved the Vampire Lady" only male vampires can make more vampires, although they are themselves confused and misled by their own magical theories about how they accomplish that result. The rate at which they can "reproduce" is slowed by virtue of their suffering a diminution of virility proportional to their potential longevity. Thus, the vampire aristocracy is slow to expand by comparison with the potential for growth that the population of common men retains.

One convenient corollary of this subsidiary hypothesis is that the activities of heterosexual vampires produce a disproportionate number of eternally-young and unusually beautiful female vampires. (They are unusually beautiful partly by virtue of being disease-free, and partly by virtue of a mysterious luster which this species of vampirism confers on human skin). The logic of the situation implies that these female vampires inevitably prefer common lovers—by reason of their virility—and that they set aesthetic standards with which common women cannot easily compete. This provides a supposedly rational basis for an assumption intrinsic to the vast majority of modern vampire stories: that supernatural lovers are intrinsically more attractive and exciting than common-or-garden partners could ever be.

"The Man Who Loved the Vampire Lady" is set in the seventeenth century of a Europe to which vampirism has been introduced in the distant past by Attila the Hun, thus altering the consequent history of the divided Roman Empire; the discovery of America has not taken place, and Great Britain remains, in political terms, part of France. The seventeenth century is selected as the most appropriate time to display the hypothesis because it was the era in our own history in which the scientific method and the scientific imagination both took wing; the story attempts to exploit the melodrama inherent in the moment when common men first begin to set aside their superstitious awe of the vampires and began to think of vampirism as a gift of nature rather than magic.

The key image of "The Man Who Loved the Vampire Lady" is the microscope. The story turns on the hypothesis that the new kind of insight that the microscope promises and symbolizes might be enough in itself—irrespective of whether anything relevant can actually be seen therein—to make the vampires fear for their empire and common men confident that it might be overturned. In order to supply the story with a human dimension it employs a central character, Edmund Cordery, who is in a crucially ambiguous position. He is a trusted lackey of the vampire aristocracy, but is secretly a revolutionary working against them; his private emotions are equally ambivalent, for he has reached his position largely as a result of having been the lover of an influential vampire lady. It is she who is delegated by her own kind to be the agent of his destruction, and his reasons for attempting to be the agent of hers are appropriately mixed.

* * * * * * *

After writing "The Man Who Loved the Vampire Lady" the author began to collect other plotworthy corollaries of the central complex of ideas. Some of these emerged while he was listening to papers and discussions at the International Conference on the Fantastic in the Arts in Houston in 1987, including those in which the editors of the present volume took part (but they are not, of course, in any way to blame for the contents of the novel—or, for that matter, the contents of this paper). Understandably, given that he was employed at the time as a teacher of sociology, offering courses in the philosophy of social science and the sociology of literature, Stableford became intrigued by the notion that different cultures might react quite differently to the introduction of biologically-based vampirism, and that African tribal societies might more easily accommodate it into their religion than European societies, thus producing a very different kind of élite. It is not entirely surprising, given this and his constant predilection for inverting and subverting other people's plots, that the core of *The Empire of Fear* is an alternative-historical African lost race adventure that sets out to pervert and overturn all the key images and imperialistic values of H. Rider Haggard's *She*.

In the interests of melodrama, *The Empire of Fear* also takes care to involve some well-known characters from our own history. Richard the Lionheart replaces the "Girard" who was credited with being the ruler of "Grand Normandy" in "The Man Who Loved the Vampire Lady". Extensive off-stage roles are given to Francis Bacon and Kenelm Digby, and a less extensive (but subtly crucial) one to Simon Sturtevant. Richard reappears to play a part in the big battle that eventually settles the fate of this alternative Europe, once the central characters have returned from their African lost land with the secret of vampirism. In this part of the novel a quasi-Spanish Armada sets forth to destroy Malta, carrying an army of marines under the joint leadership of Richard and (how could any author have resisted the temptation?) Vlad the Impaler, *alias* Dracula—or, as his scribes more often signed the name, Dragulya. In order to replace the (dead) hero of the original novelette, and to reproduce his strangely mixed feelings about vampire ladies, *The Empire of Fear* also has a connecting episode in which Edmund Cordery's son Noell undergoes a crucially problematic sentimental education; this sequence also introduces the other major characters: the pirate Langoisse, his mistress Leilah, and the scholar-monk Quintus.

In order to make the plot work, the author is forced to develop an element of vampire nature that he had not brought out in the novelette: it is necessary, in order that their secrets may not be obtained from them by torture, that these vampires have an immunity to pain as well as to injury. As a result of being required to make this move, the author became intrigued by certain hypotheses regarding the evolutionary and existential costs and benefits of pain, which gave rise to important sub-themes in some of his later works, most notably *The Angel of Pain* (1991).

The Empire of Fear ends with a coda set in the present day of the alternative world, whose events mirror (in cunningly distorted fashion) the events of the opening novelette, and which includes a full account of the biochemistry of the version of vampirism used in the book. This part of the story completes the process by which vampirism—which had at first been viewed by all the inhabitants of the alternative world as a kind of quasi-demonic magic—is ultimately domesticated by medicine and biotechnology, as would be inevitable with any matter of physiology.

The author was fully aware while designing this plot of the remarkably bad press that the idea of immortality has had in fantasy and SF (see, for instance, his entry on "Immortality" in the Peter Nicholls *Encyclopedia of Science Fiction*, 1979) and he set out deliberately to reverse a commonplace plotline by which an apparently-benevolent immortality turns into a curse. In *The Empire of Fear* an apparently-monstrous immortality (or, strictly speaking, emortality) turns out to be a great boon *even to those unlucky individuals who cannot attain it.* This supremely happy conclusion (surely the happiest imaginable!) reaffirms that the eponymous empire that is cast down in the story is *not* the imperium ruled by the vampires—which is only metaphorically an "empire of fear"—but the domination of human thought by superstitious dread, which is a perfectly literal "empire of fear".

* * * * * * *

The metaphorical links between the species of vampirism envisaged in *The Empire of Fear* and AIDS left some critics less than delighted. Robert Latham, in a review in *Necrofile*, went so far as to condemn the novel as "homophobic", although that was certainly not the author's intention. One of the main characters—Langoisse—is certainly homophobic, but it may be worth noting that the effect of his homophobia is twice to deny him the vampiric immortality that is his dearest desire, once when he rudely rejects Richard's advances to him and again when his desire to revenge himself for that "insult" results in his death. Noell Cordery's attitude to homosexuality is also rather fearful, but this is a mere corollary of his general attitude to sex, which is intrinsically tormented. Given that one of the subtexts of the novel is a commentary on the essential perversity of the sexual impulse, this is not entirely surprising. (It might also be noted that it is a marked idiosyncrasy of this particular author to use decidedly unheroic protagonists with whom it is often difficult to sympathize; as to whether this reflects some deep-seated self-dissatisfaction on the part of the author, we can, of course, only speculate.)

The Empire of Fear sets before the reader an uncommonly straightforward version of the metaphorical equivalence of vampirism and sexual intercourse that we find in such stories as "Le Magnolia" and "Le Verre de sang". The female vampires featured in the story habitually combine the taking of blood with sexual activity, and it is implied that this is commonplace. The female vampires can, in effect, use their sexual favors to "reward" common lovers for their donations of blood. The male vampires, however, are in a very different situation—the only reward they have to offer those whom they victimize is a remote possibility of recruitment to the vampire ranks. Although some male vampires, including Richard, do have "favorites" who serve as suppliers of blood, others—notably Dragulya—sneer at such sentimentalization and adopt a strictly pragmatic attitude to the routines of sanguinary predation.

This difference of attitude is reflected in the political ideas of the male vampires: Richard is a true believer in the divine right of kings and the (intrinsically hypocritical) chivalric ethos of feudalism, while Dragulya is the kind of cynical opportunist whose philosophies are shrewdly analyzed in Machiavelli's classic study of *The Vampire Prince*. The political allegory in *The Empire of Fear*, although fully conscious, is, however, a subsidiary theme. The main effect of the differences in sexual physiology between the male and female vampires of this alternative world is dramatically to exaggerate the differences of attitude to matters of sexuality that exist between vampire lords and vampire ladies—and which inevitably have their effect upon the attitudes of the common men and women who live, as it were, in their shadow. What relevance such a bizarre hypothetical situation might have to the differences of attitude to matters of sexuality that common men and women have in a vampireless world it is not easy to judge, but if common men and women did not have an intense and intimate interest in the creation and contemplation of such hypothetical possibilities, the sexual fantasies of common men and women would be far less rich and exotic than they probably are.

* * * * * * *

Young Blood is as different from *The Empire of Fear* as the author could contrive, although it similarly sets out, quite explicitly, to examine and exploit the sexual sub-texts that underlie modern vampire fiction. It confronts the image and the role of the Byronic vampire in a much more straightforward fashion than its predecessor, and there is no ambiguity at all about the representation of blood-drinking as an intrinsically sexual experience.

The vampire in *Young Blood* is a dark-cloaked demon lover named Maldureve, who is conjured out of the shadowy borderlands of existence by a neurotic girl. He is at once protective and threatening, exotically compounded out of her contorted anxieties and repressed desires. He is more traditional, in this respect, than the vampires of *The Empire of Fear*, but he too is modified so as to fit in more easily with a rational world-view. Like the vampires of *The Empire of Fear*, Maldureve (his name, as the text scrupulously points out, is a silly play on words) has no fangs. Such questions as his attitude to garlic and crosses, and his reflectability in mirrors, simply never arise—but he does eventually acquire the power to manifest himself by day.

The narrative of *Young Blood* is divided into three main parts, with a coda that throws the preceding events into a new perspective. Parts one and two show the fundamental situation—the visitation of the vampire—from two sharply contrasted points of view. Both are narrated in the first person, part one by Anne Charet, who assumes that Maldureve and the other apparitions that follow in his wake are objectively real, and part two by her human boy-friend Gil Molari, who takes it as axiomatic that any apparently-supernatural occurrence must be a subjective hallucination. Part three reverts to Anne's point of view, although she is now forced by circumstance gradually to modify her opinions, and the reader—having been presented with a dramatically different but strangely-concluded account of events in part two—is bound to regard the resumed discourse in a very different light

* * * * * * *

There is, of course, a long tradition of horror stories and metaphysical fantasies that play with alternative explanations of apparently-supernatural events. Tzvetan Todorov has even taken the trouble to construct a "theory" that argues, at length and with altogether unwarranted ponderousness, the brutally simple thesis that stories in which the contest between objective and subjective interpretations remains unresolved belong to a distinct genre (the "fantastic"). In a good deal of recent horror fiction, however, the question of whether the events experienced by the characters are "real" or "illusory" simply does not matter; this is no longer a question of any real narrative importance, and is certainly not a question whose answer could any longer provide a sense of *resolution*. "And then he woke up..." is not nowadays acceptable as a method of ending a story; by the same token, the central character's realization that he or she *isn't* dreaming cannot function as a conclusion either. A modern story that focuses on the question of whether the events it describes are real or illusory has somehow to renew the sharpness of that question, and its resolution has to go beyond the simple choice of "yes", "no" or "I'm not going to tell you, so there". This is what *Young Blood* tries to do.

In order to sharpen the question of whether the vampire in *Young Blood* is real or not, the author equips the two central characters with very specific intellectual resources. Anne is a student of philosophy, who is therefore ready, willing and able to debate with herself at some length and in some depth exactly what might be implied by acceptance of the "reality" of a vampire. Gil is a research student engaged in the study of psychotropic viruses, who can hardly help but interpret bizarre experiences according to the assumption that he has accidentally become infected by his own materials. The introduction of the notion of "psychotropic viruses" also opens up scope for a conclusion in which the subjective and the objective can be interestingly intertwined, in such a way that their implied mutual exclusivity breaks down. Because of this, the eventual conclusion of the novel is not "fantastic" by default—which is what happens when an author simply abandons the reader to indecision regarding alternative readings of the events—but "fantastic" by design. There is, in the coda, a metaphysical readjustment of what have earlier been seen as alternative readings, which endeavors to bring them into an unanticipated harmony.

* * * * * * *

One of the most interesting things about the game of subjective/objective, as played in *Young Blood,* is that the metaphysical issues that arise in connection with the question of whether Maldureve is a real vampire or a hallucination induced by a psychotropic virus are inevitably reflected in the blatantly sexual sub-text. Thus, what starts out as a particular instance of perverse sexual fantasy eventually becomes extrapolated into something much more peculiar. The convoluted plot proceeds unerringly to the kind of climax specified by tradition—a final confrontation between the heroine (armed with a pointed stake) and the vampire (rendered helpless by circumstance)—but, by the time that climactic moment arrives, the question of what, if anything, the staking of the vampire might symbolize or achieve is wide open.

There is a certain level of risk involved when any male writer attempts to tell a story from the viewpoint of a young girl—especially if he is a writer who has been accused by reviewers, as Stableford has on more than one occasion, of not being able to draw convincing female characters. The hazards are redoubled when the narrative's focal point is the sexuality of the character in question, and further increased when that sexuality is supposed to be so tormented by anxiety as to have become neurotic. Noell Cordery's peculiar attitude to vampire lovers, although unprecedented in maters of mere detail, can easily be likened to the attitudes of countless heroes of Gautieresque erotic fantasy, but Anne Charet's peculiar attitude to Maldureve and his various natural and supernatural "rivals" does not readily fall into any pre-existent literary category. The closest analogues—which the author undoubtedly had in mind while constructing his plot—are probably the allegories of female maturation wrought by the inversion of traditional fairy tale themes by Angela Carter in *The Bloody Chamber* (1979).

Because of the intimacy of the narrative, *Young Blood* is much more obviously a sustained erotic fantasy than *The Empire of Fear*. It has no reconstructed history or political allegory to deflect attention away from the sexual allegory, by means of which Anne's desires and fears are transmuted into extraordinary experience. The metaphysical issues that are raised, as the two central characters strive to make sense of what is happening, introduce a certain intellectual coolness into the ongoing orgy of exotic orgasms, but the characters continually turn their philosophically-informed points of view upon their own processes of sexual and emotional development, re-emphasizing the erotic foundations of the narrative. The true irony of the coda is not what it reveals about the reality or otherwise of the events that have taken place in the course of the story, but the fashion in which it cynically re-appraises the existential significance of sex as a biological phenomenon.

Despite what the narrative voice actually says in the final paragraphs there will probably be few readers who will consider the ending to be an uplifting one, but *Young Blood*—like *The Empire of Fear*—is a science fiction novel rather than a horror story, and it maintains a commitment, however perverse, to the idea and the ideal of progress. All of the author's recent fiction is dedicated to this ideal, although some of his rhetorical strategies are undeniably peculiar.

* * * * * * *

Young Blood borrows—as *The Empire of Fear* had done in a more oblique fashion—from an ongoing critical analysis of vampire fiction, which is a notable feature of the annual International Conference for the Fantastic in the Arts. The argument of a paper presented there in 1991 by Lloyd Worley is transplanted, lock, stock and barrel (with the original author's permission and blessing), into the mouth of one of the subsidiary characters. The argument in question suggests that our continued uneasy fascination with the vampire motif may be rooted in that experience of vampiric existence that we all have as a result of spending nine months in the womb and a further nine (or more) obtaining nourishment by suckling. Whether this is true or not remains a matter of conjecture, but it is a beautiful hypothesis not only because it seems so neat but also because it seems so disturbing. The popularity of vampires in modern fiction has nothing to do with any residuum of obsolete folkloristic beliefs and everything to do with the most intimate transactions imaginable by our anxious and desirous minds.

Just as the blue blood that courses in our veins is instantly transmuted by the alchemy of oxygenation to something richly and arterially red whenever it is shed, so something else that is secret and unseen is transformed by narrative expression into that red milk upon which literary vampires feed. We know that it is a "vital fluid" of some kind, but we do not know exactly what; symbolism is the only imaginative instrument we have with which to search, and probe, and draw hypotheses. Such hypotheses cannot be tested in the scientific sense, because the only jury to which we can deliver them for consideration is the wayward tribunal of the emotions, where horror and erotic excitement substitute for reason and the balance of probabilities. Nevertheless, the process has a ritual value not un-akin to the ritual value that the operations of science and the law have, over and above their utilitarian functions.

Whatever faults *The Empire of Fear* and *Young Blood* may have, they may surely lay claim to a certain kind of intellectual seriousness. Like so many of the stories in whose footsteps they follow, they are colorfully eccentric, wildly playful and flirtatiously horrific, but they are not blunt instruments. Their narrative scalpels are aimed to uncover and display those nerves that they aspire, in their own calculatedly nasty-minded fashion, to twist.

LAST AND FIRST MAN: TOMORROW'S ADAM AND ETERNITY'S EVE

There was once a joke in common circulation which proposed that the shortest short story in the world read as follows: "The last man in the world sat alone in his room. There was a knock on the door...."

This formula does not appear to have started life as a story or a joke, but rather as a specimen of a "narrative hook" offered by the American writer Thomas Bailey Aldrich in the 1870s. By the time *The Magazine of Fantasy & Science Fiction* was founded in 1949, however, it had become a common item of literary folklore, and it provided the writers who worked for the magazine during its first ten years with a theme for frequent variation. It was often quoted and sometimes straightforwardly expanded—as, for instance, in "The Last Shall Be First" (1958) by the magazine's sometime editor Robert P. Mills.

The item's establishment as an item of popular concern within the SF field owed a considerable debt to Fredric Brown, a prolific author of brief science-fictional "Shaggy Dog stories" framed for the purpose of producing amusing or blithely awful punch lines. Brown had examined one of the many new variations that genre SF had added to the potential inherent in Aldrich's story-seed in "Knock", which appeared in the December 1948 issue of *Thrilling Wonder Stories*. The protagonist of the story is preserved by aliens as an exhibit in a zoo, following their extermination of almost all life on Earth. The story begins and ends by quoting the Aldrich hook, but the plot changes its significance considerably, by observing that the aliens had preserved a last woman along with the last man.

The unusual popularity enjoyed by further variations on this elementary theme during the 1950s presumably had two significant causes. Firstly, the growth and complication of science fiction's standard vocabulary of ideas had opened up a wealth of possibilities beyond the obvious ambiguity contained in the word "man". Secondly, the advent of the atom bomb at Hiroshima in 1945 had made it far easier to imagine that the day when the last man might find himself alone in the world might actually be close at hand.

In a science fiction story, the knocker at the door could no longer be assumed to be Death, the last woman, or some supernatural monster; it could as easily be an alien, a robot or a dog with artificially-augmented intelligence, none of which possibilities was *necessarily* menacing. In addition, the moment that marked the end of the human story could easily be dissolved by the casual invocation of a time machine. It had always been the case that the last man was potentially the first in a new order, and that his temporary isolation might simply be a desirable psychological preparation for a new beginning, but science fiction provided a host of imaginative devices by which the last man might achieve this phoenix-like renewal, even if he really were the last of his species. As the pulp magazines died, and the action/adventure formulas that had dominated genre science fiction were supplemented by shorter slicker and wittier story-forms of the kind that *The Magazine of Fantasy & Science Fiction* set out to provide, this kind of clever-variation-on-a-familiar-theme became a staple of the digest magazines. It was further employed as a throwaway device in many brief "fillers", which dutifully recorded the serial recomplication of the "shortest story ever written" joke.

This potential was already wide open to exploitation when the culmination of the Manhattan Project lent new urgency to *all* apocalyptic fantasies dramatizing the possibility that human beings might soon be the agents of their own extermination. The serious contemplation of awful possibilities always has an inbuilt tendency to progress from stark tragedy to macabre comedy, and the vocabulary of ideas developed by genre science fiction provided the means for this progress to be achieved with remarkable rapidity and considerable ingenuity. Heartfelt after-the-bomb tragedies were almost immediately supplemented by after-the-bomb jokes, whose black humor often took the form of importing some manifest absurdity into the predicament of the last man.

* * * * * * *

Romances tracking the ordeal of the sole survivor of a catastrophe had, of course, been around for a long time before the advent of the atom bomb. The Biblical version of the Deluge allowed Noah to preserve his entire family, but not all the parallel myths and reca-pitulations thereof were as generous. There were always commenta-tors who took the minimalist approach to catastrophist fantasy even while they admitted that the "last" men of the distant past must have found mates somehow.

The most extreme formula of catastrophist fantasy eventually became so familiar as to constitute a dire cliché. Its modern form is the most commonly-repeated device of what Brian Aldiss dubbed "Shaggy God" stories: the story in which the two people who sur-vive what appears to be a futuristic catastrophe turn out in the end, as they contemplate their new safe haven, to be named Adam and Eve.

It was inevitable that imaginative literature would be haunted from its inception by the anxious contemplation of future Deluges occasioned by the fatal discordance of reckless human pride and stern divine dictatorship. Whenever writers contemplated the state of their own world and compared it to the imaginary Golden Ages wrought by historical nostalgia, they were bound to worry that some such day of reckoning might be close at hand. A rash of such fanta-sies appeared when the ideals of the Enlightenment seemed to have foundered in the aftermath of the French Revolution, spearheaded by Jean-Baptiste Cousin de Grainville's *Le Dernier homme* (1805).

The collective anguish of those who followed rapidly in Cousin de Grainville's footsteps is deemed to be evidence of a crucial divi-sion of human consciousness by Ryszard Dubanski in "The Last Man Theme in Modern Fantasy and Science Fiction" (1979). Ac-cording to Dubanski, these works and their modern equivalents trace "the development of an awareness of the unlimited potentialities and possibilities of experience inherent in the modern world"; for him, the last man is the ultimate individual, stripped of all the social props that connect the stream of private thought and feeling to the ocean of collective consciousness. What Dubanski says is correct, but we must not forget that the last man is not merely *separate* but also *summary*; the microcosm of his isolation continues to reflect and embody the macrocosm that produced him. The fate of the last man is not only a judgment of him as an individual; it is also a judgment of mankind as a whole. In the evolution of last man fanta-sies we can track the progress of man the individual *and* the pro-gress of the greater whole from which he is outcast.

When Thomas Campbell's last man of 1823 instructs the sun to "Tell the night that hides thy face/Thou saw'st the last of Adam's race,/On Earth's sepulchral clod,/The darkening universe defy/To quench his Immortality/Or shake his trust in God!" he is not only asserting a distinctly Protestant faith in his own contract with the deity; he is also underlining the fact that God has made special provision for the entire species and that the end of life on earth is merely a prelude. When Mary Shelley's last man of 1826 reports that "Neither hope nor joy are my pilots—restless despair and fierce desire of change lead me on" he is not only asserting that each individual human being is ill-equipped to live without companionship but that whatever psychological pressure (e.g. Frankensteinian obsession) or force of circumstance (e.g. widowhood) forces us towards loneliness is better combated by "fierce desire of change" than timid hope; unlike Campbell, Mary Shelley was not prepared to reckon the French revolution a potentially-fatal fracture in history.

Even in the early nineteenth century, the last man motif was ripe for infusion by a more ironic spirit. Thomas Hood's last man of 1826 (whose parodic aspect refers to Campbell) achieves that status by appointing himself prosecutor, judge, jury and executioner of a beggar who has dared to rob the abundant dead, then realizes to his distress that, were he to hang himself, "There is not another man alive/In the world, to pull my legs!" In carrying his individual folly to the bitter end he is also, quite blatantly, carrying forward the spirit of his age and offering a sharp admonition to the presumed self-satisfaction of the poem's readers.

Hood's last man is more directly deserving of his sorry fate than Campbell's or Shelley's, but the very essence of Diluvian fantasy is that the world's destruction is *always* deserved, and that the individual cannot avoid responsibility, either for the sins of his fellows, or his own isolation. The decline of belief in God neither ameliorated nor displaced this kind of guilt, and often served to enhance it. The virtue of Noah's obedience came into question while the culpability of those denied access to the Ark still remained.

The exaggeration of the sense of guilt contained in those last man stories that passed beyond the scope of Campbell's steadfast piety is startlingly obvious in the novel that concluded the list of last man fantasies penned in the nineteenth century: M. P. Shiel's Millennial fantasy *The Purple Cloud* (magazine publication 1900; book 1901). Here Adam Jeffson (who is, in symbolic terms, the Biblical Job as well as his namesake) rages against the role apparently allotted to him by his eventual discovery of the last woman, of restoring a race "to bear the wrongs, Inquisitions, rack-rents, Waterloos [and] unspeakable horrors" that had festered in the world eclipsed by the cloud. The madness that consumes Jeffson in his solitude is more extreme than that which descended upon Mary Shelley's survivor; the faith that saves him is not only required to be far more sophisticated than Campbell's stubborn orthodoxy, but also far more refined in its definition of the change that is fiercely to be desired if the world is, indeed, to be allowed the grace and favor of further human habitation.

* * * * * * *

The twentieth century began—as might be expected given the tendency of imaginative writers to attribute quasi-mystical significance to round numbers—on a more hopeful note. George C. Wallis's "The Last Days of Earth", which appeared in the July 1901 issue of *The Harmsworth Magazine* immediately after the conclusion of the serial version *The Purple Cloud* in *The Royal Magazine*, begins on the afternoon of Thursday July 18th, 13,000,085 A.D. and ends with the spaceship carrying the last man and his bride hurtling into the unknown with all potential open. The story was not influential in itself but many others were to follow in its train. Until the advent of the atom bomb, the main tendency in the popular futuristic fiction of the new century was to assume that the future of the human race was to be measured in millions of years, its limit set (if at all) by the lifespan of the sun.

At such a distance of imaginative contemplation it became easy enough to write such heartfelt requiems as Lowell Howard Morrow's "Omega, the Man" (1933), whose last man is an explicit embodiment of all the noble savagery of a humankind produced, perfected and ultimately passed over by the implacable thrust of Darwinian evolution—a process that ground so slowly and so exceeding small as to make the mills of God seem lightning-fast and lightning-furious by comparison. Soon after their initial foundation, the science fiction pulps began to entertain such improbable novelties as Wallace West's "The Last Man" (1929) and its tongue-in-cheek companion-piece, Thomas B. Gardner's "The Last Woman" (1932). This was perhaps the first instance of the tit-for-tat exchange of ideas that became fundamental to the ideology of the *Magazine of Fantasy & Science Fiction*.

The pulps also opened up scope for calculated assaults on the arrogance of such contemporary thought as would not admit the force and implication of Darwinian arguments. Frank Belknap Long's romance of evolutionary supersession "The Last Men" (1934) is one such tale. The *real* implicit message of science fiction, however, was—and still is—that nothing is inevitable, and that no matter how extreme the plight of the last man might seem to be, the infinite future still lies before him, ripe for exploitation if only he can summon up the requisite ingenuity. In this respect, Charnock Walsby's slight comedy "The Last Man" (1941) is as typical in its silliness as it is in its seriousness, although the most impressive early tale of this kind (and the only one that is still remembered) is Alfred Bester's "Adam and No Eve" (1941). This is an *authentic* last man story, which flatly refuses to cheat but nevertheless insists that what has been might one day be again, and that there is *always* scope for purposive action in the face of ultimate disaster.

There were, of course, premonitory tales of atomic Armageddon in the pre-war science fiction pulps. Some had a certain urgency about them even before Hiroshima, and some had a measure of irony as well, but the pragmatic world-view fervently impressed upon the pulp genre by Hugo Gernsback and John W. Campbell Jr. forbade such near-nihilism as was to be found, for instance, in Alfred Noyes' *The Last Man* (1940)—the novel that introduced the notion of the "doomsday weapon". By the time he wrote *The Last Man*, Noyes—who had earlier been enthusiastic in his championship of science—had been converted to a religious orthodoxy every bit as stubborn as Thomas Campbell's, reflected in the bizarre climactic twist that provided his last man with an abbey full of Benedictine monks as well as a last woman, so that he and she might have more elaborate spiritual guidance than had been laid on in Eden for Adam and Eve. After 1945, however, even American science fiction writers could see that alarmists like Noyes might have a point—and when Walter M. Miller eventually came to chronicle the future history of the Abbey Leibowitz in *A Canticle for Leibowitz* (1960), he could hardly help but set that institution adrift upon a relentless tide of lachrymose black humor.

* * * * * * *

The story that set the tone for *The Magazine of Fantasy & Science Fiction*'s sarcastic variations on "the shortest short story in the world" was Damon Knight's "Not with a Bang" (1950). Here, the last man struggles to overcome the reluctance of the last woman to begin the repopulation of the world without their first being married—an impractical proposition in the absence of a last clergyman. She relents when he offers her the best wedding-ceremony that can be contrived in the circumstances, but his plans are thwarted when he suffers a paralyzing seizure in a washroom. He realizes that no help can arrive because the paragon of propriety will *never* be able to pass through a door marked MEN.

Although this story is no more than a joke, it has become a classic of sorts, so frequently reprinted that it is probably familiar to most followers of the genre, irrespective of whether they were able to catch its original appearance in 1950. Perhaps better than any work since Thomas Hood's, it succeeds in passing judgment on a key folly of its time, achieving a neat satirical coup in fitting the punishment of world destruction to the crime of sexual prudishness—thus, of course, reversing the conventional symbolic decoding of the Biblical myth of the Fall.

It was readily appreciated, of course, that the cavalier absurdity of "Not with a Bang" overlay more serious issues. A sharper problem of propriety was posed by Sherwood Springer's "No Land of Nod" (1952), in which the last man's only surviving companion is his daughter. This situation was not without its Biblical precedent either, in the story of Lot, whose family was by no means as extended as Noah's when he was delegated to survive the destruction of Sodom and Gomorrah by fire. Springer's story was not published in *Fantasy & Science Fiction* but Ward Moore's dourly scathing "Lot" (1953) and its sequel "Lot's Daughter" (1954) were.

The by-now-inevitable companion-piece to "No Land of Nod" and "Lot" was supplied to another periodical by Wallace West, who had seen the trick worked before. In West's "Eddie for Short" (1953) the last woman has only a fetus for company, and no way of knowing, initially, whether it will offer her a slim chance of further conception. Incest also became the final duty in a *Magazine of Fantasy & Science Fiction* story that set out to parody all the newly-hatched clichés of science fiction simultaneously: "The Last Word" (1955) by Chad Oliver and Charles Beaumont. Presumably by coincidence, "The Last Word" appeared in the issue immediately before Richard Matheson's sarcastic but strangely sentimental account of a companionless last man's feebly heroic attempts to use science fiction as a prop for his sanity, "Pattern for Survival" (1955). Like "Not with a Bang," this story enjoyed a long afterlife by virtue of frequent reprinting and was adapted to provide one of several last man stories featured in the TV anthology series *The Twilight Zone*.

By the time that "Pattern for Survival" appeared, a whole decade had passed since Hiroshima. Tales of atomic holocaust had become very commonplace indeed, although the peril in which the world actually stood militated against their reduction to mere cliché.

Repetition became ritualized as necessary alarmism, rather than becoming contemptible through overfamiliarity. So intense was the sensation that humankind would deserve its fate, were the fateful button to be pressed, that many writers took a morbid glee in chronicling the obliteration of civilization and the end of the species. In Ronald Duncan's *The Last Adam* (1952) the last Eve fails to tempt the sole male survivor to play his allotted role, although she employs devices that the heroine of "Not with a Bang" could never have contemplated for an instant. In Mordecai Roshwald's *Level Seven* (1959), the last survivor of the holocaust passes the time writing witty parables and mordant poems, before confronting the final irony that the recorded music to which he is listening (Beethoven's *Eroica*) will go on playing long after there is no one to listen to it, its power to move and inspire rendered futile by the lack of anyone capable of emotion or inspiration. In both these stories—as in many others—the final sin is surrender; humankind, having possessed so much, has, in the end, nothing to offer but casual relinquishment; each last man's final gesture encapsulates the dismal failure of all that went before.

* * * * * * *

It is arguable that the atom bomb cast such a long shadow over the latter half of the twentieth century that no further evolution of the last man story has been possible since the 1950s, and that the specters that might be hovering outside his door had been thoroughly catalogued by the end of that decade. Perhaps this is true—but that does not mean that there is no more to be said about such fantasies, nor that the analysis of the ones that existed at the time can be completed by reference to the impact of Hiroshima and the perfection of science fiction's literary methodology. At least one more aspect of these stories requires further comment.

The irony that inhabits most of the last man stories of the 1950s is not entirely a matter of justice. Even at the beginning of the modern tradition, at least in the more elaborate works of Cousin de Grainville and Mary Shelley, there was a careful recognition of the fact that individualism *is* attractive. The separation of the individual from the collective was, after all, a voluntary matter—a heroic adventure as much as a surly flight—and some last man stories do pay homage to this awareness. The last man can, at least some of the time, take pleasure in his isolation. Occasionally, he is permitted actively to rejoice in his ownership of the world—but not for long.

It is possible that no daydream is more common than the fantasy of having the world to oneself, to do with as one might wish. This can, of course be accomplished by less drastic means than the explicit banishment of all others—by imagining oneself invisible, or capable of stopping time, so that one can be isolated and perfectly free even though everybody else still exists—but the fantasy of being the last person alive is the end and anchorage of the spectrum. In this sense, as well as the one already cited, the last man is also the first. The ruined world is a wonderland of opportunity and he is its emperor. No matter how sharp the pain of his solitude might be, he has fabulous compensation in terms of his possession and dominion. Mary Shelley's hero could not feel entirely comfortable with that dominion, even for an instant, but M. P. Shiel's could—and the fact that it eventually drove him mad did not *entirely* devalue the delight he took in the furnishing of his magnificent palace at Imbros.

Of all last men, Adam Jeffson is the most frankly Neronic, not merely capable of burning his acquisitions but of fiddling wildly while they burn, but there is a smattering of imperial decadence in every *honest* last man. This achievement is, however, drastically reduced by the ironic fact that possession is mainly a form of display. Who can know better than the last man that most of the things we own have no utilitarian value at all? Who can feel more keenly than he the frustration of having fine possessions *that no one is able to admire?* If the last man is Everyman by virtue of summarizing the hollow achievements of his age, he is also Everyman by virtue of embodying the universal need for *approval.* Everyone who falls prey, even occasionally, to the daydream of universal possession must also be able to identify with the frustration of its futility. The last man owns everything, but, without anyone else to see his triumph, he also owns nothing. This aspect of the last man's story affects the significance of the impending knock on the door almost as much as the possibilities that the sound opens up for the continuation of human history. Perhaps the final irony of "Not with a Bang" is not that the anti-hero will never possess the anti-heroine, but that she will never bear witness to his possession of anything else.

Even if this point is conceded, however, it might be argued that the acute sense of the essential paradox of individualism that is to be found in the best last man stories takes too little heed of the joys of solitude. Last man stories are, of course, not alone in that. Look up 'alone' in the index to any dictionary of quotations and you will be directed to a whole series of poetic plaints from Coleridge and Byron to T. S. Eliot, all proclaiming that isolation is Hell—but if it were, who would be a poet? And if it were, how could Jean-Jacques Rousseau ever have asserted, with all apparent conviction, that the best education a boy can attain is to be found in the luxurious pages of *Robinson Crusoe*?

If isolation is hell, it is only hell because we make it so, because we cannot bear to live with ourselves. Last man stories do acknowledge, at least some of the time, that news of permanent solitude is not all bad—and in that sense, if in no other, they can be reassuring as well as challenging. In a way, the most peculiar thing about last man stories is that so few of them *are* reassuring, and that such self-indulgence as they may occasionally show is so often employed as an overture to insanity.

We are now long past the time when desperate optimists hoped that every man's death might be a gateway to heaven, and that the even the death of the world need only be reckoned a test of faith for the last man: a temptation to the sin of despair that must and ought to be resisted. We understand now that such an extreme temptation could only have been worked by a Devil who had come to the brink of despair himself, and all but given up the game of temptation. Nowadays, we expect more ingenuity from the devil as well as from the last man—but the increase in our intelligence does not necessarily make us feel any better.

For all its ingenuity and plausibility, Alfred Bester's "Adam and no Eve" has no more power to console us than Frank Tipler's fervent assertion that we will all be resurrected by the ultimate computer at the Omega Point. For all its honesty regarding the heady delight that a man might take in the inheritance of all the works of man, and for all the fervor of its own conclusion that the deistic thrust of evolution can answer all doubts as to the ultimate kindness of Fate. Shiel's *The Purple Cloud* cannot console us either. If we are to add up the sum of all the last man stories so far written, we cannot deny that their aggregate effect is not merely tragic but also tired. Despite that the last shall also be first, in more ways than one, last man stories assure us that there is ultimately nothing for the last man to find in the contemplation of eternity's eve but *weltschmerz*.

* * * * * * *

It is, of course, possible that things will change now that the Cold War is over. Perhaps, as the threat of nuclear holocaust recedes, it will be possible for fantasists to discover and produce new kinds of last man stories. Perhaps it will be possible for them to set out new summaries of the failure of the contemporary world and new accounts of the way in which human extinction might serve the bitter ends of cosmic justice. Perhaps, even if they cannot become cheerful, last man stories will at least contrive to remain ingeniously witty.

On the other hand, it might be the case that the end of the Cold War, coinciding as it does with humankind's first tentative steps into space, will make the notion that there could ever be a last man seem increasingly absurd. Perhaps, sooner than we might suppose, we will all come to agree with Frank Tipler that, not only will there be humans at "the end of time," but that all the human beings who ever existed will be there, and that they will easily contrive to turn "the end of time" into a new beginning, without the merest trace of a whimper. Perhaps, then, last man stories will contrive to shake off the last remains of Decadent sensibility and offer us radically new accounts of the rebirth of everything.

I cannot tell which of these possible scenarios will come to pass. I can, however, set down one further addition to the stock of last man stories written in the wake of the shortest short story ever told, which must of necessity come down on one side or the other. I hope there is a sense in which that action will provide a firmer—and perhaps better—conclusion to this analysis than any conventional summary could.

THE LAST MAN

The last man in the world sat alone in his room, waiting for the knock at the door.

While he waited, the last man in the world thought about all the stories and anecdotes he had read or heard in which the last man in the world was sitting alone in his room when the fateful knock came.

He thought about the horror story versions in which the hearer of the tale was supposed to imagine that the knocker was Death, or the Devil, or some other horrible and hellish entity come to judge him on behalf of the malign Fate that had already annihilated all his human fellows.

He thought about the science-fictional versions in which the knocker was far more likely be a loyal robot, or a helpful alien, or an intellectually-augmented dog, any one of which would probably prove to be an invaluable companion and ally in the desperate years to come.

He thought about the happy non-sexist versions, in which it was the last woman who had beaten a path to his door, ready to play Eve to his Adam and start the whole story over again.

He thought about the militant feminist versions in which it was still the last woman who had come to the door, but in which she wasn't in the least ready to play Eve to his Adam, being rather more inclined to complete the job that malign Fate had begun, by sending him the same way that all other males of the species had gone—to oblivion.

With infinite care, the last man rehearsed a whole series of potential scripts. He intended to be ready for absolutely anything.

He knew exactly what he would say to Death. He knew exactly what he would say to the Devil. He knew exactly what he would say to a loyal robot. He knew exactly what he would say to a helpful alien—in sign language, if necessary. He knew exactly what he would say to an intellectually-augmented dog. He knew exactly what he would say to a would-be Eve, and he knew exactly what he would say to a wouldn't-be Eve.

He was prepared for every possible eventuality, except one.

The last man in the world sat alone in his room, waiting.

The knock on the door never came.

* * * * * * *

Somewhere—perhaps not very far away—the last woman in the world was sitting alone in her room, thinking deeply and remorsefully about the awful malignity of Fate.

There was a lock on the door—but she knew exactly what she would say and do if ever it were broken.

END OF STORY

It remains possible, of course, that I will write further last man stories in the future. Nothing is ever finished, until it's finished. If last man stories prove nothing else, they certainly prove that.

END OF ESSAY

THE ART OF THE GHOST STORY

In *Appearances of the Dead: A Cultural History of Ghosts* (1982) R. C. Finucane describes the manner in which attitudes to ghosts have changed over the centuries, reflecting the gradually-diminishing dependence of our beliefs and social practices on tradition. He observes that preliterate societies usually take the goodwill of their ancestors seriously enough to maintain routine communication with the dead, whose accumulated wisdom is invaluable, although their opinions are usually critical of alleged deteriorations of moral standards.

In Western Christendom these sociably assertive ghosts gradually gave way to "purgatorial ghosts" who were imagined to be doing painful penance of some kind, and were preoccupied with matters of vengeful justice and legitimate inheritance, frequently denouncing criminals and revealing hidden treasures. In more recent and more skeptical times, phantoms of this kind have also built up a profitable sideline as comforters, reassuring the clients of professional intercessors as to the reality of personal immortality and soothing the regret of loss.

Finucane argues that the growth of individualism in Western society, and the consequent disintegration of extended families, made the original social functions of ghosts redundant. It was, he suggests, inevitable that ghosts would begin to fade away, becoming tenuous and enigmatic where once they had been insistent and obvious. As Philippe Ariès points out in *L'Homme devant la mort* (1977), however, this fading process coincided with the development of a new horror of death: a fascinated post-Enlightenment existential anxiety, whose emergence was marked by "the eroticism of the macabre". Although people had always been afraid to die, Ariès argues, it was only when they were simultaneously disturbed by the revelations of anatomy and the advancement of egotism that anxiety "crossed the threshold into the unspeakable, the inexpressible". It was the crossing of this threshold that gave birth to the modern ghost story, and remains fundamental to its artistry.

It is, of course, necessary to distinguish between literary fictions and the anecdotal kinds of ghost story that persist today in such popular items of urban folklore as the tale of the vanishing hitch-hiker. The primary purpose of accounts of "real" ghosts is to maintain a defiant challenge to the skeptical orthodoxy that defeated credulity—after a long battle—in the Enlightenment of the eighteenth century; the anecdotal ghost story is a defensive weapon against the despotism of reason, carefully preserving a reservoir of the inexplicable against the deadening oppression of outright materialism. The literary ghost story is much more aggressive in its intent, even when its apparitions are so faint as to be almost illusory; its objective is no mere statement of the trivial fact that there are matters beyond the reach of our understanding, but a heroic attempt to discover a voice for the unspeakable, a form for the inexpressible. This is, admittedly, a paradoxical task—but in fiction, nothing is impossible.

The ghosts of tribal societies usually had their own Underworld, where they could be visited, or from which they could be recalled, albeit with difficulty. As Western society has progressed, however, and routine intercourse between the living and the dead has been discontinued, the ghosts that humans encounter have been conceptualized with increasing frequency as those spirits who are for one reason or another unable or unwilling to pass on to their own place. It is these unlucky spirits in whom writers of fiction have been most interested, and in whose characterization literature has played the most crucial part. This was an inevitable development, because such spirits are, by definition, the spirits whose stories are incomplete. Having departed life before bringing their personal narratives to a satisfactory closure, they stand in dire need of the further extrapolation and final relief that fiction alone can provide. The art of the ghost story lies in the technique and moral propriety of this process of extrapolation and climactic achievement.

Loitering spirits of this kind are usually anchored, sometimes to their burial places, but more often to their erstwhile homes, or to particular rooms within those homes. Until the end of the nineteenth century, such haunted rooms were usually to be found in the mansions of the aristocracy, where the relevant manifestations remained family affairs, but, as the traditional aristocracies of Europe have evaporated, aristocratic ghosts condemned to this kind of penal servitude inevitably came into confrontation with a new breed of *nouveau riche* strangers. (The shift in attitude this entails is neatly summarized—poignantly as well as wittily—in Oscar Wilde's *fin-de-siècle* account of "The Canterville Ghost".) In the twentieth century, ghosts and their anchorages have spread out across the whole of the social spectrum. The evidence of the relevant fiction suggests that the dead are as uncomfortable as the living in cheap modern housing, that their long-standing reputation as uniquely bad neighbors has been equaled, if not surpassed, by the people along the street.

* * * * * * *

The first invasion of fiction by a host of phantoms occurred in the pages of the horror stories that were produced in great profusion in Germany at the end of the nineteenth century, the Gothic novels that deluged England in the same period, and the French *romans noirs* that followed in their train. With only a few exceptions, the longer ghost stories of this period were generally considered—even by their authors—to be conspicuously lacking in artistry. Once he had kicked the habit, Balzac steadfastly refused to acknowledge the *romans noirs* he had written in his younger days, lest they detract from his respectability; he was not alone.

By the middle of the nineteenth century, English Gothic novels had been relegated to the lowest stratum of popular fiction—the so-called "penny dreadfuls"—and French *romans noirs* to the lowest ranks of the *roman feuilleton*; even at that level Ponson du Terrail quickly abandoned the apparitions of *La Baronne trépassée* (1852) for the picaresque adventures of Rocambole. The dominant opinion then was that the ideal vehicle for literary ghosts was the *conte*, and it was in this form that more exquisite literary ghosts began to appear in some profusion. In France the way was led by Théophile Gautier—the first writer to make full use of Ariès' "eroticism of the macabre", although Charles Nodier had laid some groundwork in "Smarra" (1821)—and Erckmann-Chatrian. In the British Isles the first habitual writers of ghost stories were Charles Dickens and the Irishman Joseph Sheridan le Fanu.

Peter Penzoldt points out in his analytical study of *The Supernatural in Fiction* (1952) that le Fanu was the originator of a literary method subsequently brought to perfection by M. R. James. James described the essence of this method as the development of an appropriate "atmosphere" and the creation of a "nicely managed crescendo"; Penzoldt elaborates the latter phrase in a meticulous dissection of several of James's classic tales, showing in each case how a sequence of four "allusions"—each longer than the previous one, and separated from it by a shorter textual bridge—has a subtly different impact on the protagonist and the reader, leading them to a climax that shocks the character while answering the anticipations of the audience.

Penzoldt carefully refrains from drawing attention to the double meaning explicit in the word "climax" or making any analogy between James's "nicely managed crescendo" and any other form of human activity, but no attentive reader of le Fanu could fail to notice an ideative and methodological connection that is eloquently summarized by Robert Scholes in "The Orgastic Pattern in Fiction":

"The archetype of all fiction is the sexual act...what connects fiction—and music—with sex is the fundamental orgastic rhythm of tumescence and detumescence, of tension and resolution, of intensification to the point of climax and consummation. In the sophisticated forms of fiction, as in the sophisticated practice of sex, much of the art consists of delaying climax within the framework of desire in order to prolong the pleasurable act itself. When we look at fiction with respect to its form alone, we see a pattern of events designed to move towards climax and resolution, balanced by a counter-pattern of events designed to delay this very climax and resolution."

For reasons that Ariès makes clear, and which literary interest in ghosts in need of narrative closure only serves to emphasize, there is no form of fiction that manifests this pattern more plainly than the ghost story. For reasons that Scholes makes clear, and which the same literary interest serves to explain more fully, the most sophisticated, the most artistic, forms of the ghost story are those that cleverly "delay climax within the framework of desire" by constructing "a nicely managed crescendo" within an appropriate "atmosphere".

With the notable exception of the exiled Vernon Lee, the pioneering English ghost story writers treated erotic subject-matter in a typically coy and prudish manner, but the story-structure they took aboard is designed to carry and magnify exactly that erotic charge which its content nervously eschews. There is an obvious irony in the fact that two of the finest ghost stories written in England before World War I—Robert Hichens' "How Love Came to Professor Guildea" (1900) and Oliver Onions' "The Beckoning Fair One" (1911)—are tales of insistent ghostly seduction, whose fretful protagonists inevitably choose death over dishonor. The parallel American tradition that extended from Edith Wharton and Henry James is equally cautious in its deployment of erotic imagery, but is possessed nevertheless by a subtle prurience. The French tradition, on the other hand, always manifested a refreshing frankness and casual cynicism, rooted as it was in such explicit erotic fantasies as Gautier's "La Morte amoureuse" (1836) and "Arria Marcella" (1852) and the tradition of ghostly *contes cruels* launched by Maupassant in "La Chevelure" (1884) and "La Morte" (1887).

Thanks to the intercession of Charles Baudelaire, French writers appreciated the significance of Edgar Poe's pioneering tales of hallucinatory erotic obsession long before Poe's own countrymen took up that thread of his work, and such *fin-de-siècle* writers as Marcel Schwob, Jean Lorrain, and Rémy de Gourmont followed Poe's example to spectacular effect. Although the English and American traditions have recovered the lost ground in the twentieth century, and the relentless pressure of American popular culture has had as considerable an effect on French horror fiction as other genres, the most artful modern French fiction dealing with *revenants* still obtains benefits from the depth of this native tradition. Its legacy can be seen in novels produced in the 1990s by such writers as Alain Dorémieux and Jean-Marc Ligny, as well as in the pages of *Ténèbres*.

* * * * * * *

The social role traditionally attributed to ghosts in oral cultures continues to echo in modern fiction; many literary hauntings begin as family affairs, although few nowadays remain thus confined. Such tales may heighten the post-Freudian awareness that the tightness of the nuclear family is easily capable of generating inadmissible sexual tensions, in addition to those specified within the marital contract, but they also serve to remind us of the duties that the nuclear family has renounced in shedding its extensions. Indeed, as our awareness of the past increases in sensitivity, and we become better able to place our own lives in the context of a far-reaching pattern of social evolution, the notion of ghosts left over from distant times has increased in importance once again.

As Western culture has obliterated more and more tribal societies, whether by means of actual genocide or coca-colonization, a burden of guilt has accumulated, by degrees, that is aptly expressible in a renewed ability to hear the voices of the ancestral spirits whose children have been murdered or stolen. This process has helped to swell the ranks of literary ghosts whose traditional censoriousness is newly alloyed with righteous anger. The social conscience they represent is not easily fused with the personal existential anxiety specified by Ariès, and it is partly for this reason the literary ghosts of the latter half of the twentieth century have expanded to fill a much broader spectrum than their forebears.

Given this expansion of the ghost story spectrum, it is not surprising that the nineteenth century prejudice against ghostly novels has decayed. Although the ghostly *conte* retains its own special artistry, maintaining its progress while naturalistic short fiction seems to be in decline, the position of clear dominance it maintained for more than a century is nowadays challenged by novels possessed of a far greater sophistication than the Gothic extravaganzas and *romans noirs* of old. Although the substance of the ghostly *conte* can be elaborated in several different ways, the central role in the modern ghost novel is often played by a particular location. Rather than being stories of intimate interactions between living and dead individuals, ghost novels tend to be tales of collective haunting: a subject-matter that has evolved rapidly in response to the changing role of the house in modern society.

In modern haunted house stories the lurking presences are often represented as not merely unrelated to the current occupants but utterly alien. The modern nuclear family is likely to move on a regular basis as its needs change, and each house in a sequence is likely to reflect the increasing economic prosperity that modern individuals desire and expect. Precisely because each consequent house-purchase represents an adventurous reach into unknown territories of desire, however, each step on the "property ladder" is fraught with anxiety and danger; nowadays, it is not only people who don't pay their exorcists who have their houses repossessed. Relatively few haunted house stories are straightforward accounts of economic disaster, but the fact that modern house purchases are key symbols of socioeconomic advancement adds a vital new factor to the symbolism of suburban hauntings. The impersonal malignity of so many modern haunters is akin to the objectivity of balance-sheets and the brutality of numbers that refuse to add up in the calculator's favor.

Whether Freud was right to insist that our attitudes to money are conditioned by our attitudes to sex or whether it is really the other way around, there is no doubt that our attitudes to money and sex are interlinked and interdependent. Because the artistry of long ghost stories necessarily involves a greater complexity than of shorter tales, the eroticism of the macabre identified by Ariès as the existential core of modern attitudes to death tends to be extrapolated by the finest ghostly novels into an elaborate pattern exploring the sociological and economic contexts of desire; groundbreaking examples include *The Haunting of Hill House* (1959) by Shirley Jackson, *The Shining* (1977) by Stephen King, *The House Next Door* (1978) by Anne Rivers Siddons, and *The Businessman* (1984) by Thomas M. Disch.

* * * * * * *

The most striking development in contemporary English-language fiction about ghosts is most clearly seen within the sudden deluge of horror marketed for juvenile readers that took place in the 1990s. To some extent this was a "dam-burst" effect, resulting from the fact that the gradual relaxation of the censorship applied to children's books crossed a threshold that permitted a long-pent-up demand to be lavishly met. The distinctive nature of ghost stories written for children even before the dam broke is, however, interesting in more ways than one. Although the erotic and economic elements are not entirely absent from ghost stories aimed at older children, they are usually diminished considerably in favor of an educational aspect. A sense of history is something that children develop in stages, and ghosts in children's fiction very often serve as stimuli to the development of a keen appreciation of the ways in which the present differs from the past, and of the debts that the present generation owes to the endeavors of their forebears.

The socially active ghosts of tribal societies were also enthusiastic for their contributions to the commonweal to be recognized, but the value of those contributions was defined by the extent to which the accumulated wisdom of the tribe was still useful. The significance of the continued presence of the dead was defined by social continuity. The literary ghosts of modern children's fiction are, by contrast, significant precisely because the generations to which they belonged brought about permanent and decisive changes; the anachronism of their attitudes is a testament to progress. The point of this testament is not simply to remind modern children how lucky they are by comparison with the children of former eras, but also to remind them of the importance of making progress in their own lives.

The essential subject-matter of all children's fiction is "growing up", and the foremost insistence of all children's fiction is that growing up is a matter of moral as well as material progress. The principal functions of ghosts in children's stories are to assist in the development of intellectual and emotional independence and to encourage a greater and more focused sense of social responsibility. There are, of course, several strategies by which these ends may be furthered. Parents, like priests, have until recently been grotesquely enthusiastic employers of moral terrorism, attempting to encourage good behavior with the threat that bad behavior will be punished with the utmost supernatural severity, but the recent upsurge of ghost stories for children has coincided with an abrupt decline in that policy. The deployment of a ghost as a *deus ex machina* to punish bad characters is still a common feature of the cruder kinds of adult horror story, and is certainly not unknown in children's fiction, but modern children's fiction is more likely to feature friendly ghosts, which take the side of young protagonists against evils that are either far more inhuman or all-too-firmly embodied.

This new pattern is interesting not merely as a challenge to the artistry of writers for children (although it hardly requires saying that children's fiction has at least as much artistry in it as any other kind) but because it represents a significant trend. At present, benign ghosts are a minority among the host of revenants besieging adult fiction, but their numbers are growing and there is every reason to expect the tide to increase—not merely because the readers of children's ghost stories may carry their expectations forward as they age, but because the assumptions inherent in that kind of fiction are true. It *is* because the generations who came before us contrived such dramatic changes that we owe them such a huge debt of gratitude. Seen from an objective point of view, ghosts really ought to be reminders of past progress as well as vortices of present anxiety.

* * * * * * *

If we are to write ghost stories in future, and if we are to write them as artfully as we can, we must bear in mind that there is nothing final about the state of mind described by Ariès, and that there are very good reasons for hoping that its effects will be temporary. The great majority of the ghost stories of the past two centuries have not merely been horror stories but stories focusing, analyzing and extrapolating a particular species of horror. There can be no reversal of the evolution of individualism, but that does not mean that the ego has reached a terminus of terrified isolation and irresponsible lust that is capable of no further modification. Quite the reverse: the task now before the individual is to accept and adapt to that circumstance, to make it happy as well as productive. The revenant dead are not the best symbols of the forces that stand in the way of that process of necessary maturation, nor even of the dread that we might be incapable of reaching for further goals.

We have now entered into an age when the appropriate attitude to death is not to lament its inevitability but to work towards its conquest. It seems probable that no one now alive will become emortal, but it is a hope that we may legitimately entertain for our children's children. We may be the last generation condemned to be recalled as an orderly company of mortals, and even if it turns out that we are not, the emortals who will emerge soon enough will remember us as dwellers upon a crucial threshold and openers of the way to the Land of Infinite Promise. Perhaps, therefore, we ought to exercise our own imagination a little more cleverly than to bring back our own forebears again and again and again as bitter complainants or vengeful accumulations of malice.

The artistry of the contemporary ghost story ought, I believe, to concentrate on an aspect of the genre's evolution that is too frequently overlooked, or dismissed as a minor concern. The ghost stories of M. R. James are "warnings to the curious", doggedly insisting that people who search too assiduously for knowledge will be damned by their discoveries, but, as the tradition M. R. James helped to found has been carried forward, it has gradually been transmuted into a celebration of the process of discovery, whereby a better understanding of where ghosts are coming from—and how, and why—is exactly what allows the matters outstanding between them and us to be settled. The discoveries in question have too often been nonsensical, credited to ancient, arcane and arbitrary authorities rather than to the scientific method, but, now that the twenty-first century has dawned, we really ought to expect that more and more people will consent to be dragged, without kicking and screaming quite as loudly as before, out of the seventeenth.

The horror that haunts the present, although it will not be generally realized until a few more of us have caught up with the day before yesterday, is not that we must die, and die alone, with nothing between us and the grave but the haphazard service of a few fleshy appetites, but that we might not have arrived on Earth quite soon enough to avoid the inevitability of death. That is a realization of a kind very different from the one that has so far animated the artistry of the ghost story; anyone who can find a means of its expression that is both eloquent and elegant will be remembered with respect and admiration by the future generations we shall serve as ghosts.

THE GOTHIC LIFESTYLE FROM BYRON TO BUFFY

That life imitates art more assiduously than art imitates life was obvious long before Oscar Wilde formulated the dictum in "The Decay of Lying". It had first become obvious a century earlier, during the heyday of the Gothic novel. The attachment of that label to the horror novels of the late eighteenth century had as much to do with the lifestyle fantasies in which Horace Walpole indulged at Strawberry Hill and William Beckford at Fonthill Abbey as with the content of their pioneering literary exercises. Gothic literary fantasy and Gothic lifestyle fantasy subsequently found a definitive common focus in the image of Lord Byron, who served as a role model for a host of literary villains and a considerable company of *angst*-ridden young men. As one sarcastic commentator, the Earl of Lytton, was later to write:

"Youths in the fresh exuberance of life supposed it beautiful and heroic to put on a woe-begone expression of countenance, and pretend that their existence was blighted in its bud. They affected to be sated and worn out by premature vice, and darkly hinted that their conscience was tortured by the stings of unutterable crimes."

So tight was the feedback loop that linked Byronic literary fantasies and Byronic lifestyle fantasies that two of Byron's most intimate acquaintances, Lady Caroline Lamb and John Polidori, thought it the most natural thing in the world to express their spite against him in the form of Gothic fiction. Polidori's novelette "The Vampyre" (1819), which pilloried Byron in the character of Lord Ruthven—a name borrowed from Ruthven Glenarvon, the eponymous anti-hero of Lamb's novel—established a literary stereotype of astonishing hardihood, which picked up mass and velocity throughout the nineteenth century. Bram Stoker's *Dracula* (1897) added such a powerful new charge that its central motif became a significant item of twentieth century folklore and a central icon of resurgent Gothic lifestyle fantasies. The purpose of this paper is to offer a synoptic account of the convoluted chain of influences that extends from Byron to contemporary Gothic lifestyle fantasies, with particular reference to the deployment of the vampire icon.

* * * * * * *

Just as there is a sense in which all fiction is fantasy, so there is a sense in which all lifestyle is fantasy. Just as most fiction is stubbornly mundane and slavishly mimetic, however, so the great majority of lifestyles are cravenly subservient to convention and custom. The lifestyle fantasy that made the true relationship between life and art obvious had to rip through the dull camouflage of normality, and had therefore to be calculated as a reckless challenge defiantly opposed to commonplace social norms.

Lifestyle fantasy is essentially a pick-and-mix business, varied by idiosyncratic taste and constrained by financial means. Even at the beginning of the nineteenth century, there was a wide spectrum of overlapping oppositional lifestyles, but it is the elements that were aggregated at its farthest end that are most relevant to this paper.

The definitive feature of Gothic lifestyle fantasy is an extreme adherence to a Romantic aesthetic creed, with a particular emphasis on what that creed's detractors would be likely to see as perversities. At its purest, the Gothic pose prefers the sublime to the beautiful, the wild to the ordered, emotional excess to reasonable moderation, night to day and black to color. It is interested in the arcane, the occult and altered states of consciousness, although it maintains an abrasively skeptical attitude to all problematic phenomena. It strongly favors the cause of literary Satanism: the philosophical position summarized by William Blake's remark that Milton was "of the devil's party without knowing it", as subsequently expanded and explained in Shelley's *Defence of Poetry*.

Byronic lifestyle fantasies have been called "Satanic" by their detractors ever since their inception, and modern Satanism is certainly a pose of the same kind, but the word must not be taken to imply that Byron—or anyone else—was ever a worshipper of evil. The literal meaning of *satan* is "adversary", and the Gothic lifestyle fantasy is Satanic because it is quintessentially adversarial. Like the companionable satan of *Job*, it offers a cynical challenge to the florid claims of outrageous righteousness. Classic early works of literary Satanism, including Blake's prophetic books, Shelley's "Prometheus Unbound" and Byron's "Manfred", all feature heroic rebels against divine tyranny, but some time passed before anyone dared to tackle Milton's lame theodicy head-on by employing Lucifer himself as the hero in question.

* * * * * * *

Byron had only one serious rival among the lifestyle fantasists of his day. He once described himself, in a typical fit of sarcastic modesty, as the third most important man in Europe, the second being Napoleon and the first George Brummell. The legacy of Beau Brummell's sense of style is still faintly echoed in the modern business suit, but its logic departed when Brummell's debts forced him to follow Byron into permanent exile in 1816. He established himself in Calais, where he furnished his rooms in a bizarre but economical fashion, whose fanciful details were reported back by a string of well-connected tourists who stopped off to see him on the way to the ferry. Many British lifestyle fantasists of an adversarial stripe were to follow his example, including Algernon Swinburne, Ernest Dowson and Oscar Wilde. The necessity of such departures, whether temporary or permanent, is a testament to the awesome power and rigor of British convention, whose fierce backlash against early nineteenth-century oppositional lifestyle fantasies is nowadays called "Victorianism", although it began more than a decade before Victoria acceded to the throne.

Byronism began to lose its influence as soon as its role model had died in 1824, and was soon replaced by something far more in keeping with the Victorian temper. Ironically, the literary fantasy that provided a new role model, the pioneering "silver fork novel" *Pelham* (1828), was penned by a writer who had earlier been an enthusiastic Byronist, more than ready to step into the breach when Caroline Lamb required comforting after her former lover's funeral: Edward Lytton Bulwer (he later changed his signature to Bulwer-Lytton). *Pelham* includes one of those admiring accounts of the exiled Beau Brummell's lodgings, based on Bulwer's dutiful pilgrimage there, but its substitution of a more cheerful and languid kind of foppery for what its author did not hesitate to call "the Satanic Mania" was compromised by the fact that Bulwer could never quite let that mania go. It was one of his several revisitations of Gothic literary fantasy that laid the groundwork for the rebirth of Gothic lifestyle fantasy.

The crucial difference between Byron and Bulwer may be found in the fact that, whereas Byron annoyed the hell out of Caroline Lamb by casting her aside like a worn-out sock, it was Lady Caroline who annoyed the hell out of Bulwer by subjecting him to a similar indignity, presumably because he was neither mad enough, bad enough nor dangerous enough to be worth knowing. The life-style fantasists who were to look upon Bulwer's *Zanoni* (1842) as deliriously thirsty men might greet a watery mirage were, however, far more interested in what the two men had in common.

Zanoni is a Rosicrucian romance, whose eponymous hero and his mentor Mejnour are the last survivors of a once-numerous brotherhood of occult scientists. When Zanoni elects to trade in his immortality and magic power for the love of a good woman, Mejnour takes on a new apprentice, an English artist named Glyndon—but Glyndon fails the tests that are set for him by his tutor and exits his vocation, pursued by the accusing hallucinatory stare of the monstrous Dweller of the Threshold. Glyndon, like Bulwer himself, dared not cross the threshold that separates conventional lifestyle fantasy from the allure of the occult and the adversarial—but there has never been any shortage of Byronic fools avid to rush in where angelic Victorians feared to tread.

* * * * * * *

Such was the restraint of Victorian England that *Zanoni*'s early influence was most obvious in France, where it combined fruitfully with the influence of another English-speaking writer, Edgar Poe. Poe was always a misfit in his native land, but the French took a very different view of him. The fact that Charles Baudelaire became his translator was an extraordinarily lucky break for both of them; between them, they prized Gothic Lifestyle fantasy loose from its aristocratic roots and made it available to men of more slender means.

Poe was schooled in England between 1815 and 1820. Although he was only a precocious eleven-year-old when he returned to the USA, he had been indelibly marked by Byronism. Byron and Coleridge remained the key influences on his work, and Poe's literary fantasies paid effusive homage to lifestyle fantasies that he could not afford to support.

"The Murders in the Rue Morgue" describes how the eccentric C. Auguste Dupin and a kindred spirit indulge themselves in "the expense of renting, and furnishing in a style that suited the rather fantastic gloom of our common temper, a time-eaten and grotesque mansion, long deserted through superstitions into which we did not inquire, and tottering to its fall in a retired and desolate portion of the Faubourg St Germain". There the two men live a secluded life, admitting no visitors and going out only by night. "It was a freak of fancy in my friend," the narrator observes, "to be enamored of the night for her own sake; and into this *bizarrerie*, as into all his others, I quietly fell; giving myself up to his wild whims with a perfect *abandon*. The sable divinity would not herself dwell with us always; but we could counterfeit her presence. At first dawn of the morning we closed all the massy shutters of our old building; lighted a couple of tapers which, strongly perfumed, threw out only the ghastliest and feeblest of rays. By the aid of these we then busied our souls in dreams—reading, writing or conversing until warned by the clock of the advent of the true Darkness."

There is an element of parodic humor in this description, but that sarcastic playfulness—a key feature of the great majority of Gothic lifestyle fantasies—merely serves to mask the self-indulgent sincerity of the fantasy. Baudelaire, who also lived in penury, having been prevented by a wicked stepfather from coming into his legitimate inheritance, identified very strongly with Poe, but Poe was not the only significant influence on Baudelaire's own literary and lifestyle fantasies. Two years after the first publication of "The Murders in the Rue Morgue" Jules-Amadée Barbey d'Aurevilly published *Du dandyisme et de G. Brummel* (1843), which combined a fantasized biography of Byron's accomplice with an elaborate analysis of the philosophy of dandyism. After reading it, Baudelaire immediately announced that henceforth his only colors would be black. He wore black clothes and he wrote black comedy, fervently dedicating himself to the sarcastically serious business of being a soul in torment and unleashing the full heroic fervor of his imagination against the draconian threats of *ennui* (morbid tedium) and *spleen* (acrimonious melancholy). His classic collection *Les Fleurs du mal*, first issued in 1857 and immediately prosecuted for obscenity, includes the first fully-explicit work of literary Satanism, "Litany to Satan".

Like Poe, Baudelaire died wretched, destitute and almost universally despised, but his rehabilitation was swift. Théophile Gautier, introducing the third edition of *Les Fleurs du mal*, redefined him as the great pioneer and paradigm example of the "Decadent style". According to Gautier, the Decadent style is "ingenious, complicated, clever, full of delicate hints and refinements, gathering all the delicacies of speech, borrowing from technical vocabularies, taking color from every palette, tones from all musical instruments, contours vague and fleeting, listening to translate subtle confidences, confessions of depraved passions and the odd hallucinations of a fixed idea turning to madness". Such a style is "summoned to express all and to venture to the very extremes", preserving a particular fascination for "the phosphorescence of putrescence". Gautier was, of course, referring to Baudelaire's literary style, but it only required the slightest shift of emphasis to convert the glowing reference into advocacy for an adversarial lifestyle.

Meanwhile, Bulwer's influence was also at work in Paris. The man who played the leading role in re-adapting *Zanoni*'s literary fantasy into lifestyle fantasy was Alphonse-Louis Constant, a failed *littérateur* who had also dabbled unsuccessfully in politics before finding his métier in 1851, when he adopted the pseudonym Éliphas Lévi. Éliphas Lévi quickly established himself as the great pioneer of modern occult scholarly fantasy. *Dogme et rituel de la haute magie* (1854-56; tr. as *The Doctrine and Ritual of Transcendental Magic*) became the principal source-book of all subsequent practical handbooks of "high magic", including those used by the "Rosicrucian lodges" that sprang up in some profusion in *fin-de-siècle* Paris. The principal English contributors to this tradition of scholarly fantasy were A. E. Waite, who was Lévi's translator before taking up the torch on his own account, and the prolific exhibitionist Aleister Crowley. The success of Lévi's *Histoire de la magie* (1859; tr. as *The History of Magic*) prompted the poverty-stricken historian Jules Michelet to dash off the highly imaginative potboiler that was to become the most influential scholarly fantasy of its era: *La Sorcière* (1862), the ancestral text of all lifestyle fantasies involving witchcraft.

Zanoni was not the only source of Constant's ambition to become a wholehearted lifestyle fantasist, but Éliphas Lévi certainly thought of Bulwer as his closest kindred spirit. He visited London in 1854 and 1861, subsequently offering carefully sensationalized accounts of the relationship he developed with Bulwer, although he did not actually meet his hero until he went to Knebworth House to give Bulwer complimentary copies of his books during his second visit. Bulwer obligingly borrowed colorful details from these presentation copies for inclusion in his last full-blown occult romance, *A Strange Story* (1862).

We cannot know, of course, how earnest Lévi's impostures were, although the history of charlatanry testifies to the propensity that even the most cynical scholarly fantasists have for falling victim to their own patter. There is, however, no doubt that the feedback loop that connected Bulwer's literary fantasies with Lévi's lifestyle and scholarly fantasies still spins like a tornado in the present day. The great majority of modern lifestyle fantasists retain a quasi-Victorian insistence on the virtue of their poses: an insistence as typically Bulwerian as the guarded ambivalence of their claims.

* * * * * * *

A generation after his death, Baudelaire became the figurehead of the French Decadent Movement. The lifestyle fantasy longingly described by Poe and lightly refined by Baudelaire was further elaborated by the central prose document of the movement: Joris-Karl Huysmans' *À rebours* (1884). The hero of *À rebours*, Jean Des Esseintes, has secluded himself in a house in an unfashionable district of Paris in order that he may restrict his intercourse with other human beings to the appreciation of their works of art—which is, he confidently asserts, the only kind of human contact worth having. With the aid of modern artifice he can reproduce in the comfort of his own home any experience worth having; for instance, all that is worthwhile about a sea voyage can be synthesized with the aid of suitable dress, fishing-tackle, a few sound-effects, a briny odor and a copy of Poe's *Narrative of Arthur Gordon Pym*.

Des Esseintes' opinions as to which works of art are worth keeping are calculatedly heretical (praising Baudelaire's prose-poetry above all else), as are his comments on morality, which casually overturn all the commonly-accepted precepts of his day. His greatest triumph of inversion comes, however, when he mistakenly assumes that a doctor's prescription for a strength-building diet is a prescription for an enema and begins taking his daily nourishment via the wrong end of the alimentary canal. His final decision to embrace the Catholic Church is not a repentance; he commits himself to God because he knows full well that belief in God is absurd, and that the religious life is therefore the ultimate lifestyle fantasy. *À rebours* is, of course, a comedy (although some of its readers contrive not to notice its hilarity), but its whimsical fantasies are appealing, at least to that alienated minority of human beings whose tastes and opinions run contrary both to those of the majority and those of the majority-sanctioned cultural élite.

Huysmans was a close friend of Jean Lorrain, who was described by the principal chronicler of the French Decadent Movement, Rémy de Gourmont, as "the last disciple of Barbey d'Aurevilly". Lorrain had grown up on the coast of Normandy, where the lavishly Decadent lifestyle adopted by the exiled Swinburne was still the subject of popular rumor, and where he became acquainted with another exile of similar stripe, Lord Arthur Somerset. With Somerset's encouragement, Lorrain set off for Paris, intent on becoming a gentleman of letters, but his hopes were dashed when he discovered after his father's death that the lavish inheritance he had long expected had all been spent. Forced to make a living from his pen, he worked with such fervor that he was tempted to make use of the only drug then being touted as a powerful stimulant: ether. He damaged his gut so irreparably that he was in agony until he died, in 1906, after perforating his ulcerated colon while attempting to give himself a palliative enema. In the meantime, ether filled his house in the Rue de Courty with the hallucinatory phantoms he described in his story cycle *Contes d'un buveur d'éther*, which give due credit to the exotically morbid décor he established therein. He became the ironic archetype of a Decadent lifestyle fantasist.

Another of Huysmans' acquaintances was Berthe Courrière, the sometime mistress of Rémy de Gourmont and an enthusiastic acolyte of the most flamboyant and most successful of Alphonse-Louis Constant's imitators, the self-styled Rosicrucian magus Joséphin Péladan. Péladan was the most spectacular of the lifestyle fantasists of *fin-de-siècle* Paris, his celebrity extrapolated by a prodigious number of literary and scholarly fantasies. He and other people to whom Berthe Courrière introduced Huysmans cropped up, lightly disguised, in Huysmans' quasi-documentary novel of fashionable Parisian Satanism, *Là-Bas* (1891). This was Huysmans' second crucial contribution to the development of modern Gothic lifestyle fantasy: the cornerstone of the modern mythology of the Black Mass.

* * * * * * *

The repercussions of Huysmans' thought-experiments in lifestyle fantasy were widespread. Huysmans was not present when Jean Lorrain persuaded Marcel Schwob to bring Oscar Wilde to dinner in the Rue de Courty—Anatole France, who was to bring French literary Satanism to its magnificent climax in *The Revolt of the Angels* in 1914, completed the party of four—but Wilde was a great admirer of *À rebours*, and paid homage to it in *The Picture of Dorian Gray*; it was the model of the "yellow book" that inspires Dorian to make the most of his unprecedented opportunity to live his life as an incorruptible work of art.

The fragile English Decadent Movement labored under the handicap of Victorian standards of decency and was conclusively slain by Wilde's condemnation to two years hard labor and universal ignominy; its supporters instantly relabeled themselves Symbolists, having learned from Stéphane Mallarmé that that was the safest route to near-respectability. While it flourished, however, the English Decadent Movement produced one marvelously extravagant lifestyle fantasist in Count Stanislaus Eric Stenbock, author of the stridently homoerotic *Studies in Death* (1893), who delighted in boasting that he slept in a coffin and shared his dinner-table with a pet toad. Other literary fantasies it inspired included Arthur Machen's paean to escapism, *The Hill of Dreams,* and Edgar Jepson's heretical fantasy *The Horned Shepherd*—both of which first appeared, absurdly, not in John Lane's *Yellow Book* but in *Horlick's Malted Milk Magazine*, whose editorship had briefly fallen into the unlikely hands of A. E. Waite. Its most spectacular products were, however, *hommages* to Poe penned by M. P. Shiel and collected in *Prince Zaleski* and *Shapes in the Fire*, both issued by Lane with Aubrey Beardsley decorations.

C. Auguste Dupin's most famous English descendant is, of course, Sherlock Holmes, whose lifestyle as described in *A Study in Scarlet* (1887) had marked Decadent touches. Under the influence of the terminally tedious Dr Watson and the pressure of fame, however, Holmes became a less flamboyant character, whose nocturnal habits and drug-addiction were de-emphasized. No such domestication spoiled Shiel's Zaleski, who easily outdid all his rivals in status and style. His home was "a vast tomb of Mausoleums in which lay deep sepulchres.... Even in the semi-darkness of the very faint greenish lustre radiated from an open cDepartmentenserlike *lampas* of fretted gold in the centre of the domed encausted roof, a certain incongruity of barbaric gorgeousness in the furnishing filled me with amazement. The air was heavy with the scented odour of this light, and the fumes of the narcotic *cannabis sativa*." Whereas Holmes favored the musical distraction of the violin, Zaleski was the spiritual forefather of modern Gothic rock. "One side of the room was occupied by an organ whose thunder in that circumscribed place must have set all these relics of dead epochs clashing and jingling in fantastic dances."

* * * * * * *

So closely was the French Decadent movement tied to the notion of the *fin-de-siècle* that its fashionability did not survive the dawn of the new century, although its lessons in lifestyle fantasy had been thoroughly absorbed by many of those who came after, most obviously the surrealists and the pioneers of the Theatre of the Absurd. The Léviesque Order of the Golden Dawn spawned numerous successor organizations in Britain, most notably the splinter-groups set up by Aleister Crowley and Violet Firth (alias Dion Fortune), but they never came close to replicating the spectacular success that Péladan had briefly enjoyed in Paris.

The last cobwebs of European Decadence were blown away by the Great War, and its brief resurrection in the cabarets of Berlin was soon stamped out by Hitler's Brownshirts. The flickering flame of Gothic literary fantasy was transplanted to the most inhospitable soil of all, the USA. Two groups of self-styled Bohemians, one located in the north-east and one in the south-west, had imported Decadent ideals into America as a protest against the gathering forces of Prohibition—which were, of course, as enthusiastic to ban intoxicating literature as intoxicating liquor. European émigrés like Ben Hecht, author of *Fantazius Mallare*, and George S. Viereck, author of *The House of the Vampire*, were joined in this cause, albeit half-heartedly, by James Huneker, Edgar Saltus, and Ambrose Bierce—but such is the irony of fate that the only two recruits who are remembered today were the two who elected to ply their trade in the most despised of all the media available: the pulp magazines. The man who became both the foremost theorist of American Decadent literature and the foremost American exemplar of the Gothic lifestyle, was the New Englander H. P. Lovecraft, although the last and most extreme practitioner of Decadent poetry and prose was Lovecraft's Californian correspondent Clark Ashton Smith.

Like Edgar Poe, Lovecraft was a gentleman fallen on hard times. He died prematurely in 1937, never having seen his works published in volume form—but he became, and has remained, the central figure of a distinctive form of horror fiction, exemplified by the tales constituting what came to be known as "the Cthulhu Mythos". These stories, of which the best include "The Shadow Over Innsmouth" and "The Shadow out of Time", have exerted an enormous influence over the development of modern horror fiction. Bizarrely, one of Aleister Crowley's most dedicated followers, Kenneth Grant, expended a great deal of effort in identifying a close symmetry between the entities described in Crowley's scholarly fantasies and those described in Lovecraft's literary fantasies. The syncretic amalgam thus produced has had some slight influence upon the development of modern Satanist ritual, and a great deal more on the development of what is now the most obvious "literary" correlate of contemporary Gothic lifestyle fantasy: the lyrics of British and American Gothic rock bands and their counterparts in German "dark wave" music.

* * * * * * *

It was another despised American medium, the cinema, which crystallized the image of the aristocratic vampire into its contemporary form. Tod Browning's *Dracula* (1931), with Bela Lugosi in the lead, was parent to a host of cheap schlock-horror movies, which soon degenerated into frank absurdity, but its central character retained his iconic force. Browning subsequently cast Lugosi in a remake of his silent movie *London After Midnight* called *Mark of the Vampire* (1934), in which Lugosi's masquerade as a Byronic vampire is supported by Carol Borland, playing a *femme fatale* in a costume that was to become equally stereotypical. When comedic parodies of horror film cliché such as Charles Addams' cartoons were readapted for television in the 1960s, in *The Addams Family* and *The Munsters*, the costume-designers were still tightly constrained by the dress-codes established by Browning via Lugosi and Borland.

Like the vast majority of characters stamped from mock-Byronic moulds, Dracula was an out-and-out villain, but the charismatic quality of his villainy survived every indignity that Hollywood could heap upon it. Lugosi ended up posthumously playing the lead in Ed Wood's *Plan 9 from Outer Space*, while the amateur who took his place used a Dracula cape to conceal his true identity, but even that could not diminish his prior achievements to negligibility. The cycle began again in Britain when Christopher Lee took the title role in the Hammer version of *Dracula* (1958), which likewise spawned an endless series of sequels, imitations and parodies while similarly retaining, in spite of everything, a defiant iconic grandeur. The morality of the vast majority of these execrable movies was steadfastly Victorian, but it was their Byronic aspects that proved attractive to a new generation of lifestyle fantasists. At first, such fantasies were a mere matter of appearance, but they soon began to go beyond that, aided and reinspired by a new wave of literary fantasies, and by new fashions in yet another widely-despised medium of mass culture.

From its very inception, rock music was stigmatized by its detractors as "the devil's music". Most performers reacted, predictably enough, by refining their images to deflect the criticism, but hardline aficionados of the genre always knew that there was an ideological as well as a commercial meaning to the phrase "selling out". Those rock musicians who not only maintained but sought to exaggerate their adversarial poses provided the bedrock of popular culture's unheralded dark companion: unpopular culture, which is defiantly opposed both to the mass appeal of popular culture and to the snobbery of high culture. Even rock musicians who became rich and famous sometimes pretend to have kept faith with their roots by employing their sudden wealth in extremes of Decadent excess that easily outstrip the relatively modest hypothetical fantasies of Jean Des Esseintes.

In 1967 the Rolling Stones attempted to release an album called *Their Satanic Majesties Request and Require*, although they compromised with the management of Decca by removing the last two words. Their next album, *Beggars Banquet*, was spearheaded by a track that they wanted to call "The Devil is my Name", although the powers-that-be at Decca used their veto again to make it "Sympathy for the Devil". Mick Jagger, Keith Richards and Brian Jones had all become peripherally involved in a vogue for Satanic lifestyle fantasy that was then at its zenith in California, centered on the Church of Satan founded by Anton LaVey, author of *The Satanic Bible* (1969). All three were scheduled to appear in *Lucifer Rising* a film written and directed by Kenneth Anger—Jagger was to play Lucifer—but the movie was never completed and the Stones settled for a more orthodox career-path. The torch they dropped was, however, immediately picked up by heavy metal pioneers Black Widow and Black Sabbath.

The subculture associated with heavy metal music has remained avid to appropriate any and all symbols of defiant opposition, usually but not always in a spirit of pure showmanship. The genre's devotees modelled their dress code on the Hell's Angels of California, and the stage shows of artists such as Alice Cooper borrowed extensively from French *grand guignol* theatre. It is hardly surprising that such tactics attracted witch-hunts from the people whose ideas they were designed to affront, nor that the attacks in question soon plumbed the depths of absurdity when the members of Judas Priest were hauled into court, charged with implanting subliminal exhortations to suicide in one of their albums. In 1981 *Welcome to Hell* was the debut album of the English band Venom, who continued their career with *Black Metal*, a label gladly adopted by an apocalyptic Satanist subgenre pioneered in Norway—although American acts like Deicide, whose eponymous first album was released in 1990, preferred the label "death metal".

The main problem with heavy metal music as an expressive medium is that it is very noisy, not just in the literal sense but in the technical sense defined by Simon Reynolds in his book *Blissed Out* (1990):

> If music is like a language, if it communicates some kind of emotional or spiritual message, then noise is best defined as interference, something which blocks transmission, jams the code, prevents sense being made. The subliminal message of most music is that the universe is essentially benign, that if there is sadness or tragedy, this is resolved at the level of some higher harmony. Noise troubles this worldview. That is why noise groups invariably deal with subject-matter that is anti-humanist—extremes of abjection, obsession, trauma, atrocity, possession—all of which undermine humanism's confidence that...we can become the subjects of our lives, and work together for the general progress of the commonwealth.

Given this, it is only to be expected that the heavy metal scene is the chief modern location for explicit Satanism, but not all Satanist rock music is heavy metal. The Satanist church founded by Anton LaVey was set solidly in the theatrical and libertine tradition of the eighteenth century Hellfire clubs, whose sole *raison d'être* was wild partying. Set firmly and wholeheartedly within this ideological milieu, *Burn, Baby, Burn!* (1993) and subsequent albums by The Electric Hellfire Club deploy the technology and techniques of disco music to produce music designed for Dionysian dancing rather than headbanging. The Electric Hellfire Club make prolific use of samples plundered from horror movies: a method of creating ideative links that had earlier been exploited by the avant-gardist British band Bauhaus, and became a key feature of the musical rhetoric informing Gothic rock music.

The Goth subculture, which first emerged out of the punk era of the late 1970s, is most obviously demarcated by its striking dress code. This involves all-black attire, occasionally ameliorated by a dash of red velvet and lavishly augmented with heavy faux-silver jewelry. Dyed-black hair, often wildly splayed, is customary and make-up tends to the garish, particularly about the eyes. The principal model for this look was Siouxsie Sioux of Siouxsie and the Banshees, who discovered its apparatus in the London boutique run by Malcolm McLaren and Vivienne Westwood, especially those stocks-in-trade that had previously been sold though mail-order catalogues catering to rubber, leather and bondage fetishists. Already considerably influenced by horror movies, these stylistic elements were further complicated by items modelled on cinematic images of sinister and sexy vampires.

The cultural affiliations of the Goth pose were neatly summarized by a satirical account of "Gothic Party Time" offered by punk band Action Pact in 1983. Edgar Poe and Dorian Gray are guests at the party in question, although Aleister Crowley is the star—but the host, significantly, is Nosferatu: the vampire. In its earliest phase, a London club called the Batcave provided the main focus for the growth of Goth subculture, and London-based bands like Bauhaus, Alien Sex Fiend and Sex Gang Children were its early idols. It was Bauhaus who identified the cinematic vampire as the key icon of Gothic existentialist fantasy in the ironic nine-minute anthem "Bela Lugosi is Dead" (on *Press the Eject and Give Me the Tape*, 1982).

The Leeds-based Sisters of Mercy eventually became the definitive British Goth band, providing a paradigm for the mood of the music and its manner of presentation. The black-clad band played in semi-darkness, obscured by the liberal outpourings of a smoke-machine, while front man Andrew Eldritch intoned his lyrics in a deep and conspicuously raw baritone voice. The other significant British Goth bands of the late 1980s were The Mission and Fields of the Nephilim. East German "dark wave" music evolved in parallel, with early exemplars like X-mal Deutschland and Calling Dead Red Roses establishing a distinct base that was even more conscious of its cultural roots. Various occult societies—including the Vril society, named after the occult force featured in Bulwer's *The Coming Race*—constituted the only kind of underground tolerated by the communist regimes of Eastern Europe, and the record label on which most German dark wave music was and is released adopted the name of Dion Fortune. Dark wave music was, however, very heavily influenced by the leading British bands once it became commonplace for German bands to sing in English. Many other vocalists modelled their style and their material on the key British exemplars, Andrew Eldritch and Carl McCoy, front-man of Fields of the Nephilim; some of them followed McCoy's example in using a voice-distorter to make their lyrics more guttural than nature would permit.

Andrew Eldritch's lyrics never exhibited any conspicuous interest in fantastic imagery, but the songs written by his principal rivals, McCoy and Wayne Hussey of The Mission, were often infused with occult and mystical imagery. McCoy became increasingly vociferous about his strong interest in the occult—heavily influenced by Kenneth Grant's syncretic amalgam of Aleister Crowley and H. P. Lovecraft—and his allegedly-devout paganism, which came increasingly to the fore in the songs he wrote. Fields of the Nephilim's most successful single, "Moonchild", was named for Crowley's most substantial literary fantasy, and the lyrics of the ambitious concept album *Elizium* (1990) resemble those penned by Artaud Franzmann, front man of the German dark wave band The Garden of Delight, in fusing the imagery of Lovecraft's Cthulhu Mythos with Sumerian mythology as well as Crowleyan occultism. This link, forged by identifying Cthulhu with the Sumerian Tiamat, a symbol of Chaos, had first been made in a 1977 scholarly fantasy by-lined "Simon", which purported to be a translation of the *Necronomicon*—an imaginary book in which the secrets of the Cthulhu Mythos are contained.

* * * * * * *

The partial reliance of Goth dress-codes on the imagery of Hammer films might have remained superficial had it not been for a sudden flood of novels in which Byronic vampires were redefined as tormented heroes rather than villains. Although pioneered in Europe by Jane Gaskell's *The Shiny Narrow Grin* (1964) and Pierre Kast's *Les Vampires de l'Alfama* (1975), revisionist vampire stories enjoyed their most spectacular success in America, spearheaded by Anne Rice's series begun with *Interview with the Vampire* (1976) and Chelsea Quinn Yarbro's series begun with *Hôtel Transylvania* (1978). Apologetic exercises in vampire existentialism poured forth in awesome profusion throughout the 1980s and 1990s; millions of readers were able to find therein an ennobling echo of their own confusions, appetites and anxieties.

The most remarkable spin-off of Anne Rice's literary stardom was the rapid infection of American Gothic subculture with vampiric lifestyle fantasies. In Britain too, long-standing literary and cinematic fan clubs like the Dracula Society and the Vampire Society were abruptly supplemented with Goth/vampire fusions like Thee Vampire Guild. The invasion of the Vampire Society by extreme lifestyle fantasists eventually caused its disintegration and the death of its fanzine *The Velvet Vampyre*. In the meantime, the Newcastle-based Goth/vampire fanzine *Bats and Red Velvet* became the nation's primary showcase for Gothic music, issuing a sampler CD with every issue once it had abbreviated is name to BRV. The more traditionally-minded members of the Vampire Society retired from the London scene to leave the field clear for the London Vampire Group, whose most adventurous members hosted the Vampyria events at the London Hippodrome, founded the glossy magazine *Bloodstone* and eventually contrived to release the anthology *In Blood We Lust: Depraved Sexual Fantasies for Vampires,* in spite of the extreme difficulty of finding a printer willing to produce it.

While a second generation of British Goth bands and European dark wave bands rose to prominence in the 1990s, frequently deploying vampire imagery in their lyrics, Britain produced its own native versions of Anne Rice and Chelsea Quinn Yarbro in the Goth novelists Storm Constantine and Freda Warrington—although such fellow travelers as Kim Newman remained content with more moderate poses. Thee Vampire Guild produced three compilation albums of vampire rock under the title *"What Sweet Music They Make...",* featuring such bands as Inkubus Sukkubus, Nosferatu, Corpus Delicti, The Dark Theater, London After Midnight, Midnight Configuration, Morticia and Lestat before its founder Phill White departed in search of dark stardom as the front man of the band Narcissus Pool. The use of vampire imagery briefly became a significant marketing tool even for bands and record labels whose use of such imagery was purely tokenistic.

* * * * * * *

If one considers the *"What Sweet Music They Make..."* series as a semi-coherent set, one can readily discern the partly-entwined connecting threads that bind modern vampire fiction and modern vampire rock together into the core of Gothic lifestyle fantasy. Its existential thread involves a virtual inversion of traditional existentialist characterizations of *angst*, further complicated by the way in which that reconfigured *angst* is ameliorated by more assertive elements. Its erotic thread celebrates the heightening of erotic excitement that can be achieved by certain kinds of exoticism, further complicated by the acute awareness that this particular kind of sexual exoticism is implicitly predatory or sacrificial (depending upon the point of view). The sadomasochistic aspects of vampiric sexual relationships are not seen in terms of destruction but in terms of recruitment, the threat of extinction being largely displaced by the promise of a perpetuation that is only partly misfortunate.

All this is, of course, pure fantasy. Although there is a kind of vampirism that is easily available to anyone who cares to take it up and can find a compliant partner, the kind to which modern vampire fiction refers is far more ambitious. The lyrics of vampire rock music are not about blood-drinking *per se*, but blood-drinking as a symbolic unholy communion, which promises both an advanced form of sexual intimacy and privileged access to an altered state of being, to which common notions of life and death cannot be applied. This is, of course, a calculatedly ironic perversion of the mythology of romantic love that currently possesses (or obsesses) Western sexual relationships, which also pretends that "falling in love" is a heady transportation to a higher state of being.

Identification with the imagined existential plight of vampires serves an elementary function of fantasy fiction that J. R. R. Tolkien called "Recovery"; by removing us from the most fundamental conditions of reality, it allows us to cease taking those fundamental conditions for granted, and thus helps us to see them more objectively and more clearly. There is a sense in which all literary and lifestyle fantasies are similar in offering scope for a Tolkienian Recovery of a distanced view of reality, but the fact that they are similar does not make them equal. If the aspect of reality with which we are concerned is mortality, and the *angst* associated with awareness of mortality, removal to an imaginative standpoint from which mortality is banished (whether that of orthodox religion or that of science-fictional emortality) is crude and unhelpful. If we desire to get a clearer sight of the *angst* that actually afflicts us—with a view, of course, to being better able to cope with it—the imaginative assumption of a markedly different but no less acute form of hypothetical *angst* might be far more serviceable than merely trying to envisage a state of being that is merely *angst*-less.

We already know, of course, that the people most inclined to grapple with *angst* are adolescents; it is those newly arrived on the threshold adult awareness and adult responsibility who come fresh to the age-old conflict. Young people are not the only ones who stand to benefit from kinds of Recovery that readily extend (if only tentatively) into lifestyle fantasy, but they are the ones with the most to gain. It is only to be expected that the most dedicated fans of

Anne Rice novels and vampire films are young, and that the young people who accept the kind of sentimental education offered by these cultural resources should delight in finding that education echoed, amplified and dramatized by appropriate music. The music in question is various, but its core examples are haunting without being feeble, melancholy without being dreary, exotic without being esoteric, and insistently stimulating without being crudely repetitive.

We must remember, however, that Tolkienian Recovery is a two-stage process, which not only leads us there but back again. Whatever benefits might be gained from the vicarious experience of vampire *angst* must, if they are to be authentically valuable, be applicable in everyday life. We must remember, too, that the vast majority of the *angst*-ridden lack the courage for any but the most tentative exercises in literary and lifestyle fantasy. Unpopular culture is, by definition, the province of the fortunate few. The pusillanimous masses will always have to be content with popular culture, and the portentously uptight with high culture.

It is for this reason that any rebirth of a Byronic Satanic Mania was always bound to be followed by a Bulwerian remove to a more cheerful kind of foppery and a carefully-rebalanced view of occult mysteries. The vast majority of couch potatoes who cannot stomach "depraved sexual fantasies for vampires," even in the realm of fantasy, require representation by heroes who can take on the revivified Dracula and win—and by far the most ingenious and successful of these heroes is the TV version of Buffy the Vampire Slayer.

Buffy's flirtation with vampiric lifestyle fantasy—brazenly explicit in the history of her passionate but decisively frustrated affair with Angel—is certainly *angst*-ridden, but Buffy's fate is not to succumb to her demons, or even to learn to live with them; it is to overcome them, and to keep on overcoming them, week by week, as they continue to rise in awful profusion from the Hellmouth that sits beneath every significant locus of adolescent life. While today's Glyndons approach that threshold only to turn tail in stark terror, pursued by the intimidating gazes of its dark dwellers, Buffy crosses it with a courage and skill that few other travelers of the long and winding road have ever displayed. In the true spirit of comic-book superheroism, her scholarly companion Giles is reduced to the status of a humble sidekick, alongside the apprentice witch Willow and the hapless male bimbo Xander.

The parasitism of the TV show upon the adversarial Gothic fantasies it purports to re-oppose is wittily acknowledged by its attribution of the Gothic dress-code to a series of *doppelgänger* figures: to

Willow's vampire *alter ego*, called into being by Cordelia's reckless wish; to Faith, the flawed slayer called prematurely into being by Buffy's temporary death; to the insane *femme fatale* Drusilla, and so on. The one person who observes the Gothic dress-code throughout is Angel, who contains his own doppelgänger by virtue of his status as a paradoxically ensouled vampire, living in perpetual hazard of being forced by passionate fulfillment to revert to type. Like Bulwer's Pelham before her, Buffy has renounced Byronism and is thus entitled to dress more colorfully—but, like Pelham's creator and everyone else possessed of an imagination, she can never entirely escape the urgency of Byronic allure: there is a sense in which her role as a vampire slayer is the most eloquent contemporary witness of the protean invincibility of the vampire icon. Although she strives with all her might—and some success—to avoid being reckoned mad or bad, Buffy is definitely and defiantly dangerous to know. Who, in her right mind, would want to be any other way?

RE-ENCHANTMENT IN
THE AFTERMATH OF WAR

The most important events in the history of the twentieth century were the two "world wars" waged between 1914-18 and 1939-
45. They provided dramatic interruptions to every human concern,
especially in Europe, which provided both conflicts with their most
significant arenas. The imprints left by the wars on naturalistic fiction are easy enough to see, as are some of the imprints left on
imaginative fiction, but there are others not so obvious; the purpose
of this article is to call attention to one of the latter.

In Britain, as in several other European countries, the two decades prior to 1914 had seen a rapid growth in speculative fiction
based in anticipations of future social and technological progress,
but the Great War of 1914-18 brought the evolution of such fiction
to an abrupt halt. There was a dramatic loss of faith in all aspects of
progress, which was made even worse than it might otherwise have
been by the unfortunate prevalence within pre-war British scientific
romance of future war stories that had represented war as a means of
progress—and had, in the process, provided the slogans used in Britain to recruit the war's cannon fodder: the notion of a "war to end
war" and a "war to save civilization".

While the war was actually being fought, a certain flickering
optimism survived, although it required an enormous propagandistic
effort to keep the flame alight, but almost all hope for the future was
inevitably invested in a mere return to "normality" rather than any
progressive transformation. For the vast majority, the goal of life in
1917 was a return to the conditions of life that had pertained in
1913, or even earlier, not a movement towards any new and unprecedented state. Once the armistice had been signed, the fact that
millions of lives had been squandered—not merely without any
measurable gain, but with such irretrievable economic losses that the
economic heart of the world had been transplanted from Europe to

America—became painfully obvious, and the accounting of that loss became a major theme in the literature of the next decade.

Almost all of the future war novels written in Britain during the 1920s took it for granted that a second world war would obliterate European civilization, but most took the bitter view that some such outcome was probably inevitable. The view became widespread that technological progress was intrinsically bad, because it would continue to provide means for us to destroy ourselves more easily and more cruelly; one of the most fervent popularizers of this view was Bertrand Russell, who set it out uncompromisingly in his ideological reply to J. B. S. Haldane's optimistic *Daedalus; or, the Future of Science* (1923), entitled *Icarus; or, Science and the Future* (1924). Britain has lived with the legacy of that pessimism ever since; though gradually modified by opposition, it has never entirely dwindled away.

The effect of the Great War on other kinds of fantastic fiction is not so obvious to the historian, partly because one of the logical corollaries of the abovementioned effect was the encouragement of an attitude of mind that dismissed all forms of "wish-fulfillment" fiction as ridiculous and stupid, utterly unworthy of intelligent consideration. Fantasy *fiction* came to be widely regarded as essentially childish. I have emphasized the word "fiction" because the effect did not apply to fantasies that pretended to be real, which enjoyed a spectacular boom during and after the war. The hunger for miracles rapidly reached such a pitch that Arthur Machen's slight story of "The Bowmen" (1914)—in which the archers of Agincourt emerge from the depths of time to provide what meager cover they can for the British retreat at Mons—was willfully misrepresented by countless readers as actual reportage, giving birth not merely to the specific consolatory myth of "the Angels of Mons" but to dozens of others of a similar ilk. The boost given by the Great War to fantastic *faiths* such as spiritualism eventually produced such extraordinary items of spin-off as the 1920 *cause célèbre* surrounding the ineptly faked photographs of the Cottingley fairies. While the war was in progress, though, faith seemed the only permissible antidote to the grim realism of everyday life on the Home Front; mere fabulation seemed suspiciously akin to moral and intellectual treason.

The end of the war and the consequent resurrection of the publishing industry witnessed a considerable demand for light popular fiction of a kind that certainly warrants description as escapist, but in Britain that demand was focused almost entirely on naturalistic and determinedly insular genres such as love stories and polite detective fiction. When the USA, which had been relatively untouched by the war, came under the threat of the moral tyranny of Prohibition during the 1920s, the ideological counter-assault produced a barrage of defiantly frivolous fantasy fiction, spearheaded by such writers as James Branch Cabell and Thorne Smith, while such pulp fantasists as Abraham Merritt and Edgar Rice Burroughs undertook odysseys in exotica more colorful than any that had ever been wrought before; in Britain, by contrast, any attempt to widen the horizons of fiction beyond the calculatedly trivial was an uphill struggle.

The battle to re-open space within British fiction for fantastic tropes was waged by writers of both sexes, but female writers played a particularly significant role. In particular, there was a small group of female writers who produced vividly eloquent accounts of a world impoverished by atrophied imagination, which stood in dire need of careful re-enchantment. In this article I shall focus most closely at four such novels: *Living Alone* (1919) by Stella Benson; *These Mortals* (1925) by Margaret Irwin; *Lud-in-the-Mist* (1926) by Hope Mirrlees, and *Lolly Willowes; or, The Loving Huntsman* (1926) by Sylvia Townsend Warner.

All four of these books marked significant points in their writers' careers. The first- and last-named were first major publications, and Irwin's was a second; her earlier novel *Still She Wished for Company* (1924) is also a fantasy of only slightly lesser relevance. For Mirrlees, by contrast, her one and only fantasy novel was almost a last publication; it marked a pause in a seemingly-promising career that was not resumed for more than thirty years. All of the authors except Mirrlees went on to build substantial careers on the basis of their naturalistic fictions, but only one made any significant contribution to fantasy fiction in later life, that being Sylvia Townsend Warner's magisterial collection *The Kingdoms of Elfin* (1977), issued after an interval of half a century.

Although the four novels cited are, in my opinion, the most important, three other first major publications by female writers, which might have also been included had this study been broader in scope, are *Martin Pippin in the Apple-Orchard* (1921) by Eleanor Farjeon, *The Venetian Glass Nephew* (1925) by Elinor Wylie, and *The Burning Ring* (1927) by Kay Burdekin. Wylie's later works also concentrated on more naturalistic subject-matter, while the cost of Farjeon's continued interest in fantasy was her long relegation to the field of children's fiction—to which her work was ill-fitted, on the grounds of both sophistication and style. The cost of Burdekin's was a fall from fashion so precipitate that she had to re-invent herself as "Murray Constantine" (whose career proved equally meteoric).

The overall picture constituted by these works is, therefore, that their production was a keenly-motivated but entirely thankless task, at least at the time. The only one of the books to have been significantly rehabilitated, even today, is *Lud-in-the-Mist*, which owes its modern reputation to the freak of chance that brought it to the attention of Lin Carter while he was editing the Ballantine "Adult Fantasy Series"—the enterprise that laid the groundwork for the commercial fantasy genre whose marketing potential was belatedly discovered in the 1970s.

* * * * * * *

Living Alone, expanded from a brief sketch that originally appeared in the *Athenaeum,* is far more clearly marked as an ideological product of the war than the later items of the quartet. The story is actually set in London during the war years, and it describes the transformation of a young woman's tediously oppressive everyday life by a healthily chaotic infusion of magic.

The story begins with the disruption of an unbearably prosaic committee meeting by a mysterious stranger, who turns out to be a witch. The witch's intervention is unwelcome to the majority of the committee members, but fascinates the novel's heroine, Sarah Brown (who shares more than her initials with the author). Sarah follows the witch to the exotic "House of Living Alone", where she meets other magically-talented individuals. Her life is decisively changed by this shift in circumstance, and she embarks on a series of strange encounters and vivid adventures. These include an aerial combat between two broomstick-riding witches, an air raid whose bombs provoke a few of the dead to rise from their graves in deluded expectation of the Last Judgment, and a visit to a "faery farm".

These experiences revitalize a spirit that had been all-but-annihilated by the erosions of the war and the necessities imposed by the war on those trying to maintain the pattern of everyday life in a beleaguered (but uninvaded) country. At the end of the novel, Sarah's magical moral rearmament provides her with the impetus to get out of England altogether; she sets sail for a new life in America. Sarah takes the witch (who has never acquired a personal name) with her on the ship, but her magical *alter ego* takes to her broomstick in order to go home before passing through immigration, because magic—which thrives on the wrath of the Law—is not suited to a land of Liberty. When Sarah disembarks in New York, she enters a new phase of her life, which is literally, but no longer metaphorically, disenchanted.

If any reader were still in doubt, this conclusion provides the final evidence that the novel requires to be construed as a quirkily allegorical item of spiritual autobiography. Its function as psychological therapy is clearly spelled out in the poem that serves as a headpiece, "The Dweller Alone", which begins: "My Self has grown too mad for me to master./Craven, beyond what comfort I can find,/It cries: *"Oh, God, I am stricken with disaster."*/Cries in the night: *"I am stricken, I am blind..."* The novel's more general concerns are exhibited in a romantic subplot, which tracks the problematic relationship of the magically-talented Private Richard Higgins and his imp-tormented lover Peony. This part of the story, in which Sarah is a mere observer, endorses conventional notions of the life-enhancing power of sexual communion, but the main narrative seeks a more self-sufficient destiny for the heroine. Her need, and destiny, is ultimately to find her way to a House of Living Alone unequipped with supportive phantoms.

In common with many other fantastically-transfigured spiritual autobiographies, *Living Alone* has a considerable power to move those readers who are capable of empathizing with the existential plight of its heroine; in that respect it is a glorious celebration of the power of the imagination and a fine argument for the psychological utility of escapism. The novel's narrative trajectory re-emphasizes—as, arguably, all great works of fantasy must and do—that the purpose of fantasy is to be triumphantly self-defeating. Its elaborations and embroideries of everyday life are recommended as a means rather than an end. The only triumph that the novel can envisage is however, a purely personal one; it offers little expectation of Britain's recovery from its historical plight—although the witch returns, and while its native faery folk remain, hope remains for Britain too.

* * * * * * *

Although Margaret Irwin's first-published novel was the heart-felt but scrupulously cautious timeslip romance *Still She Wished for Company* (1924), it is possible that *These Mortals* had been written earlier, but had its publication postponed because it was too unorthodox to be risked without the way being prepared. The novel tells the story of Melusine, the daughter of the enchanter Aldebaran.

Aldebaran—who may well be based on Shakespeare's Prospero, given that another of the bard's fairy plays provided the novel's title—has withdrawn in disgust from the world of mortal human beings. Like Prospero's daughter Miranda, Melusine has been raised in virtual isolation, with no companions but magical ones. Having no idea why her father felt his compulsion to withdraw, she becomes exceedingly curious about the world of human beings, and eventually runs away to make her own exploration of it. Her magic boat brings her, along with three animal friends—a cat, a snake and a raven—to the shore of a kingdom ruled by Eminondas and Adelisa. Melusine's diamond-studded shoes and extraordinary beauty command the instant respect of the royal couple, who lodge her with their daughter Blanchelys and nurse the hope that she might eventually marry their son Pharamond.

Melusine finds the wayward affections and hypocritical affectations of the people who now surround her very difficult to comprehend. She can find nothing to admire in such paragons of courtly insincerity as the fashionable Sir Diarmid and the seductive Lady Valeria. Her ability to turn herself into a moonbeam allows her to wander invisibly about the court, but her clandestine observations only add to her puzzlement. She discovers by degrees that the marriage of Eminondas and Adelisa has more hatred in it than love, that Pharamond is a drunken libertine, and that Blanchelys is a vain fool. The only admirable person she can find is Garth, the king of a distant country, who has been cast into prison by Eminondas for refusing to marry Blanchelys.

Melusine falls in love with Garth and rescues him from his prison, but finds that he cannot accept the kind of love she offers and she must instead accept him on *his* terms. Unfortunately, his notions of propriety prove stifling and oppressive, and she quickly comes to feel wretched. Eventually, she is abandoned to live in the forest with a woodcutter's family, nursing a baby whose arrival has been a complete surprise to her, while Garth returns to Blanchelys, made captive by a magic spell unwisely gifted to the princess by Melusine.

With the help of her animal friends, Melusine eventually contrives to win Garth back, but their final flight to an unknown destination falls some way short of the conventional happy ending with which fairy tales are traditionally supplied. Insofar as the enterprise is a parable of disenchantment, however, its argument is strikingly similar to that of *Living Alone*. The real point is that the foolish mortals she encounters are making a dire mistake in adopting a crassly "realistic" attitude to the gifts that Melusine brings from Aldebaran's world: their disenchantment is unjustified because they had never known the true value of enchantment. Melusine's, on the other hand, is a much more careful and potentially rewarding disenchantment, which might yet allow her to contrive a worthwhile life.

The country to which Melusine is brought by her magical boat resembles the kind of quasi-Medieval kingdom that features in most traditional fairy tales, but it is really an allegory of the 1920s. Signaled by such quirky anachronisms as the fact that Pharamond plays golf, the contemporary relevance of the plot is to be found in the moral environment of the court: an arena in which human relationships have been reduced to a kind of game. The tragedy of Melusine's disillusionment is the tragedy of the post-war world's disillusionment, and the story is, in essence, a plea for the void to be re-filled, not by magic *per se* but by a sense of honor and an authentic enthusiasm for commitment. The explicit moral of the story, stated at the beginning when Aldebaran summarizes of the condition of mortal men—"All the intricacies of their laws, their societies, their towns, their nations, amount only to this: that each individual human being dreads solitude and tries to circumvent it"—echoes the starting-point of *Living Alone*, but the underlying argument of both stories is that this should not and need not be so, if only people could rise above the limitations of their disenchantment to find a better spiritual harmony and to strike a better balance between realism and imagination. Melusine's personal success comes *after* her escapist flight, when she finds a new accommodation with the reality-principle, symbolized by her child; the relative modesty of her final achievement is calculated to encourage the supposition that it is a path others might follow.

* * * * * * *

Lud-in-the-Mist is similar to *These Mortals* in using a profoundly disenchanted fairy-tale kingdom as a stand-in for 1920s Britain. Lud-in-the-Mist—named after a mythical British king whose name was appropriated by anti-technological rioters during the industrial revolution—is the chief market-town of the tiny "free state" of Dorimare, whose geographical situation is the confluence of two rivers: the broad and navigable Dawl, which gives Lud-in-the-Mist the privileges of trade, and the narrow and problematic Dapple, which rises in the Debatable Hills. The Debatable Hills, also known as the Elfin Hills, lie far to the west, marking Dorimare's border with a Land of Faerie that has been all-but forgotten when the story begins. For Dorimarites, the reader is told, "fairy things had always spelled delusion". Lud-in-the-Mist's burial ground is, tellingly, known as the Field of Grammary (Gramarye being a traditional synonym of Faerie).

Like *Living Alone* and *These Mortals*, *Lud-in-the-Mist* is careful to provide a teasing summary of its theme before its story gets under way, this time enigmatized in the form of a riddle inscribed on a fan painted with wind-flowers and violets: *"Why is Melancholy like Honey? Because it is very sweet, and it is culled from Flowers."* In deciphering the problematic "solution" to this riddle, it is useful to recall that a river is also a "flow-er"; when the plot gets under way it is the Dapple that brings the fairy fruits that begin to divert the townspeople from their stubbornly prosaic existence with melancholy sweetness. It is young folk who are seduced by consumption of the forbidden fruit into leaving home to seek their fortune in Faerie, but the older generation is not entirely protected by its members' refusal to taste it, for even they can recall the temptations of "the Note": elfin music heard as if from afar.

Lud-in-the-Mist's mayor, Nathaniel Chanticleer—who has been tempted by the Note in his time, but has resisted its wiles—becomes increasingly troubled by mysteries before the pattern of his life is shattered when he is framed as a distributor of the forbidden fruit by the sinister doctor Endymion Leer. Although he contrives to clear his name, the breach in his fortunes is decisive, and he undertakes a journey up the Dapple into the Debatable Hills and beyond, in the hope of recovering the townspeople who have been wooed away by the fruit—who include his son Ranulph. The *genius loci* of Faerie turns out to be the Puckish spirit of Duke Aubrey, a one-time ruler of Dorimare who has been demonized by the morally upright, his alleged decadence being credited to traffic with "fairy things". Chanticleer has not only to make Dorimare's peace with Aubrey, but also his own—and neither reconciliation is easily set on a sound basis. The moral boundaries remain blurred throughout; Leer's concealed villainy is no more complete than Aubrey's concealed virtue.

More hope is tacitly offered in *Lud-in-the-Mist* than in *These Mortals* for a reconciliation of the post-war world with the enchantment that it has banished, but the difference between the two novels is relative. They refer to the same tragedy, and although they stress that the amelioration of that tragedy cannot be an easy one, they both attempt to map out a path to salvation that is collective as well as personal. Here, as in the other novels under consideration, escapist flight is seen as a means rather than an end, offering no solution in itself and assistance only as a transitory phase. Chanticleer always intends to come back from the Land of Faerie, and to bring others back with him if he can. Not only that, but, after his return, he attempts to make changes in Lud-in-the-Mist that will help to ensure that the problems do not arise again, by allowing the Dapple and the distant strains of the Note to have just sufficient effect to be life-enhancing without being excessively seductive. He knows that it will be a difficult balance to strike, but he does not think it impossible of attainment.

Nathaniel Chanticleer is the only protagonist in the group of four novels who cannot be easily regarded as an alter ego of his tale's teller, which may not be unconnected with the fact that his book is the only one to have ended a career rather than beginning one. By the same token, he is the only one who reaches a conclusion within the text—though not, of course, until he has been allowed a rich and fruitful life between chapter XXXI and Chapter XXXII, "The Conclusion"—but it has already been established in the early pages that the burial ground in which he will end up is the Fields of Grammary. The recording of his epitaph provides the author with an opportunity to remind us that "that the Written Word is a Fairy, as mocking and elusive as Willy Wisp". And so it is, no matter how the tastes of the reading public might resist the notion in stressful times.

* * * * * * *

Like *Lud-in-the-Mist, Lolly Willowes* has a much older protagonist than *Living Alone* or *These Mortals*, and, like Mirrlees' novel, it pits that protagonist against a demonized adversary. In another way however, it bends the sequence back upon itself, sharing with *Living Alone* an insistence that any reconciliation that is to be found between the modern world and the mythical past is a purely personal matter, which requires a phase of transition rather than a permanent settlement.

Lolly Willowes (the name by which she is known is an amiable but slightly diminishing contraction of Laura) is a passive spinster who lives a humdrum life of exploitation by her relatives, passed on from her elder brother to others in need of help in child-rearing. Her various hosts are very willing to accommodate her within their families for as long as she is useful, but when she has outlived her usefulness as a maiden aunt she is effectively cast out, eventually being despatched to retirement in a cottage in the Chiltern village of Great Mop.

In Great Mop, whose local inn is called the Reason Why, she engages in a desultory and ultimately unsatisfactory pursuit of new social relationships, but it is not until she is taken to the Witches' Sabbath by Mrs Leak that she begins to find a rewarding way of existing in the world—and not without difficulty even then. She is at embarrassed at first by the merriment of the Sabbath, for which she feels ill-fitted, and is not initially pleased to make the acquaintance of Satan, but she eventually comes to appreciate his role as a "loving huntsman" who is still prepared to take an interest in her, and to provide a function for her to fulfill.

Unlike Mirrlees' Duke Aubrey, who was unjustly demonized for sins that amounted to little more than a fondness for wine, women, song and magic, Warner's Satan really is the Devil, although he has more in common with the pagan god Pan than the anti-god of Christian mythology. When Lolly first goes looking for him, she searches in Folly Wood, but she soon learns that he is ever-present, and that he purchases many more souls, far more cheaply, than she had been brought up to imagine. His principal attraction, to begin with, is that his game, however crooked, is the only one in town, but she soon learns to cultivate a proper appreciation of "his satisfied but profoundly indifferent ownership" of her soul.

To the extent that Warner's devil provides Lolly with real rewards, they are closely akin to the rewards sought by Sarah Brown, or Melusine, or the young ladies of Miss Primrose Crabapple's Academy in Lud-in-the-Mist; they are poor enough in material terms, but they have considerable sentimental value. Life within his harem, in the coven, is only a little less stultifying than the life from which Lolly has escaped, but there is a valuable personal component to their relationship that she never contrived to find in her few mundane—and conspicuously desultory—admirers.

Like Irwin's Melusine, Lolly Willowes finds that, although one can make progress on the journey, the end of the rainbow remains frustratingly out of sight, but she learns to strike a balance between hope and expectation. One suspects, of course, that sequels to *Living Alone* and *Lud-in-the-Mist* might have revealed that Sarah Brown fared less well in America than she hoped when she set off from Southampton, an that Nathaniel Chanticleer might have had more problems than are suggested by the casual gap separating the penultimate chapter of his story from its conclusion—and, if so, Lolly Willowes is a thoroughly appropriate conclusion to the quartet I have constructed from these four novels. Each of the four is, in its own peculiar fashion, an insistently realistic work, conscientious in not claiming too much, but equally conscientious in celebrating the true value of that which is there to be claimed, if only petty prejudices and unjustified moral oppressions could be set aside.

* * * * * * *

The most important male writers who contributed to the same narrow literary subset to which the four described works belong were David Garnett, author of *Lady into Fox* (1923), Gerald Bullett, author of *Mr. Godly Beside Himself* (1924), and Lord Dunsany, whose most relevant works were *The King of Elfland's Daughter* (1924) and *The Blessing of Pan* (1927). Garnett and Bullett both wrote occasional subsequent fantasies, although they had greater success with naturalistic works; Dunsany became the leading fantasy writer in the British Isles, mainly because he was far less concerned with commercial and critical success, although the fact that he was Irish rather than English was also a significant contributory factor.

The chief difference between these four works by male authors and those analyzed above is an expectable masculine assertiveness, although this is not necessarily symptomatic of a greater confidence in the possibility of recovering a more life-enhancing relationship between the private imagination and the public demands of quotidian reality. The waning of that hope is expressed as clearly in the biographies and career-paths of the male and female writers alike as it is the relative subtlety of the of four novels chosen as primary exhibits. There is, however, a particular plaintiveness in the novels by female writers that probably captures the mood of the post-war decade with a unique clarity. Their encapsulation of the "spirit of the age"—or, more accurately, the dispiritedness of the age—is exceptionally neat, perhaps because it is a trifle more objective, coming as it does from outside the ranks of potential combatants, but from deep inside the ranks of actual victims of the deprivations and corrosions of war.

As I have already argued, close inspection of these works sustains the argument that great works of fantasy fiction are self-defeating, in the sense that their arguments never give way to the supposition that escapism can be permanent or absolute. But sensitive reading also sustains another argument, which is that the greatest works of imaginative fiction use fantasy as an instrument of use-

120

ful revelation, stripping away the life-denying veils of illusion in which "real life" and "naturalistic fiction" are sometimes protectively decked.

In the wake of World War I the world needed the education that might have been provided by works like *Living Alone, These Mortals, Lud-in-the-Mist* and *Lolly Willowes*, and the fact that the four books failed to attract or retain much of an audience is a sad reflection of the world's inability—only slightly less now than then—to come to sensible terms with that need. We have a great deal more fantasy fiction now than our forebears had then— enormous quantities of it mass-produced by female writers—but one would have to search long and hard to find four novels produced in the last decade that have a sense of mission as delicate or as dedicated as these. Had there not been a second world war, the scars left by the first might not have remained so livid and so numb, but, even though we have now enjoyed a much longer interval of relative peace and prosperity, very few of us have found the kind of healthy balance between the demands of mundanity and the opportunities of imagination that these novels tried hard to promote.

DEAD LETTERS AND THEIR INHERITORS

"Ruin is the destruction toward which all men rush, each pursuing his own best interest in a society that believes in the freedom of the commons. Freedom in a commons brings ruin to all."
    (Garrett Hardin, "The Tragedy of the Commons" p.1244)

* * * * * * *

"Science fiction, even at the popular level, should always be exploratory and it should always be ironic; it should celebrate the process of scientific discovery and enlightenment, and it should brutally examine any and all idols of contemporary thought in the cynical hope of finding feet of clay.

"Science fiction should never lend its inventive energy to the cause of daydream wish-fulfilment, although its most precious inventions will inevitably be plundered wholesale for exactly that purpose; its plots should never be populated with straw men whose narrative function it is to be blown away, and its heroes should never be content to become rich or to achieve the kinds of sexual success that are stereotypical of romantic fiction or pornography.

"In every science fiction story the question ought to be raised as to whether the hero might be utterly misguided in everything he believes and is trying to achieve; every time a problem is solved, and every time a conclusion is arrived at, a cunning and skeptical observer should start pointing out the new problems that have thereby been created and the new conflicts that have been opened up.

"Any science fiction story that does not annoy at least half its readers ought to be reckoned a failure; any science fiction reader who ends a story feeling comfortable and satisfied ought to throw it away and go looking for something that will mock, insult and disturb him—*not* in the way that a conventional horror story disturbs him, by assuming that any disruption of the everyday world is *ipso facto* evil, but in the authentic science-fictional way, which is to

122

suggest that there is nothing more ridiculous, degrading and unworthy of the commitment of an intelligent person than normality—except, of course, for a conventional eucatastrophe."
(Brian Stableford, "How Should a Science Fiction Story End?"
p.15)

* * * * * * *

The notion that the present world order is bound to be devastated in the relatively near future by an all-encompassing ecocatastrophe has been a fundamental assumption of Brian Stableford's science fiction since the very beginning. Almost all of his Earth-set novels deal with the aftermath of some such crisis. Their main focus is, however, on processes of post-catastrophic reconstruction, whose architects are intent on avoiding any repetition of disaster. This usually involves the emergence of a post-human condition whose central feature is extreme longevity—a condition that he describes, following the example of Alvin Silverstein, as emortality. ("Immortality" is here construed as providing total immunity against death, while mere "emortals", although free of the ravages of age and disease, remain perennially vulnerable to violent annihilation.)

The basic future-historical template of Stableford's emortality stories was first set out in a futurological "coffee-table book" *The Third Millennium: A History of the World, AD 2000-3000* (1985) whose text he wrote in collaboration with David Langford. This describes, in some detail, the ecospasmic Crash that puts a grim end to the world's population explosion in the twenty-first century, then outlines in a more languid fashion the salvation of humanity by the careful application of sophisticated biotechnologies. Although the book was an item of hackwork, whose well-intentioned text was rudely butchered by its packager, Stableford continued to use its vision of the future, and simple variants thereof, as a template for many of the short stories he began to write when he returned to SF writing after a five-year absence in 1986. As time went by, the tacit histories backgrounding these stories diverged considerably from one another, and from their original, partly by virtue of the attention Stableford paid to current developments in biotechnology and partly by virtue of purely idiosyncratic additions.

Ten years after the publication of *The Third Millennium,* Stableford prepared an outline for a series of six novels that would map out a revised and updated historical template. Although all six volumes were to be expansions of pre-existent works whose backgrounds were only loosely related (one of which had not been published) the prospectus promised to revise the stories in question to make their backcloths fully consistent. Because the series failed to find a publisher in the UK and its eventual US publisher cautiously insisted on commissioning one volume at a time—beginning with the one that he considered to be the most commercial rather than the earliest-set—the bibliography of the series has become slightly confused. The sequence as originally envisaged began with the novel now titled *The Cassandra Complex* (2001) and continued with *Inherit the Earth* (1998), *Dark Ararat* (forthcoming), *Architects of Emortality* (1999), *The Fountains of Youth* (2000), and *The Omega Expedition* (forthcoming). Given that none of the books so far published has appeared under the title on the typescript, the titles of the unpublished books must be regarded as speculative.

A detailed account of the situation of this series of novels within Stableford's massive literary output, or its significance within his long and checkered career, would be far too tedious for users of a volume such as this to bear, but it would be impossible to present a competent analysis of their manner and method without saying something about the exceedingly peculiar situation of biotechnology within the general field of science fiction—something of which Stableford, who has made a few slight contributions to the mapping of the genre's history, is obviously aware.

The first notable example of speculative fiction in which biotechnology plays a crucial role is *Mizora*, published in 1890 under the pseudonym of Princess Vera Zaronovitch. In Mizora the male of the species is extinct, having been made redundant by new reproductive technologies. Related technologies have freed the Mizorans from dependence on crop plants and animal husbandry, all food being synthetic. Advanced medical technology has resulted in the conquest of disease and the extension of the human lifespan. Princess Zaronovitch takes it for granted that all these advances are implicitly good: perfect foundation-stones for a Utopian society. Within the course of the next hundred years, however, she proved to be in a minority so tiny that its enumeration does not require all the fingers of a single hand.

Tissue culture experiments carried out by Alexis Carrel and others in the early part of the twentieth century prompted J. B. S. Haldane to produce *Daedalus; or, Science and the Future*, a lecture read at Cambridge University on 4 February 1923 and reprinted as a pamphlet. Haldane proposes that the technologies that will remake human society in the second half of the twentieth century will be "biological inventions", the most important of which will be synthetic food. He declares that advances in the understanding of basic biological processes will produce many technological applications of which the world stands in dire need but sounds a cautionary note about the manner in which they are likely to be received by the public. After offering a list of the great biological inventions of the past he observes that:

> The chemical or physical inventor is always a Prometheus. There is no great invention, from fire to flying, which has not been hailed as an insult to some god. But if every physical and chemical invention is a blasphemy, every biological invention is a perversion. There is hardly one which, on first being brought to the notice of an observer from any nation which has not previously heard of their existence, would not appear to him as indecent and unnatural. (Haldane, *Daedalus* p.44)

This passage—which Stableford is exceedingly fond of quoting—recognizes and calls attention to the great irony of biotechnological progress, which has comprehensively blighted all but a few examples of speculative fiction dealing with such innovations. Everything that we think of as "human nature"—and, indeed, almost everything we nowadays think of as "nature"—is in fact the product of biotechnological invention. Everything that we think of as good and every worthwhile human achievement owes its existence to biotechnology, and yet—paradoxical as it may seem—the grateful awe with which we cling to the produce of the biotechnological discoveries of the past has as its flip-side a deep suspicion of all further biotechnological discoveries.

Haldane's close friend Julian Huxley extrapolated the ideas contained in *Daedalus* in a satirical parable set in darkest Africa, "The Tissue-Culture King" (1926), but Julian left it to his younger brother Aldous to bring the message home in *Brave New World* (1932). The most eloquent testimony to the accuracy and force of Haldane's argument is that during the next half-century this magnificently cynical and brutally sarcastic comedy was never supplemented, let alone surpassed, by any similarly-comprehensive account of a biotechnologically sophisticated society. There seems to have been a tacit admission by almost all subsequent writers that this one novel had said all that needs to be said on the subject. In

1951, when James Blish wrote an essay on "The Biological Story" in the May 1951 issue of *Science Fiction Quarterly*, he had to begin with the lament that he had only been able to find one solitary example of a sensible application of biotechnology: Norman L. Knight's novella "Crisis in Utopia" (*Astounding Science-Fiction* July-August 1940).

The real subject-matter of "Crisis in Utopia" is not, in fact, the "tectogenetics" on which the future Utopia of the forty-second century is based but the extreme prejudice of the Utopians against the use of such technologies on the human genome. Blish points out that other pulp SF stories extrapolating biological ideas had routinely played upon the same anxiety in more brutal fashion; they were, almost without exception, exercises in teratology. Nothing changed in the next thirty years; the vast majority of SF stories about biotechnology continued to take the form of Frankensteinian fables in which the products of induced mutation and other interventions, however well-intended, run amok and have to be destroyed. Even stories about such seemingly-benign innovations as the conquest of disease and ageing routinely insisted on finding some crucial fly in the ointment.

Blish made a conscientious attempt to oppose this trend in his own work, most obviously in the mosaic novel *The Seedling Stars* (1957) and the novella belatedly expanded into *Titan's Daughter* (1961). He was not the only SF writer to follow Norman Knight's example in the 1950s and 1960s by offering scrupulous objections to a prejudice whose enormous strength was taken for granted, but he remained in a tiny minority. Such attempts received a massive setback when British journalist Gordon Rattray Taylor published a fervent exercise in alarmism called *The Biological Time-Bomb* in 1968, with a contents page listing such topics as "the new eugenics" and "the spectre of gene warfare" and a last chapter entitled "The Future, If Any". The book inspired the creation of the alarmist TV drama series *Doomwatch*, launching an epidemic anxiety that was imported into the USA by Vance Packard, who was famous as the author of a best-selling attack on the use of insidious techniques of manipulation by advertisers, *The Hidden Persuaders* (1957). Packard's *The People Shapers* (1978) arrived with a front-flap blurb promising that the developments mapped out within "will make your skin crawl" and asking such questions as "What happens to the historic concept of the sanctity of the individual if surgeons can transplant heads?"

Everything that has happened in the field of biotechnology since the genetic code was cracked in the 1960s, up to and including the current controversies regarding cloning and genetically modified food, provides conclusive evidence that Haldane was a far better prophet than he could possibly have wished. The vast majority of civilized human beings, who are in every respect the products of biotechnology and who consider the biotechnologies of the past to be entirely and definitively natural, seemingly cannot contemplate the biotechnologies of the present—let alone those of the future— without a suffering a reflexive tidal-wave of neurotic anxiety and blind, unreasoning terror. This is the context in which Stableford's work has to be seen, not merely as the reality surrounding it but as an appalling circumstance against which he has continually tried— albeit ineffectually and well-nigh invisibly—to excite justified moral outrage.

We can, of course, only speculate as to the extent to which the long-standing unpopularity of Stableford's work is due to its mere incompetence rather than his insistence on swimming against what he knows too well to be an irresistible ideological tide, but it would be kind to assume that the latter factor plays some small part. By the same token, we have no way of knowing what awful hidden perversity compels him to such madness, and it is probably kinder not to speculate. The simple fact is, however, that providing what opposition he can to the irrational follies of a sick society is what he has chosen to do—and the horrid history of similar exercises in public outrage goes at least some way to explaining the slightly bizarre manner in which he chooses to do it.

One must presume that, every time Stableford sees TV news footage of posturing idiots uprooting test-crops of genetically modified plants, or hears moral imbeciles railing against the mere idea of therapeutic cloning, he is consumed by a righteous anger that has no other vent but literary work that (as he surely knows full well) is unlikely to sell and highly likely to fall by the generic wayside even if it does. He may well feel that the handling of biotechnological themes by the vast majority of writers and journalists is a metaphorical ecocatastrophe in its own right: a tragedy of the common desire to base attitudes and decisions on ill-trained "gut instincts" and yuk factors rather than on rational evaluation, and that the over-inflated currency of biotechnological horror stories will be a significant, if minor, contributor to the impending Crash. He must know that a sarcastic refusal to flatter the petty prejudices of the squeamish majority is no way to endear himself to editors and publishers, but anyone who knows—as he clearly does—the extent of the debt that human "nature" owes to biotechnology is duty-bound to repay his fraction, with as much interest as he can muster.

* * * * * * *

The Cassandra Complex takes its title from a psychological syndrome whose sufferers believe that they can foresee a disastrous future for themselves but are impotent to prevent it. It is named for the Trojan prophetess whose true anticipations were rendered impotent by the refusal of their hearers to act upon them. (This probably does count as a curable delusion in some rare instances, but will usually pass for realism in a world where only lunatics can avoid paranoia and all ugly cygnets turn out to be mere ducks.)

The Cassandra Complex is the only element of the emortality series set before the Crash that will put an end to the population explosion, although all of its leading characters can see perfectly clearly that the Crash is inevitable. Stableford has also several written stories that make much of the equally-ironic Oedipus effect, which describes the capacity that both true and false prophecies have to pervert the future if they do provoke action, however slight. There is, therefore, a sense in which this series of novels, and the entire *corpus* of which it is a part, may be regarded as the desperate effort of a self-diagnosed sufferer from the Cassandra complex to exert an Oedipus effect.

The plot of *The Cassandra Complex*, whose elements are borrowed from the short story "The Magic Bullet" (1989), is superficially disguised as an exercise in futuristic crime fiction, although the mystery of why a once-famous but conspicuously unsuccessful biotechnologist has been kidnapped is merely a peg on which to hang a series of philosophical discussions. The first four novels in the projected series are all cast in the same mock-criminous mould, although the crimes and the processes of their detection become increasingly tokenistic and increasingly absurd until the formula reaches breaking point in the nakedly preposterous black comedy of *Architects of Emortality*.

The main characters of *The Cassandra Complex* are somewhat older than is usual in crime stories, all of them being in their sixties or seventies. This enables them to look back as well as forward over considerable historical spectra whose patterns display technology-driven social changes. As technologies of longevity become more effective in each volume of the series, these spectra are gradually elongated and elaborated, mimicking the geometrical shift of changing time-scales of the four parts of *The Third Millennium* (a literary device borrowed from Olaf Stapledon's *Last and First Men*).

The central character of *The Cassandra Complex*, the kidnapped biologist Morgan Miller, is conspicuous by his absence until the climax, when he is allowed on stage to explain everything. This too is a recurring device; the central characters of *Inherit the Earth* and *Architects of Emortality*, Conrad Helier and Jafri Biasiolo, never appear on stage at all, and all five of the preparatory volumes refer more-or-less obliquely to the absence of Adam Zimmerman, who is the true progenitor of the series in two separate but closely related senses. Within the series he is the facilitator of the economic coup that delivers the Earth into the tender care of the "Hardinist Cabal". In a wider context, the first story Stableford wrote when he returned to SF writing in 1986 was "...And He Not Busy Being Born", which is an account of Zimmerman's remarkable biography. (The final volume of the series will incorporate a heavily-revised version of this biography and will bring Zimmerman on to the stage at last.)

Even as a true progenitor, however, Zimmerman is not the character whose absence from centre-stage is most crucially important, as *The Fountains of Youth* makes abundantly clear. Although Mortimer Gray is the first-person narrator of that text, its central character—unsurpassably conspicuous by his remarkable absence—is Death. The narrative purpose served by all these absent characters is that missing persons prompt searches, the most important of which are searches for understanding.

* * * * * * *

The people of the post-Crash world featured in *Inherit the Earth* (expanded from the similarly-titled novella) have shelved the bio-technological line of approach to technologies of emortality favored by Morgan Miller in favor of nanotechnological processes of repair that currently promise life spans in the region of 150-200 years. It is widely, believed, however, that there will be an "escalator effect" by which the beneficiaries of the present generation of repair technologies will be preserved long enough to obtain a further boost from the next generation, which will in turn enable them to reap further benefits as ever-more sophisticated nanotechnologies enter the public domain.

The kidnappee in *Inherit the Earth* is Silas Arnett, a member of a group of biotechnologists who pioneered the use of what J. B. S. Haldane called "ectogenesis"—the growth of human embryos in artificial wombs—in response to a plague of sterilizing viruses that might or might not have been the final phase of the "plague wars" whose first phase had just begun in *The Cassandra Complex*. The character put under the greatest pressure by the kidnapping, Damon Hart, is the disaffected son of the leader of the group, Conrad Helier, rumors of whose death are thought by the kidnappers to have been greatly exaggerated. The movers of the plot ultimately turn out to be the descendants of the capitalist Cabal that lurks in the background of all six novels, whose stranglehold on the world economy has been further increased by their effective monopoly on the deployment of nanotechnology—a stranglehold that they intend to make absolutely secure by reining in any rogue biotechnologists capable of upsetting their apple-cart.

As in *The Cassandra Complex*, the technology of which the world's secret masters are slightly afraid turns out in *Inherit the Earth* to have more ramifications than are immediately obvious, although their potential is not spelled out in any detail until they are integrated, explicitly but unobtrusively, into the background *Architects of Emortality* (expanded from a novella entitled "Les Fleurs du Mal", which was an abridgment of a similarly-titled unpublished novel).

The novel envisaged as the third volume of the series, *Dark Ararat*, was always conceived as a sidestep, in that it will describe the landfall of the only survivor of a group of interstellar "Arks" launched at the height of the Crash, when the more anxious members of the capitalist Cabal became convinced that the world was doomed. It was placed third in the original sequence, although news of the landfall does not each Earth until part-way through *The Fountains of Youth*, because its key characters are awakened from suspended animation with memories of a world historically located between the worlds of *The Cassandra Complex* and *Inherit the Earth*, and it is therefore more closely associated with those novels than with the later triad, which deal with societies that are much more technologically-advanced.

While the first three novels in the series-as-planned were conceived by the author as mock-thrillers, the final three were conceived as comedies. For bridging purposes, however, *Architects of Emortality* retains a calculatedly absurd murder-mystery framework in which a genetic engineer specializing in flower design, named Oscar Wilde, lends his expertise as an aesthetic theorist to the investigation by Charlotte Holmes ad Hal Watson of a series of murders signed (pseudonymously) "Rappaccini". The fact that some American reviewers—and, indeed, at least one of the editors involved in the novel's progress from typescript to print—somehow failed to notice that the story is a sarcastic joke is not entirely surprising, given that *Brave New World* has always suffered from the same problem.

As in *The Cassandra Complex*, the investigation of the crime that moves the plot of *Architects of Emortality* is carefully monitored by the descendants of the capitalist Cabal, whose front organizations are now popularly known as the MegaMall. Oscar Wilde is here the only character sufficiently cursed by the Cassandra Complex to realize exactly how unlucky he is to have been born at the tail end the unfulfilled flirtation with repair nanotechnology whose early phases were mapped out in *Inherit the Earth*. The old people of this world can no longer take comfort in the illusory escalator effect, and they are already making way for a new breed of biotechnologically-created emortals, here called "naturals".

The seemingly-final conquest of death that is visible to the characters of *Architects of Emortality* is fully realized in *The Fountains of Youth*, whose central character is Mortimer Gray, the first man to set out to write a comprehensive history of death, and hence the first to provide a truly enlightened analysis of the significance of its newly minimized role in human affairs—which is, of course, by no means a total elimination. The novel is an expansion of the novella "Mortimer Gray's *History of Death*", which was itself expanded from an earlier unpublished novella.

The author's hope must have been that the mock-thriller elements of the series would have built an audience whose curiosity as sufficient not merely to see them through the carefully hybridized comedy of *Architects of Emortality* but also to encourage them tolerate the fact that the final two volumes in the series comprise an extraordinarily-elaborated and blatantly comic *bildungsroman* devoid of all the conventional melodramatic props of popular fiction. It is, of course, difficult to set exciting stories in any Utopia, and a Utopia of emortals is even less hospitable to urgent dramatic tension; Stableford presumably knew that this problem further compounded the one mapped out by Haldane, that the redoubled difficulty made the publication of an account of a biotechnologically-sophisticated Utopia into the greatest challenge available to a contemporary writer, and that, even if he ever contrived to get some such work into print, he would get no medals for it, but he went ahead anyway. Some critics might consider him brave—although none, to date, has actually said so—but the cynics who think him merely stubborn to the point of perversity are probably more accurate judges of character.

Mortimer Gray is scheduled to return as one of the central characters of *The Omega Expedition*, so that his *bildungsroman* can continue to prove a narrative frame of sorts. As a historian, he will be fascinated to meet up with Adam Zimmerman, whose appearance will permit the establishment of a bridge across the entire time span of the series. A secondary bridge will be established to *Inherit the Earth* by the reappearance of one of its minor characters, Madoc Tamlin, also awakened after a long sojourn in suspended animation.

* * * * * * *

The various versions of the Crash that feature in Stableford's stories all have one thing in common: no one is uniquely responsible for them. They are never the work of scapegoatable "villains" but the inevitable collective result of perfectly ordinary people following their individual self-interest. The ecospasms in Stableford's works always work out, on a global scale, the logic of Garrett Hardin's classic essay on "The Tragedy of the Commons", invariably taking for granted the statement that appeared as the article's summary blurb in *Science*: "The population problem has no technical solution; it requires a fundamental extension in morality".

Many of Stableford's stories deal with individuals who feel obliged to conceal actions taken to oppose or ameliorate the effects of ecocatastrophe, because they rightly fear being perceived, in terms of an obsolete morality, as "villains" by those whose individual interests they are subverting. The most obvious example of a character of this kind is Conrad Helier, who is remembered in *Inherit the Earth* as a hero only because he has taken great care to conceal the fact that he helped to spread the plague of sterility that put a stop to the population explosion before perfecting the artificial wombs that forced the business of reproduction to become subject to collective planning. Another is the architect of the Arks featured in *Dark Ararat*, who does indeed become the victim of a "revolution" by his crew-members.

Stableford is careful in his depiction of such characters not to represent them as authentically heroic, and usually suggests that their contributions to the public good arise out of the desire for self-glorification or personal enrichment rather than genuine altruism. The character who precipitates by far the most extravagant change for the better envisaged by any of his stories, Giovanni Casanova in

"A Career in Sexual Chemistry", does so entirely by accident while pursuing his own base agenda. The character who does most to help the world to recover rapidly from the most extreme of all Stableford's imagined Crashes, Cade Carlyle Maclaine in "Hidden Agendas" (1999), is generally considered—not altogether unjustly—to be a war criminal.

The vague patterns formed by the Malthusian checks in Stableford's various retrospective accounts of ecospasmic Crash usually give due credit to famine, but tend to assume that the principal destructive role has been played by genetically-engineered diseases. Oddly enough, however, his characterization of "plague wars" actually emphasizes the lack of individual accountability for the Crash, because none of the wars in question is ever formally declared and none of the plagues is ever conclusively traced to its source. Reference is frequently made to speculations about the first plague war being a campaign waged against the poor by the rich—an attempt to clear away unproductive and troublesome "underclasses"—and the second being a retaliatory strike that inevitably rebounded, but the fundamental assumption is always that the people of the future will never have anyone to blame for the birth-pangs of their new order. Even the assiduous historian of death in all its aspects, Mortimer Gray, dismisses the question as irrelevant as well as unanswerable in *The Fountains of Youth*.

Mortimer Gray belongs to a set of characters quite distinct from that comprising the likes of Conrad Helier and Cade Carlyle Maclaine. He is neither hero nor villain, either in objective terms or in terms of his reputation. He is frequently accused of being a fool, and, although he resents such accusations far more than Oscar Wilde in *Architects of Emortality*—who casually reinterprets the word to transform it into a compliment—there is some justice in it. He is a very earnest jester, but his principal reason for being is to remind the world of emortals of their extraordinary good fortune in not having to die. Similar "wise fools" occupy centre stage in such tales as "Cinderella's Sisters" (1989), "Skin Deep" (1991) and "The Cure for Love" (1993), although—like the inquisitive children in "What Can Chloë Want?" (1994), "The Age of Innocence" (1995) and "The Pipes of Pan" (1998) and the young Emily Marchant in *The Fountains of Youth*—they might perhaps be more kindly described as "clever innocents".

All writers who construct exotic worlds-within-texts find "innocents abroad" useful as main characters, because they can ask the naive questions whose answers the reader needs to know, but Stableford's use of such characters goes beyond mere matters of narrative convenience. His inquisitive innocents are figures who mirror both the negligence that can cause Crashes and the hopeful optimism that might prevent them, not merely alloyed but oddly allied. The most exaggerated adult example of this kind of character, apart from Mortimer Gray, is Adam Zimmerman.

All the Stablefordian characters cast in this peculiar mold are tentatively but boldly engaged in the problematic business of trying to contrive a Hardinesque "fundamental extension in morality". In effect, they are learning to be post-human without the benefit of pre-existent role-models. They frequently make a mess of it, but they always stick to their guns, because they take it for granted that the first and foremost virtue a post-human will require is stubbornness. How could it be otherwise, if the key to post-humanity is post-mortality?

All these characters find themselves adrift in a historical moment caught between a disaster-laden past and a hopefully-Utopian future, knowing—however vaguely—that they are the people who will have to discover the moral compass that future generations will use to guide them through a world of infinite opportunity. All but the youngest are also aware—dimly, at least—that, if they fail, then Pandora's box is likely to be unlocked again. They are not heroes, because their role is an essentially unheroic one. The most fundamental premise of the overarching project of which their individual tales are but a part is that, if world-wide disaster is the collective result of vast numbers of mostly insignificant individuals rationally and doggedly pursuing their own interests, then any recipe for the salvation of the world must involve vast numbers of mostly insignificant individuals, whose equally dogged and equally rational pursuit of their own interests must yield an arithmetical sum, within a new and fundamentally different moral context.

As to the means that might and ought to bring this about, Stableford relies on his conviction that, just as the biotechnologies of the past have remolded human "nature" for the better, so the biotechnologies of the future should bring about further improvements. The personal problems of Stableford's characters (like all real personal problems) require behavioral solutions, and the social problems of his not-yet-Utopian futures (like all real social problems) require political solutions, but the human problems featured in his stories—which is to say, the problems his characters face by virtue of being human rather than idiosyncratic members of a particular society—have biotechnological solutions because biotechnological solutions are the only kind of solutions that "human problems" have ever had or ever can have.

* * * * * * *

Stableford's fascination with Haldane's *Daedalus* and its distorted reflections in "The Tissue Culture King" and *Brave New World* (1932) has often prompted him to try to redeem the imagery of the last-named work from its horrific connotations. The most telling of those images is contained in its first chapter: the "hatchery" in which the children of the future are produced in clonal batches from artificial wombs. *Inherit the Earth* follows *The Third Millennium* in arguing that the removal of the privileges of fertility from natural wombs is highly desirable, because the one thing that must be brought under strict political control in a world of long-lived people is the dynamics of its population.

This proved, not unexpectedly, to be the most controversial contention of both books, and Stableford has tried hard in other stories—especially "The Invisible Worm" (1991), "The Age of Innocence" and *The Fountains of Youth*—to offer sympathetic accounts of alternatives to the nuclear family. "The Pipes of Pan" considers the other side of the coin, describing an absurd situation resulting from a stubborn determination to hold on to the nuclear family in the world of emortals. "The Invisible Worm" and *The Fountains of Youth* both assume that, in order to protect the right to found a family that is currently guaranteed by the UN and European charters of human rights, it will be desirable in a world of emortals for the normal exercise of that right to be posthumous.

Stableford's stories routinely assume that children will routinely be raised in aggregate households formed by groups of between eight and twelve adults for that specific purpose. Although "The Invisible Worm" suggests that an outcome of this kind might be achieved by the voluntary exercise of political will, the future history series assumes that it cannot, and for this reason the role of the Crash in that series is somewhat ambiguous. The plague wars that contrive the relatively sudden reduction of the human population provide cover for the deployment of a "plague of sterility" that facilitates the evolution of a population whose numbers are much more easily controllable.

A different apologetic case is made out in "Hidden Agendas" and its sequel, "Ashes and Tombstones", which are set in a future where the Crash is far more drastic, almost causing the extinction of the human and many other species. In this future, ectogenesis and cloning technologies become enormously valuable assets in contriving a rapid multispecific "repopulation" of the Earth, whose ironic "heroes" are genetically-engineered cockroaches. Even here, though, the Crash is slightly ambiguous; although it is certainly a disaster of epic proportions, it does clear the way for the development of a more careful—and hence more sustainable—relationship between human beings and reproductive technology.

Such ambiguities as this have long been a major feature of genre science fiction, where every disastrous cloud that stops short of total annihilation (if only by a whisker) usually turns out to have a silver lining—and it is perhaps as well, given that the destructive imagery of SF would otherwise seem nihilistic or pornographic. Stableford's knowledge of this fact is probably one of the factors that have made him so cautious in his handling of the idea of a population Crash that he has never attempted to describe it in any detail. He does, however, take the trouble to point out in the summary of the relevant chapter of Mortimer Gray's *History of Death*, that the everyday work of natural mortality produced Crash-like casualty figures on a regular basis throughout the twentieth century, with only moderate aid from murderous malice—and Mortimer Gray is in no doubt as to which ought to be reckoned the greater tragedy. It is not altogether surprising, therefore, that even the leading characters in *The Cassandra Complex*—who know that they will have to live through the impending Crash, or die trying—ultimately take the view that they have some reason to be cheerful, on account of the brief and intrinsically frustrating glimpse of the possibility of emortality that has been vouchsafed to them. Stableford presumably hopes that his audience will eventually come to a similar conclusion, although he is unlikely to be holding his breath in the meantime.

* * * * * * *

Stableford's fiftieth novel, *Year Zero* (2000), might be regarded as a brief holiday from the serious business of the future history series. It is by far the broadest of all his comedies, features by far the cleverest of all his innocent protagonists, and its plot climaxes (on 31 December 2000) in by far the most extravagant of all his imagined apocalypses. Along the way it "reveals" that the alien greys whose UFOs are currently haunting the world are trying to pick up a few existential tips from humankind before deciding how to restart the evolutionary process in their homeworld, which they have unfortunately ruined. Their ecospasm, irredeemable even by heroic cockroaches, has reduced a rich and strange biosphere to the "cyanobacterial slime" from which it began. Ours will follow suit unless the hapless heroine can find a way to thwart the Devil—who is not only alive and well but up close and personal—although she knows full well that he is only a phantom of the cerebral cortex, a mere projection of the human desire for moral order.

Similar themes, dressed in equally gaudy costumes, recur in many of the "dark fantasies" that Stableford has written alongside his science fiction. Even more ironic than the biotechnological Utopias, these fantasies provide a further reflection of the process by which the human race is pulling itself apart; given the present state of the publishing industry it seems highly unlikely that any of the short stories Stableford wrote in the 1990s will ever be collected together, but the disconnection to which their near-random scattering has condemned them may itself be seen as an echo of the process of disintegration that they attempt to map, and to which they attempt to call attention. If Stableford's science fiction is primarily devoted to his dreams of world salvation, his fantasies can easily be seen as their nightmarish flip side: the Gothic suspicion that human decadence might indeed be irredeemable, and that post-mortality is a phantom of the cerebral cortex, a mere projection of the personal desire for moral order. The intermediate Crash, on the other hand, is inevitable, as real as real can be even though it has not yet happened.

If there are two things of which we can all be absolutely certain, one is that the ecosphere will soon go postal, and the other is that the current leaseholders of the Earth will all die soon. The question that remains to be answered is whether our descendants will be deliverable thereafter. Brian Stableford hopes that they will, but does not imagine that it will be easy.

SCIENCE FICTION BEFORE THE GENRE

The word "science" acquired its modern meaning when it took aboard the realization that reliable knowledge is rooted in the evidence of the senses, carefully sifted by deductive reasoning and the experimental testing of generalizations. In the seventeenth century, writers began producing speculative fictions about new discoveries and technologies that the application of scientific method might bring about, the earliest examples being accommodated—rather uncomfortably—within existing genres and narrative frameworks.

One genre hospitable to science-fictional speculation was that of Utopian fantasy, whose usual narrative form was the imaginary voyage. The rich tradition of science-fictional travelers' tales was launched by one of the first and foremost champions of the scientific method, Francis Bacon, in *New Atlantis* (written c1617; published 1627), although the importance of technological progress to social reform had earlier been recognized by Johann Valentin Andreae's account of *Christianopolis* (1619) and Tommaso Campanella's description of *La Città del Sole* (written 1602; published 1623). Most subsequent Utopian fantasies took scientific and technological advancement into account, but relegated it to a minor role while matters of social, religious and political reform remained centre-stage. Nor were those writers who took account of scientific progress always enthusiastic about it; Baconian optimism prompted a backlash of hostility from those who perceived a threat to religious values in the secularizing tendencies of religion and the materialistic encouragements of technology.

The imaginary voyage was also the usual narrative form of scathing satirical fantasies, and scientists became satirical targets in Margaret Cavendish's *The Blazing World* (1666) and the third book of Jonathan Swift's *Gulliver's Travels* (1726). Such works helped to found a tradition of "anti-science fiction", whose reliance on similar motifs and narrative strategies has always resulted in its subsumption within the genre whose ambitions it opposes. Given the importance of skepticism and theoretical dissent to the advancement of science, and the near-oxymoronic quality of the "science fiction" label, this confusion is not entirely inappropriate.

The more extreme versions of the fantastic voyage overlapped with the standard format of religious fantasy, the dream story. Whenever seventeenth and eighteenth-century imaginary voyages found it convenient to cross interplanetary space their devices became phantasmagorical, and dreaming remained the only plausible means of gaining access to the future until the late nineteenth century. Another pioneer of the scientific revolution, John Kepler, was the first to couch an earnest scientific argument—a representation of the Copernican theory of the solar system—as a visionary fantasy. His *Somnium* (1634) also includes an ingenious attempt to imagine how life on the moon might have adapted to the long cycle of day and night.

Although most early accounts of lunar voyages are calculatedly ludicrous, the proposition that the moon and the planets were other worlds was a central contention of the heliocentric theory of the solar system. That theory became an important champion of the cause of science in its contest against religious faith, because the Christian Church had adopted the geocentric cosmology favored by Aristotle into its faith-supported world-view. Francis Godwin's farcical account of *The Man in the Moone* (1638) may, therefore, be placed among the ancestors of science fiction as confidently as John Wilkins' earnest essay celebrating the *Discovery of a World in the Moon* (1638)—to which a supplement was added in 1640 proposing that men would one day journey to the moon.

Such discussions were less risky in Protestant England than in Catholic France, but Pierre Borel's *Discours nouveau prouvant le pluralité des mondes* (1657) and Cyrano de Bergerac's flamboyant *L'Autre monde*—two fragments of which were published in 1657 and 1662—prepared the way for Bernard de Fontenelle's enormously popular *Entretiens sur la pluralité des mondes* (1686). Fontenelle's adaptation of the classical dialogue into a casual and flippant "conversation" was calculated to defuse criticism, but it helped pave the way for the development of more naturalistic speculative fictions. Throughout the eighteenth century, however, such fictions were handicapped by the lack of any plausible narrative devices capable of opening up the imaginative frontiers of space and time.

Although most satirists were satisfied with the moon as an extraterrestrial venue, a tradition of more wide-ranging cosmic voyages was founded by Athanasius Kircher's *Itinerarium Exstaticum* (1656). Cosmic tours taking in all the known worlds of the solar system became a hybrid subgenre fusing religious and scientific fantasies, usually incorporating Utopian and eschatological imagery within the same framework. Attempts to describe a universe in which the sun was merely one star had little alternative but to adopt the form of visionary fantasy, however, even when the vision took the form of a voyage through space. Such works as Gabriel Daniel's *Voyage au monde de Descartes* (1692) and Christian Huygens' *Cosmotheoros* (1698) struggled to find an appropriate narrative form.

The most ambitious cosmic visions of the eighteenth century were those allegedly experienced in 1743-5 and reported in *Arcana Coelestia* (1749-56) by the Swedish mystical theologian Emmanuel Swedenborg, strongly influenced by Swedenborg's early work in physics, geology and mathematics. In France, the tradition of cosmic voyages was encouraged by a new imaginative license—often involving the casual deployment of magical devices borrowed from Antoine Galland's translation of the Arabian Nights—associated with the fashionability of fantastic fiction. *Voyages de Mylord Céton dans les sept planètes* (1765) by Marie-Anne de Roumier-Robert was the most extravagant, employing a narrative template established by the Chevalier de Béthune's *Relation du monde de Mercure* (1750).

The gradual removal of *terra incognita* from maps of the Earth's surface helped to force Utopian and satirical images out into space, although the remoter regions of the southern hemisphere remained useful to such writers as Gabriel de Foigny in *La Terre australe connu* (1676) and Restif de la Bretonne in *La Découverte australe par un homme volant* (1781). Ludvig Holberg's *Nils Klim* (1741) pointed out another way to go, but the interior of the Earth was always a minority choice, although *Le Passage de pôle arctique au pôle antarctique* (1780) might have attracted more attention had it not remained unattributable. A more significant variation on the cosmic voyage theme was, however, employed in Voltaire's *conte philosophique Micromégas* (1752), which brought visitors to Earth from Sirius and Saturn.

Many French works, along with several translations from English, were reprinted in a thirty-six-volume series of *Voyages imaginaires* produced by Charles Garnier in 1787-89. This attempt to define and exemplify a genre might have been even more influential had it not been interrupted by the Revolution; even so, it provided a vital landmark for Camille Flammarion—who included many of its constituent works in his pioneering history of cosmological speculative fiction he constructed in *Les Mondes imaginaires et les mondes réels* (1864)—and Jules Verne, who described his own works, collectively, as *Voyages extraordinaires.*

The adaptation of traditional narrative frameworks to the work of serious speculation labored under several handicaps. Traveler's tales, even in their most earnest Utopian mode, were infected by a chronic frivolity that increased as the travels extended into regions inaccessible to ships and pedestrians. Literary dreams, even at their most gravely allegorical, were by definition mere phantoms of the imagination, demolished by reawakening. The transformation of moral fables into Voltairean *contes philosophiques* was hampered by the calculated artificiality of their traditional milieux and exemplary characters. These problems became more acute as the philosophy of progress made the future an imaginative realm ripe for exploration. Utopian speculation entered a "euchronian" mode once Louis-Sebastien Mercier had led the way in *L'An deux mille quatre cent quarante* (1771)—which soon prompted the production of more cynical accounts of futurity, such as Cousin de Grainville's *Le dernier homme* (1805)—but the only obvious alternative to dreaming as a means of gaining access to the future was sleeping for a long time. This was no help to a contemporary narrator, if the intelligence gained could not be returned to the present. The problem of designing and developing appropriate narrative frames for scientific *contes philosophiques* inevitably became acute during the nineteenth century, and was not easily solved.

* * * * * * *

The first writer to grapple with this problem in a wide-ranging experimental fashion was Edgar Allan Poe. The earliest poem by Poe to see eventual publication was "Sonnet—to Science", written in the early 1820s, and his career culminated in *Eureka* (1848), an extraordinary poetic essay on the nature of the universe newly revealed by astronomical telescopes. The imaginative thread connecting these two works ran through Poe's entire career. As his appreciation of the aesthetics of scientific discovery grew, his attempts to find literary means of communicating and celebrating the wonders of science became more varied and more inventive.

Although the prefatory essay on the necessity of verisimilitude attached to reprints of Poe's lunar voyage story "Hans Phaal" (1835; revised 1840 as "The Unparalleled Adventure of One Hans Pfaall") was not intended to be taken seriously, it highlighted the problem implicit in extending travelers' tales beyond the Earth's surface. Although balloons had enabled a few intrepid aeronauts to get off the ground, they were not a convincing means of extraterrestrial exploration, and Hans Pfaall's attempt to outdo the hero of Willem Bilderdijk's pioneering *Kort verhaal van eene aanmerklijke luctreis en nieuwe planeetokdekking* (1813) never seemed convincing even to its author. Despite its self-taunting sarcasm, however, Poe's preface became the first tentative manifesto for modern science fiction.

Poe experimented with new frameworks for futuristic speculation in "The Conversation of Eiros and Charmion" (1839), a dialogue of the dead whose protagonists recall the near-future destruction of Earth by a comet, and "The Colloquy of Monos and Una" (1841), before producing "Mesmeric Revelation" (1844), which recognizes and emphasizes the necessity of establishing a more authoritative species of visionary fantasy for science-fictional use. He also used mesmerism as a device in "A Tale of the Ragged Mountains" (1844) and "The Facts in the Case of M. Valdemar" (1845); the latter added the further device of mimicking a "scientific paper"—a prose form then in its infancy—thus paving the way for *Eureka*.

A few British writers contemporary with Poe grappled with the problem of finding appropriate narrative frameworks for bold scientific speculation, without any conspicuous success. Sir Humphry Davy's posthumously-published *Consolations in Travel* (1830) was formulated as a series of dialogues extrapolating responses to a cosmological vision. In the same year that Poe published Eureka, Robert Hunt—a significant pioneer of the popularization of science—published *The Poetry of Science*, but the metaphysical visions in Hunt's novel *Panthea* (1849) owe more to the "Rosicrucian romances" popularized by Edward Bulwer-Lytton (building on foundation-stones provided by J. V. Andreae) than to the scientific method for which Hunt gave up his own Romantic aspirations. Hunt's *Poetry of Science* inspired William Wilson to coin the term "science-fiction" in *A Little Earnest Book Upon a Great Old Subject* (1851), but the only instance of the new genre Wilson could find was R. H. Horne's *The Poor Artist* (1850), a fable in which an artist discovers the wonders of the world as beheld by the eyesights of different creatures.

Modern historians of science fiction often locate the origins of British scientific romance in the works of Mary Shelley, although the Gothic trappings of *Frankenstein* (1818) place it firmly within the tradition of anti-science fiction, and *The Last Man* (1826), a lachrymosely fatalistic disaster story, is equally antithetical to the philosophy of progress. Neither work made its influence felt immediately, but both became formative templates heading powerful traditions of imaginative fiction. The Frankenstein formula of an unruly and unfortunate artifact bringing about the downfall of its creator became established in the last decade of the nineteenth century as the principal narrative form of anti-science fiction, and still retains that status, while *The Last Man* became grandparent to an entire genre of elegiac British disaster stories, more directly fathered by Richard Jefferies' *After London* (1885). One early work derivative of *Frankenstein* that did offer some tentative championship of progress was *The Mummy! A Tale of the Twenty-Second Century* (1827) by Jane Webb Loudon, but explorations of the future remained few and tentative for many years. Notable exceptions include *The Air Battle* (1859) by "Herrmann Lang", which anticipates what was soon to become an important British genre of future war fiction, and *The History of a Voyage to the Moon* (1864), Poe's demand for more "verisimilitude" in interplanetary fiction was taken up by the pseudonymous "Chrysostom Trueman", who employed an early "antigravity" technology to transport his protagonists to a lunar Utopia.

Poe's American contemporary Nathaniel Hawthorne described imaginary scientific experiments in several of his moral tales, but his deep suspicion of the scientific world-view placed him in the antagonistic tradition; "The Birthmark" (1843) and "Rappaccini's Daughter" (1844) are early exemplars of a skeptical attitude deploring the excesses and perversions of what would nowadays be called "scientism". Other nineteenth-century American writers following in Poe's footsteps were mostly inclined to a similar caution. Fitz-James O'Brien's "The Diamond Lens" (1858) and Ambrose Bierce's "Moxon's Master" (1909) are usually read as conservative moral tales, although the latter item is flirtatiously ambiguous. Edward Everett Hale's space flight satire "The Brick Moon" (1869) is unconvincing, but Hale set an important precedent by producing the first significant fictionalization of an essay in alternative history, "Hands Off!" (1881). Frank R. Stockton took advantage of the increasing familiarity of science-fictional devices by employing them as launch-pads for playful flights of fancy in such tales as "The Water-Devil" (1874) and "A Tale of Negative Gravity" (1884).

Thanks to Charles Baudelaire, their French translator, Poe's works became far more influential in France than in his native land, and it was there that the cause of finding more appropriate narrative frameworks for science fiction was taken up most urgently and most adventurously. Jules Verne toyed briefly with Poesque short forms before deciding that the imaginary voyage offered far more scope for interstitial scientific discourse. The essence of Verne's method was the carefully-constrained extrapolation of contemporary technology, and he became famous for the application of hypothetical locomotive technologies to laborious exploration and leisurely tourism. Verne made the most convincing nineteenth century attempt to import a measure of verisimilitude into an extraterrestrial voyage in *De la terre à la lune* (1865), but his conscience forbade him to land his moon shot—because he had no plausible way to return it to Earth—and his quarrelsome travelers ended up merely making a trip *Autour de la lune* (1870).

Verne's earliest *voyages extraordinaires* included several boldly imaginative works, the most extravagant of all being *Voyage au centre de la terre* (1863) and *Vingt mille lieues sous les mers* (1870), but he became convinced that the key to success was the moderation of his imagination. His publisher, P.-J. Hetzel, apparently refused to publish an adventurous vision of twentieth-century Paris in the future that Verne penned in the early 1860s. Verne's imaginative discipline became so stern that several of the more adventurous works credited to him in his later years required imaginative injections from his enthusiastic disciple Paschal Grousset—who signed himself André Laurie—or his son Michel Verne. Jules Verne was, however, solely responsible for the extraterrestrial fantasy *Hector Servadac* (1877) and the flying machine story *Robur le conquérant* (1886). The most important of the works in which Grousset had a hand was *Les Cinq cents millions de la bégum* (1879), which contrasts Utopian and Dystopian images of technological development, while Michel's most impressive "posthumous collaboration" with his father was the fantasy of historical recurrence "L'Eternel Adam" (1910). Unfortunately, Verne's belated sequel to Poe's *The Narrative of Arthur Gordon Pym* (1837), *Le Sphinx des glaces* (1897), meticulously squeezed all the imaginative virility out of its predecessor, contriving a bathetic quasi-naturalistic reduction of all its ominous wonders.

Poe's inspiration is also manifest in the works of Camille Flammarion, another pioneer of the popularization of science. Flammarion, who also took considerable inspiration from Humphry Davy, was more imaginatively ambitious than Verne, although he struggled in vain to find narrative frameworks appropriate to his ambition. The most daring item in *Récits de l'infini* (1872), expanded for separate publication as *Lumen* (1887), is a dialogue between a human questioner and a disembodied soul, whose ability to travel faster than light has allowed him to view and remember former incarnations on a large number of alien worlds, each of which has life-forms adapted to its particular physical circumstances. No other nineteenth century work is so thoroughly imbued with a sense of wonder at the universe revealed by astronomy and the Earth sciences. Flammarion incorporated a synoptic account of *Lumen*'s schema into a painstakingly didactic account of a reincarnation on Mars in the patchwork *Uranie* (1889), and his account of *La fin du monde* (1893) is also a patchwork, concluding with a rhapsodic prose poem.

Hetzel's restraint of Jules Verne's imagination was encouraged by his desire to serialize Verne's novels in an educational magazine for young readers, and this tactic inhibited Verne's influence both at home and abroad. Although Verne's works were read by adults as well as children, the works of other "Vernian" writers—who sprang up in some profusion in France, Britain and Germany—were usually marketed as juveniles. The most prolific of Verne's French disciples were Pierre d'Ivoi and Gustave le Rouge; the most inventive writers featured in British boys' papers were Francis Henry Atkins—who wrote as "Frank Aubrey" and "Fenton Ash"—and George C. Wallis; the leading German Vernians were Robert Kraft and F. W. Mader.

The introduction of Vernian fiction into America initially followed the same path, but was always distinctive by virtue of its cultural context. Stories about young inventors comprised one of a number of marketing categories formulated by the publishers of "dime novels", alongside westerns and detective stories. Edward S. Ellis's pioneering account of *The Steam Man of the Prairies* (1868) was, in fact, a western, as were many of the items in story series featuring inventors such as Frank Reade and Tom Edison Jr. The hybridization of inventor fiction and westerns emphasized the importance of the myth of the frontier to American attitudes to technological development. The two genres retained a crucial spiritual affinity that persisted for a hundred years. Although English Vernian fiction was always enthusiastic to link technological inventiveness with imperial adventurism, it was much harder for Europeans, whose railroads were not opening a permanent way into a quasi-virginal West, to mythologize space as a "final frontier" waiting to be pioneered and conquered.

So powerful was the myth of the West as a place where the future was to be found and made, however, that American Vernian fiction soon began to outstrip the ambitions of European Vernians. Writers like Frank R. Stockton, in *The Great War Syndicate* (1889) and *The Great Stone of Sardis* (1898), and Garrett P. Serviss, in *The Moon Metal* (1900) and *A Columbus of Space* (1909), helped pave the way for the development of popular science fiction of a distinctively American kind.

* * * * * * *

British speculative fiction received a vital boost in 1871 when *Blackwood's Magazine* published George T. Chesney's account of "The Battle of Dorking". This account of British defeat following a German invasion provoked numerous replies in kind, founding a genre of future war stories that remained prolific until the outbreak of the actual Great War in 1914. Its early practitioners favored mock-nonfictional formats, often following Chesney's example—which was subtitled "Reminiscences of a Volunteer"—in presenting their accounts as "memoirs", but as time went by the accounts of future conflict became increasingly novelistic. Another important precedent set in 1871 was the initially-anonymous publication of the most science-fictional of Bulwer-Lytton's occult romances, *The Coming Race*, featuring a technologically-advanced subterranean Utopia. Samuel Butler's flamboyant Utopian satire *Erewhon* (1872), including a parody of Darwinistic evolution applied to machinery, provided a further stimulus, as did the first translation of Verne's *Journey to the Centre of the Earth*.

Britain might have been more hospitable to scientific speculation had it not been for the fact that the standard format of Victorian fiction was the three-volume novel beloved of the circulating libraries. Building descriptions of significantly different other worlds, whether futuristic or alien, requires a great deal of narrative labor, but the task is better suited to sketchy outlining than to detailed elaboration. Such three-decker futuristic fantasies as Edward Maitland's *By and By* (1873) and Andrew Blair's *Annals of the Twenty-Ninth Century* (1874) foundered under their own ponderous weight, in stark contrast to the deftest of the Poesque tales produced in America, which occupied the opposite limit of the broadening spectrum of speculative fiction.

The future war story popularized by Chesney offered a solution to the awkward problem of how to make technological advancement dramatic. From the point of view of progressively-minded writers, the device involved the unfortunate cost of concentrating heavily on

146

military technology, but that was not initially a deterrent. The crucial point in the evolution of future war stories arrived when they made the leap from propagandistic pamphlets to serialization in a host of new popular periodicals, which entered into a fierce circulation war in the 1890s. A relatively pedestrian account of "The Great War of 1892" compiled by military experts, including Rear-Admiral Colomb, which was serialized in 1891-92, was immediately upstaged by George Griffith's lurid account of the exploits of heroic "Terrorists" armed with airships, submarines and high explosives in *The Angel of the Revolution*, whose anti-imperialistic sentiments immediately called forth a right-wing backlash in E. Douglas Fawcett's account of the exploits of *Hartmann the Anarchist*. All three of these works were reprinted in book form in 1893, after which the steady trickle of future war stories became a flood.

Griffith's casual deployment of as-yet-non-existent arms and armor was rapidly standardized, and the escalation was such that when Griffith began his last future war story in 1906, *The Lord of Labour* (published posthumously in 1911), his weapons of choice were nuclear missiles and disintegrator rays. Other journalists persuaded by their editors to write future war serials included Louis Tracy, author of *The Final War* (1896), and William le Queux, author of *The Invasion of 1910* (1906), both of whom went on to write scientific romances of other kinds. One of the most adventurous early contributors to the new genre, M. P. Shiel, also made his entry by this route with "The Empress of the Earth"—reprinted as *The Yellow Danger* (1898)—although he was the chief British disciple of Edgar Allan Poe.

Although the expansion of the future war genre into a much broader speculative genre of "scientific romance" was tentatively begun by others, it was not until H. G. Wells got involved that anyone replicated Poe's determination to explore the utility of a whole range of narrative frameworks. The sudden surge of new periodicals provided the perfect arena for Wells to conduct his experiments in speculation. The earliest were cast as brief journalistic essays, of which the most adventurous was "The Man of the Year Million" (1893), but, as soon as he began to adapt the ideas in these essays into fictional form, he discovered the limitations of such travelers' tales as "Aepyornis Island" (1894) and such visionary fantasies as "The Remarkable Case of Davidson's Eyes" (1894).

By the time Wells made his third attempt to fit an appropriate fictional frame around a speculative account of the future evolution of life on Earth—initially published as "The Chronic Argonauts"

(1888)—he was very conscious indeed of the necessity of replacing dreams as a means of exploring possible futures. The idea of mesmerically-induced "true visions" no longer commanded the least shred of plausibility, so he took advantage of articles by C. H. Hinton collected in *Scientific Romances* (1886), which had popularized the idea of time as a "fourth dimension", to provide an apologetic jargon for a new facilitating device: *The Time Machine* (1895). This imaginative exercise had little in common with Jules Verne's modest extrapolations of locomotive technology, as Verne was quick to recognize and complain, but Wells had not taken the trouble to make his time machine seem plausible to sympathetic readers because he expected them to take the notion seriously as an actual possibility; he knew how necessary some such device had become as a means of opening the future to serious speculative scrutiny.

Wells's time machine became the first of a series of facilitating devices that opened up the farther reaches of time and space to a kind of rational enquiry that had previously been severely handicapped by its reliance on obsolete narrative frameworks. The crucial invention of *The Time Machine* was the establishment of a paradigm example of a whole new class of narrative devices. The antigravity technology of Cavorite, employed by Wells in *The First Men in the Moon* (1901) was the most obvious equivalent of the time machine, and its most necessary supplement. The publication dates of these two works defined the brief interval in which Wells produced all his important scientific romances; not only did he never use the time machine or Cavorite again but he never invented or used any significant facilitating device after 1901.

As soon as the twentieth century had begun, moved by the earnest passion of his strong socialist convictions, Wells gave up wide-ranging exploration of the infinite range of future possibility in favor of a much less interesting quest to discover and comment upon the particular form that the future actually would take. The first philosophical novel subjecting the possibilities of futuristic fiction to scrupulous analysis, Anatole France's *Sur la pierre blanche* (1905), hailed Wells as the only writer prepared to venture into the future as an open-minded explorer rather than a vulgar prophet intent on painting his own hopes or anxieties on its blank canvas, but, by the time that judgment appeared in print, it was no longer true. Even so, Wells single-handedly laid the groundwork for the distinctive methods of modern science fiction, which employed the narrative technique he had developed in *The Time Machine*, gaudily seasoned with melodrama, to reinvigorate the narrative framework of the moral *conte philosophique* far more effectively than anyone had previously contrived.

The Island of Dr Moreau (1896), *The Invisible Man* (1897) and *The War of the Worlds* (1898) are all painstaking moral fables, albeit of an unprecedentedly zestful and unusually realistic kind, cleverly assisted by the narrative labor that made their central devices plausible. Wells's other moral fables in melodramatic guise include "The Star" (1897) and "The Empire of the Ants" (1904), but he always remained willing to develop such fables in more traditional forms, as he did in *The Wonderful Visit* (1895), "The Man Who Could Work Miracles" (1898) and "The Country of the Blind" (1904). He also remained content, as and when the mood moved him, to employ perfectly straightforward visionary fantasies, as in "Under the Knife" (1896)—although "The Crystal Egg" (1897) does make use of a facilitating device of sorts.

Precedents had been set for Wellsian speculative fiction by such cautionary tales as Grant Allen's "Pausodyne" (1881) and "A Child of the Phalanstery" (1884), and by such extended *contes philosophiques* as W. H. Hudson's *A Crystal Age* (1887) and Walter Besant's *The Inner House* (1888), but Wells imported such powerful narrative energy and sturdy conviction into his works that he transformed the methodology of speculative fiction, with almost instantaneous effect. Indeed, he demonstrated far more potential than he sought to exploit, even in his brief fervent phase. Although his demonstration that moral fables could be couched as gripping and violent thrillers was welcome news to at least a few would-be moralists, *The Island of Dr Moreau, The Invisible Man* and *The War of the Worlds* spawned far more imitations whose writers were only interested in the melodramatic potential of monster-makers, alien incursions and scientifically-assisted criminals.

Wells's work was, therefore, a revelation to writers of action-adventure fiction enthusiastic to work on wider stages in a more spectacular manner than naturalistic fiction would ever permit, as well as to speculative fabulators. There was, inevitably, a certain parting of the ways between writers whose primary interest was in futuristic and other-worldly costume drama and writers who were seriously concerned to explore future possibilities associated with the advancement of science and technology, but the overlap between the two remained considerable, and the artful combination of the two kinds of ambition has always been able to exploit a powerful synergy.

It is perhaps regrettable that Wells never followed up his most useful discoveries. With one exception—the awkward but enterprising mock-naturalistic novella "A Story of the Days to Come" (1897)—his post-*Time Machine* ventures into the future all fell back on more traditional modes of presentation, including suspended animation in *When the Sleeper Wakes* (1899) and visionary fantasy in *The Dream* (1924). Nor did he make any further use of his new means of space travel, tending to fall back on Vernian space-guns in other interplanetary tales (he could never bring himself to accept the potential of rockets). When Wells did use pseudoscientific facilitating devices after 1901, in fact, he did so in a tokenistic fashion whose casualness was almost insulting, as in *In the Days of the Comet* (1906).

Although his work grew out of the same milieu as the future war subgenre, Wells was a latecomer to that branch of speculative fiction, and he was virtually alone among its writers in deploring the destruction that such a war might bring. His anticipation of tank warfare in "The Land Ironclads" (1903) was followed up by an account of *The War in the Air* (1908) as witnessed by its potential victims. These two stories now seem far more prophetic than the jingoistic flood of novels that took it for granted that "the war to end war" would be won by the British—and thus provided the slogan under which the actual Great War could recruit its canon fodder—but in this respect too, Wells relented; his atomic war story *The World Set Free* (1914), was the first of several works in which he welcomed the prospect of a destruction of civilization, on the grounds that nothing less would clear the way for socialist reconstruction. There was, however, no shortage of twentieth century writers ambitious to write the "Wellsian" works that Wells himself would not.

* * * * * * *

Wells's influence at home and abroad was mediated by local circumstance. In Britain the extension of scientific romance beyond the margins of future war fiction was exploited by future war chroniclers like Fred T. Jane and M. P. Shiel, in the apocalyptic fantasies *The Violet Flame* (1899) and *The Purple Cloud* (1901). George Griffith, a relentless borrower of other writers' ideas, soon progressed to interplanetary romance in *A Honeymoon in Space* (1901), although he also became a prolific writer of "karmic romances" in a vein popularized by Edwin Lester Arnold and Henry Rider Haggard.

The broader horizons of scientific romance attracted a host of assiduous new recruits. Robert Cromie—who felt that Wells had stolen the thunder of his interplanetary romance *A Plunge into Space* (1890), which had employed an antigravity device similar to Chrysostom Trueman's—offered his own take on the implications of Darwin's theory of evolution in *The Crack of Doom* (1895). William Hope Hodgson embedded a cosmic vision in *The House on the Borderland* (1908) before publishing the far futuristic phantasmagoria *The Night Land* (1912), which outdid *The Time Machine* in supplying an account of the death of the Earth as anticipated by the theory of Lord Kelvin (which held that the sun's heat was generated by the energy of its gravitational collapse, and could not last more than a few million years). J. D. Beresford followed the fine evolutionary fantasy *The Hampdenshire Wonder* (1912), tracing the career of a superhuman born out of his time, with the elegiac disaster story *Goslings* (1913) and a series of visionary *contes philosophiques* collected in *Signs and Wonders* (1921).

Many members of the new generation of professional writers created by the new periodicals dabbled in scientific romance as they dabbled in detective fiction and adventure stories. The most notable were Arthur Conan Doyle, whose tentative pre-Wellsian *The Doings of Raffles Haw* (1891) was far surpassed by his series chronicling the adventures of Professor Challenger, begun with *The Lost World* (1912) and *The Poison Belt* (1913), and Rudyard Kipling, whose "With the Night Mail" (1905) and "As Easy as A.B.C." (1912) imagine the dramatic transformation of future society by air transport and air power. Minor writers who helped formularize genre templates included C. J. Cutcliffe Hyne, who employed the Frankenstein formula in numerous stories published under the pseudonym Weatherby Chesney, and the disaster-story writer Fred M. White.

This activity was curbed as the popular periodicals moved beyond their experimental phase, having discovered that other genres were more popular with larger audiences; the long-anticipated Great War delivered an abrupt *coup de grace*. The bitter legacy of disenchantment left by the war lasted far longer than the fighting, very obviously reflected in such dire anticipations of the destruction of civilization by war as *The People of the Ruins* (1920) by Edward Shanks and *Theodore Savage* (1922) by Cicely Hamilton. Although those writers of imaginatively-ambitious scientific romance who survived the war tried to continue their work in that vein they found it very difficult to do so, and the most adventurous scientific romances of the early post-war years—E. V. Odle's *The Clockwork*

Man (1923), Edward Heron-Allen's *The Cheetah Girl* (1923) and S. Fowler Wright's *The Amphibians* (1925)—were released into a hostile environment whose inhospitability was not to relent until the 1930s.

In France the continuing influence of Poe, Verne and Flammarion was quickly combined with Wellsian elements by such writers as J. H. Rosny *aîné*, the pioneer of the novel of prehistory. Rosny had already adapted that subgenre to more adventurous speculation in the alien visitation story "Les Xipéhuz" (1887), as well as dabbling in Flammarionesque visionary fantasy in "La Légende sceptique" (1889), but the influences of Flammarion and Wells are fruitfully combined in "La Mort de la terre" (1910) and *Les Navigateurs de l'infini* (1925). Albert Robida, who had built a career as a writer and illustrator by cleverly satirizing Jules Verne and future war fiction, also became more adventurous towards the end of his career, in such novels as the time-reversal fantasy *L'Horloge des siècles* (1902). Flammarionesque notions of serial extraterrestrial reincarnation remained important in French speculative fiction, providing a logic for the striking visionary fantasy *Force ennemie* (1903) by John-Antoine Nau—which won the first Prix Goncourt—but they were melodramatically combined with Wellsian influences in such novels as Octave Joncquel and Théo Varlet's "Martian epic", *Les Titans du ciel* (1921) and *L'Agonie de la terre* (1922). In France as in England, however, the Great War was a drastic interruption inhibiting the genre's development and lending encouragement to its skeptical and pessimistic elements.

Elsewhere in Europe, where no traditions of scientific romance had taken root before the importation of Verne and Wells, the Great War had even more dramatic effects. Although the German Wellsian, Kurd Lasswitz, produced three speculative novels, including the monumental *Auf Zwei Planeten* (1897), his influence—and that of the highly imaginative Paul Scheerbart, whose *Astrale Novelletten* were collected in 1912—was effaced by the war and its aftermath. The Russian revolutions of 1917 interrupted a burgeoning tradition including such innovative works as Valery Brussof's futuristic fable "Respublika yuzhnavo kresta" (1905) and rocket pioneer Konstantin Tsiolkovsky's ground-breaking account of extraterrestrial colonization *Vne zemli* (1916). The futuristic socialist rhetoric of Alexei Tolstoi's *Aëlita* (1922) founded a very different tradition, although Mikhail Bulgakov managed to produce the fine Wellsian satire "Rokovy'e yaitsa" (1922) before being silenced.

Because the USA came late into World War I and was remote from its battlefields, the interruption of the domestic tradition of American speculative fiction was much less pronounced. Even more important, the effect of the war on American attitudes to technological progress was much less caustic. As in Europe, the development of late nineteenth-century American speculative fiction had been handicapped by the lack of convincing narrative frames. Tentatively adventurous works by Edward Bellamy, including *Dr. Heidenhoff's Process* (1880) and "The Blindman's World" (1886), and Edgar Fawcett, including *Solarion* (1889) and *The Ghost of Guy Thyrle* (1895), were hamstrung by their formulation as visionary fantasies. Bellamy overcame the barrier in his best-selling Utopian romance *Looking Backward, 2000-1887* (1888), whose last chapter defiantly cast aside the conventional apology that it was all a dream, but Fawcett never could, even though he took the trouble to preface *The Ghost of Guy Thyrle* with a defiant manifesto for a new genre of "realistic romances".

As in the UK, it was an explosion of new periodicals in the 1890s that opened up market space for experimental exploitation by such writers as Jack London, whose Wellsian short stories, including "A Thousand Deaths" (1899) and "The Shadow and the Flesh" (1903), paved the way for the prehistoric fantasy *Before Adam* (1906) and the apocalyptic fantasy *The Scarlet Plague* (1912). Like Wells, London was a committed socialist, and his political fantasy *The Iron Heel* (1907) carried forward a skeptical tradition founded by Ignatius Donnelly's spectacular dystopia *Caesar's Column* (1890), the most extreme of many reactions to Bellamy's account of a peaceful evolutionary transition from capitalism to socialism.

The ready availability in the USA of cheap paper made from wood pulp encouraged the rapid growth of "pulp magazines" specializing in garish melodramas, which inherited the commercial genres identified by the dime novels. One of the many new subgenres developed in this medium consisted of uninhibited extraterrestrial adventure stories, pioneered by Edgar Rice Burroughs' extraordinarily influential "Under the Moons of Mars" (1912; reprinted as *A Princess of Mars*). This was an unashamed dream story, which did not trouble to establish a plausible mechanism for its hero's abrupt transplantation to the plant Mars. Although the image of Mars presented in the story owed something to speculative descriptions offered by the astronomer Percival Lowell in such books as *Mars as the Abode of Life* (1908), Burroughs used the ideas he borrowed as a backdrop for a fantasy of extraordinary derring-do.

Almost all of the colorful fantasies written in imitation of *A Princess of Mars* were essentially dream stories, although relatively few of them were as scornful of facilitating devices—even Burroughs, when he began to write a similar series set on Venus, condescended to employ a spaceship. Many of the writers, having read H. G. Wells, were enthusiastic to deploy pseudoscientific jargon in support of their facilitating devices, and some went so far as to use it to attain and define new imaginative spaces. J. U. Giesy employed a variant of Flammarionesque reincarnation to transport the hero of *Palos of the Dog Star Pack* (1918) across interstellar distances. Ray Cummings pioneered the microcosmic romance in the hybrid Wells/Burroughs pastiche "The Girl in the Golden Atom" (1919). Ralph Milne Farley extended the idea of radio broadcasting to include matter transmission in *The Radio Man* (1924). Once their preliminary journeys were complete, however, pulp fantasies of this kind became straightforward costume dramas in which stereotyped heroes fought sneering villains and grotesque monsters in order to win the hands of lovely heroines.

Burroughs' chief rival as a pulp fantasist was Abraham Merritt, an unashamed master of purple prose who was even less concerned to cloak his facilitating devices in scientific jargon. Even so, his ground-breaking story "The Moon Pool" (1918) gave a new gloss of plausibility to the folkloristic notion that our world is juxtaposed with far more fantastic "parallel worlds", which can be reached via magical portals. This device was immediately borrowed by other pulp fantasists, most notably "Francis Stevens" (Gertrude Barrows Bennett), who elaborated it considerably in the futuristic *The Heads of Cerberus* (1919).

Pulp-dependent writers who were ambitious to produce morally challenging works, including Jack London and Upton Sinclair, usually had to issue their political fantasies in other formats, although Victor Rousseau Emanuel—who used his forenames as a pseudonym in the USA—was able to serialize *The Messiah of the Cylinder* (1917), a ringing ideological reply to Wells's *When the Sleeper Wakes*, and George Allan England serialized the political fable *The Golden Blight* (1912) before becoming the third major pulp fantasist with a trilogy of post-holocaust romances begun with *Darkness and Dawn* (1912-13; collected in book form 1914). England was, however, unable to serialize his angry condemnation of predatory capitalism *The Air Trust* (1915).

It was the gaudy exotica of pulp fiction rather than these more earnest speculative fictions that provided the backcloth for Hugo

Gernsback's invention of the new genre of "scientifiction", although the popular science magazines in which it was first featured, including *The Electrical Experimenter* and *Science and Invention*, were not themselves pulps. Scientifiction was a didactic enterprise intended to spread enthusiasm for the various technological devices (including radio sets) that Gernsback imported and sold. Although it was extremely crude in literary terms, and had no more interest in moral fabulation than any other kind of pulp fiction, it had perforce to develop new methods of story-telling in order to fulfill its didactic purpose.

The format that early writers of scientifiction found most useful was a variant of the conversation piece: anecdotal tall tales spiced with technically-inclined questions. Series of this type, in which zany scientists and inventors would explain their new ventures to curious innocents, included Gernsback's own accounts of "Baron Munchhausen's New Scientific Adventures" (1915-17) and Clement Fézandié's "Doctor Hackenshaw" series (1921-25); they established a method of using a mock-comedic mask for the exposition of extravagant ideas that was carried forward into genre SF when Gernsback founded the first scientifiction magazine, *Amazing Stories*, in 1926. Gernsback was, however, almost as great an admirer of Burroughs and Merritt as he was of Jules Verne and H. G. Wells; he encouraged both American writers to produce more speculatively-inclined works so that he could publish them, and when their responses were lukewarm he encouraged other writers to take over that particular crusade.

While it was still gestating in its pulp womb, therefore, American science fiction had already brought about a zygotic fusion of British scientific romance and American otherworldly exotica, lightly leavened with casually extravagant tall tales of scientific miracle-making. It was from this point that the collaborative work of horizon-expansion, social extrapolation, and moral re-sophistication, which has been the labor and triumph of modern science fiction, began anew.

SCIENCE FICTION AND ECOLOGY

Introduction

Ecology is the study of organisms in relation to their environment—not merely the physical components of the environment but the other organisms whose lives overlap theirs, particularly those on which they feed and for which they in their turn provide sustenance. The central thread of ecological analysis is the food chain, which extends from the "primary producers" that fix solar energy into variously extended pathways whose links are herbivores, predators, parasites and saprophytes. Such chains are often elaborately intertwined.

The physical environment may be considerably modified by side-effects of the food chain; most importantly, the atmospheric oxygen on which all respiration depends is a product of photosynthesis by plants and algae. Because the manner in which organisms obtain their sustenance from one another exerts a powerful selective pressure, the evolution of the Earth's biosphere has produced organisms that exploit the feeding habits of other organisms in order to secure their own reproductive fortunes; thus, plants routinely produce seeds with edible packaging, or use nectar to inveigle insects into becoming pollen-disseminators. Such "symbiotic" patterns of mutual dependency are a further augmentation of the complexity and intricacy of ecosystems.

Although the word was coined by Ernst Haeckel in 1873, ecology did not become established as a formal discipline until the 1920s, one notable early work on the subject being Charles Elton's *Animal Ecology* (1927), but some slight awareness of the fragility of human dependence on the natural environment is an inevitable corollary of agricultural endeavor. A good deal of religious ritual and magic in ancient agrarian societies appears to have been devoted to the task of attempting to ensure bountiful harvests and success in hunting, and to alleviate diseases caused by parasitic infestation.

156

The evolution of scientific ecology can thus be seen as a process of demystification—which, in common with similar historical developments, has not been entirely effective.

The attribution of magical or mystical significance to ecological relationships is reflected in some imaginative literature that predates the evolution of ecological science. A striking example of this kind of proto-ecological mysticism can be found in the fiction of the naturalist W. H. Hudson, whose pastoral Utopia *A Crystal Age* (1887) describes a future in which a much more intimate and harmonious relationship between human beings and their environment. His later novel *Green Mansions* (1902)—a transfigurative response to Joseph Conrad's "Heart of Darkness"—proposes that the ultimate horror at the core of human nature is not the barbarism that lies beneath the surface of civilization but the fact that all extant cultures, no matter how "advanced," have sacrificed an intimate bond with the nurturing aspects of Mother Earth, which is symbolized within the plot by the ill-fated Rima, the last of her magical kind.

Once Elton had popularized the idea of ecology, and such corollary notions as the "Eltonian pyramid"—the incremental reduction of biomass of in each successive phase of a food-chain—the aesthetic component of ecological analysis soon began to affect the way writers of speculative fiction dealt with interspecific relationships. J. D. Beresford's "The Man Who Hated Flies" (1929) is an early "ecological parable" about the inventor of a perfect insecticide, whose annihilation of insect populations disrupts processes of pollination, thus precipitating massive crop failures and threatening the extinction of many other species, including humankind. Although the phenomenon was not to acquire a name until the 1960s, this was one of the first literary accounts of what would now be termed an "ecocatastrophe."

Many human societies had, of course, lived through such self-inflicted ecocatastrophes in the past—usually as a consequence of deforestation or soil laterization associated with population growth—but had usually failed to realize where the responsibility for such disasters actually lay, presumably castigating their priests and magicians for want of any rational analysis or constructive response. The problematic aspects of the tendency of populations to increase faster than their resources could be renewed was first noted by T. R. Malthus in his *Essay on the Principle of Population as it Affects the Future Improvement of Society* (1798), which played a significant role in enabling Charles Darwin to formulate the theory of evolution by natural selection, but the effect of such ideas on literary images of catastrophe was initially muted. Disaster stories and apocalyptic fantasies, even when they involved biological agents, like the plague in Mary Shelley's *The Last Man* (1826), tended to retain an implication of divine judgment—an implication that has been very difficult to discard while the language employed to describe disasters is shot through with religious metaphors. Such terms as deluge, Armageddon, doom(sday), judgment (day), holocaust and apocalypse still provide the basic vocabulary of catastrophist fiction.

Speculative Ecology and the Construction of Alien Biospheres

When Johannes Kepler wrote an account of astronomical observations made from a viewpoint on the moon in support of the Copernican model of the solar system—published as *Somnium* (written 1609; published 1634)—he could not resist the temptation to add a few hundred words to the end of his essay pointing out that life on the moon would have to be adapted to very different physical conditions from those supporting life on Earth. Although it was not soon followed up, this set the precedent for much of the work done by early writers of scientific romance and SF that touched on ecological issues. H. G. Wells's Martians in *The War of the Worlds* (1898) are compelled to invade Earth by virtue of a resource crisis on their own world, and other literary images of Mars drawing on speculations by the astronomer Percival Lowell similarly focus on an ecological decadence brought about by a long-term decline in the water and air supply.

The War of the Worlds became a highly influential exemplar for twentieth-century SF, but what most subsequent writers found valuable in it was the melodramatic currency of the alien invasion. It was the priorities of melodrama that shaped the animal population of Edgar Rice Burroughs' Barsoom and other pulp magazine planetary romance; the logic of the Eltonian pyramid was ignored as alien worlds were populated with hosts of monstrous predators and parasites devoid of any plausible ecological context. The advent of specialist pulps made little difference at first; the pulp SF writer most interested in the mass-production of exotic life-forms, Stanley G. Weinbaum, demonstrated a rudimentary awareness of ecological issues in such stories as "The Lotus Eaters" (1935), "Flight on Titan" (1935) and "The Mad Moon" (1935), but died before he could extend that line of thought any further.

This situation began to change when John W. Campbell Jr. took over as editor of *Astounding Stories* in 1938 and began to pressurize his writers to put more thought into the aspects of rational plausibility relevant to their fictional constructs, including the ecological issues relevant to "world-building." One consequence of this demand was that some of *Astounding*'s writers realized that the intellectual labor devoted to ecological questions could work to their advantage, by generating puzzles to be solved, hence supplying useful plot ideas and convenient story arcs. The opportunity was taken up, albeit tentatively, by Clifford D. Simak in a loosely-knit series including "Tools" (1942), and by Eric Frank Russell in "Symbiotica" (1943), before Hal Clement integrated it into his literary method in such stories as "Cold Front" (1946).

A few stories, including William Tenn's "The Ionian Cycle" (1948), employed the ecological puzzle formula in other venues, but it was fundamentally unsuited to the action-adventure pulps and was marginal even in *Astounding*, where Campbell was careful to maintain a melodramatic component in all but the shortest works he published. It was not until the pulps were replaced by more sophisticated digest magazines in the 1950s that ecological puzzle stories became a standard feature of the genre, and they remained problematic because of the immense difficulty of reflecting the actual complexity of ecosystems in literary images.

It was in the 1950s that significant pioneers of ecological SF, including Simak and Clement, hit their stride, but the difficult nature of the work forced them to take their work in two sharply divergent directions. Simak conserved the puzzle aspect of stories founded on ecological ideas by focusing on relatively simple alien interspecific relationships whose elucidation could provide a satisfactory sense of narrative closure. In order to make such devices relevant to his human characters, however, he frequently configured his stories as ironic parables; examples include "You'll Never Go Home Again" (1951) and "Drop Dead" (1956). Clement, on the other hand, made the puzzle element subsidiary to scrupulously detailed exercises in ecospheric construction, in novel-length works such as *Mission of Gravity* (1953) and *Cycle of Fire* (1957).

It was Clement's endeavors—paradigmatic of what came to be called "hard science fiction"—that revealed the true complexity of the dual task facing conscientious world builders: the logical ingenuity that needed to be put in "behind the scenes" in planning an alien ecosphere, and the narrative ingenuity that needed to be put into constructing a coherent image of the ecosphere in the reader's mind as the story was laid out. It was immediately obvious to Clement's admirers that only a tiny minority of readers would ever be sufficiently interested to appreciate the hard speculative labor and exhaustive exposition required by novels of this kind, because the aesthetics of fully-developed accounts of alien ecology were intrinsically esoteric. Only a handful of writers have ever attempted to apply a rigorous Campbellian conscience to the construction of alien ecospheres. Clement's most notable early follower was Poul Anderson, who began such work tentatively in such stories as "Question and Answer" (1955) and "A Twelvemonth and a Day" (1960), carefully maintaining the melodramatic component as he laid groundwork for more ambitious works such as *Fire Time* (1974) and *The Winter of the World* (1975). Later writers who have worked in the same vein—entirely for art's sake, given the esotericism of the subgenre—include Robert Forward, in the Rocheworld series begun in 1982-83, and Larry Niven in *The Integral Trees* (1984) and *The Smoke Ring* (1987).

Unsurprisingly, the path followed by Simak in his ecological puzzle stories was more inviting and more typical. Stories in a similar vein include Jack Vance's "Winner Loses All" (1951)—a rare example of a story with no sentient characters—James H. Schmitz's "Grandpa" (1955), Brian Aldiss's series tracking the exploits of a Planetary Ecological Survey Team (1958-62) and Jack Sharkey's similar series begun with "Arcturus Times Three" (1961). The establishment in the 1950s of a galactic empire of "Earth-clone" worlds as a standard framework for science-fictional thought-experiments relieved writers of the necessity of devising ecospheres as radically different from ours as those designed by Clement and Forward, but conscientious writers of modern planetary romance still had to think carefully about extrapolating the consequences of any subtle differences they introduced to make their not-very-alien worlds more interesting. As issues raised by ecological science overflowed into the political arena and began to influence other philosophical fields the standard of expectation applied to serious SF inevitably rose.

When paperback books took over from magazines as the economic core of the genre, ecological puzzle stories were routinely expanded to novel length, but they retained a fabular element flamboyantly displayed in such extended examples as John Boyd's *The Pollinators of Eden* (1969), Neal Barrett's *Highwood* (1972), Michael Coney's *Syzygy* (1973) and *Hello Summer, Goodbye* (1975), John Brunner's *Total Eclipse* (1974), Frederik Pohl's *JEM* (1979) and Gordon R. Dickson's *Masters of Everon* (1979). As the standard size of paperback novels grew, so did the ambitions of this kind of story, as exemplified by Brian Aldiss's Helliconia trilogy (1982-5), Donald Kingsbury's *Courtship Rite* (1982), Paul J. McAuley's *Four Hundred Billion Stars* (1988) and Sheri S. Tepper's *Grass* (1989). By the end of the 1980s SF novelists had abundant narrative space in which to establish elaborate images of distant Earth-clone worlds, and many—especially those with biological training—were able to take advantage of to develop images of ecospheres that were similar to, but significantly not quite the same as, Earth's. Notable examples include Joan Slonczewski's *A Door into Ocean* (1987) and *Daughters of Elysium* (1993), Alison Sinclair's *Blueheart* (1996), Larry Niven's *Destiny's Road* (1997) and Neal Asher's *The Line of Polity* (2003). The increasing interest in ecological issues in the political arena assisted writers in constructing such works—no matter how extreme their length—as parables offering valuable lessons to the hapless custodians of the ecosphere whose model was being so profligately cloned.

Ecological Mysticism in Science Fiction

Clifford D. Simak's contribution to ecological pulp SF was not confined to puzzle stories set in alien ecospheres. He also wrote a pastoral Utopian series, launched with "City" (1944), in which humankind's desertion of Earth paves the way for a replacement society of dogs and robots that is more harmonious in an ecological as well as a political sense. The idea that a redemption of the Earth's ecosphere from the threats posed by human activity could only be achieved by a drastic retreat from modern technology took rapid hold in the late 1940s, infecting many disaster stories—including stories of the aftermath of nuclear holocaust—with a sense that a decisive interruption of technological progress might be a blessing in disguise.

Such morals were most explicitly drawn out in a number of scientific romances produced by British-born writers as that genre was about to be eclipsed by imported SF, most notably Gerald Heard's "The Great Fog" (1944), in which a god-substitute called "Mind" sends a mildew-generated fog to slow down the progress of a civilization that has run out of control. Similar notions also took root in the American SF, in spite of the fact that Campbell and his authors had followed the example set by Hugo Gernsback in committing themselves firmly to the cause of scientific and technological progress.

The pulp genre had been infiltrated almost from its inception by such skeptics as David H. Keller—whose account of "The Metal Doom" (1932) represents the demise of industrial technology as a good thing—and Campbell had been sufficiently worried about the debilitating effects of humankind's potential over-reliance on machinery to pin his own ultimate hopes for the future on transcendent mental evolution. Campbell's "Forgetfulness" (1937, originally by-lined Don A. Stuart) features a pastoral Utopia, and his sympathy for the kind of nostalgic pastoralism cultivated by Simak made *Astounding* much more hospitable to ecological parables demanding a retreat from technological excess than it might have been, given the apparent contradiction of his fervent propagandistic support for atomic power and space technology.

The temptation to remystify ecological relationships by imagining some kind of quasi-godlike intelligence manifest within them was irresistible. C. S. Lewis's religious fantasy *Out of the Silent Planet* (1938) offered a view of Martian ecology very different from that of Lowell and Burroughs, crediting its harmony to the active involvement of a spiritual overseer, and sentient ecospheres are featured in such genre SF stories as Murray Leinster's "The Lonely Planet" (1949). The French Jesuit Pierre Teilhard de Chardin had already worked out an evolutionary schema in which the destiny of the ecosphere was to fall increasingly under the way of a superimposed "noösphere" until a harmonious integration was achieved, but the notion had to await posthumous publication in 1955. By then, Clifford Simak had pioneered the employment of ecological relationships as substitutes for traditional religious imagery in *Time and Again* (1951), where alien "symbiotes" provide stand-ins for souls and the raw material of potential noöspheres.

The late 1950s saw a remarkable resurgence of ecological mysticism in genre SF as human explorers and colonists were routinely humiliated by the belated discovery of sophisticated ecosystems blessed with quasi-supernatural harmony. Notable examples include Richard McKenna's "The Night of Hoggy Darn" (1958; revised as "Hunter Come Home," 1963), Robert F. Young's "To Fell a Tree" (1959) and Mark Clifton's *Eight Keys to Eden* (1960). This trend reflected an upsurge of explicit ecological mysticism in the burgeoning environmentalist movement; for instance, the Findhorn Foundation, inaugurated in 1962—named for a bay on the East Coast of Scotland where its first experimental Utopian community was based—followed a creed based on the assumption of an "intelligent nature" in which God is incarnate and everpresent. The remystification of ecological relationships was fundamental to two of the best-selling SF novels of the 1960s, both of which take the form of messianic fantasies focusing on the reverent ritualization of water relations: Robert A. Heinlein's *Stranger in a Strange Land* (1961) and Frank Herbert's *Dune* (1965). Piers Anthony's *Omnivore* (1968) and its sequels transform the fundamental pattern of ecological relationships into a mystical trinity. Herbert's *The Green Brain* (1966) echoes and amplifies Heard's "Great Fog" in featuring a active revolt of intelligent nature against the ecological heresies of humankind.

The notion of ecospheres so completely integrated that their core consists of vast more-or-less godlike organisms became very popular, reflected in such stories as Stanislaw Lem's *Solaris* (1961; tr. 1970), the Strugatsky brothers' *The Snail on the Slope* (1966-68; tr. 1980), Ursula le Guin's "Vaster than Empires and More Slow" (1971), Gordon R. Dickson's "Twig" (1974) and Doris Piserchia's *Earthchild* (1977). The idea that life on Earth could and perhaps should be viewed in this way had been broached by Vladimir Vernadsky in *The Biosphere* (1926; tr. 1986) but had passed unheeded at the time; it made a spectacular comeback, however, in James Lovelock's "Gaia hypothesis," set out in *Gaia: A New Look at Life on Earth* (1973). Although not mystical in itself, the language in which the Gaia hypothesis was couched lent tremendous encouragement to those who desired to construe it as if it were, so Lovelock's tentative assertion that the ecosphere could, in some respects, be usefully viewed *as if* it were a single organism was routinely extrapolated into a literal personification. The notion was rapidly fed back into SF in such works as John Varley's *Titan* trilogy (1979-84), whose sentient super-organism is named Gaea.

For many people, the word "ecology"—and such associated terms as "green"—had by this time come to symbolize a kind of harmony with the natural environment that modern civilization had sacrificed on the altar of technology, greatly to humankind's spiritual detriment. Furthermore, the term had begun to broaden out in such works as Gregory Bateson's *Steps Towards an Ecology of Mind* (1972) to signify a worldview rather than a mere branch of science, whose essential "holism" was appropriate to the study of mental as well as biological phenomena. Arne Naess's "The Shallow and the Deep: Long Range Ecology Movements" (1973) proposed a wide-ranging pursuit of "ecocentric wisdom" whose ambition were resummarized in *Ecology, Community, and Lifestyle: Outline of an Ecosophy* (1989), which was rapidly followed by Warwick Fox's

Towards a Transpersonal Ecology (1990)—a prospectus for "utopian ecologism"—and Freya Mathews' *The Ecological Self* (1991).

Such developments as these helped fuel the demand for a renaissance of pastoral nostalgia, whose plaints became increasingly eloquent in such heartfelt SF stories as Richard Cowper's trilogy begun with *The Road to Corlay* (1978), John Crowley's *Engine Summer* (1979) and Kate Wilhelm's *Juniper Time* (1979), then increasingly earnest in such scrupulously meditative works as Norman Spinrad's *Songs from the Stars* (1980), Russell Hoban's *Riddley Walker* (1980), Ursula Le Guin's *Always Coming Home* (1986) and Judith Moffett's *Pennterra* (1987). The case for an actual technological retreat was forcefully made in Ernest Callenbach's bestselling Millenarian tract *Ecotopia: A Novel About Ecology, People, and Politics in 1999* (1978), which describes the secession from the USA of the western seaboard states, whose new masters establish a new low-tech society based on the principles of "alternative technology" laid out in such texts as Ernst Schumacher's *Small is Beautiful* (1973). Ecotopia's established religion is a straightforward ecological mysticism whose rituals licensed the popular description of environmentalists as "tree-huggers."

Callenbach's new term caught on to the extent that Kim Stanley Robinson produced a showcase SF anthology entitled *Future Primitive: The New Ecotopias* (1994), which collects works operating on the assumption that contemporary "megacities...serve not as models for development but as demonstrations of a dysfunctional social order" and constitute an "attempt to imagine sophisticated new technologies combined with habits saved or reinvented from our deep past." The muted ecological mysticism celebrated in the anthology is, however, less ambitious than the transcendental varieties featured in more lyrical works such as Ursula le Guin's *The Word for World is Forest* (1972), Hilbert Schenck's *At the Eye of the Ocean* (1980) and Somtow Sucharitkul's *Starship and Haiku* (1984). The ultimate extension of that mystical strand tends to fuse the perspectives of Lovelock and Teilhard de Chardin, most forthrightly in the prospectus for the hyper-Gaian "Galaxia" set out in Isaac Asimov's *Foundation's Edge* (1982).

The transplantation of ecological concepts to other fields was continued, rather whimsically, by Ursula le Guin's essay on "The Carrier Bag Theory of Fiction" (1986), which draws a basic distinction between "techno-heroic" tales of hunters and uncombative novelistic accounts of gatherers. The essay was, however, reprinted in the altogether earnest *The Ecocriticism Reader: Landmarks in Liter-*

ary Ecology (1996) edited by Cheryll Glotfelty and Harold Fromm, which became the bible of an Association for the Study of Literature and the Environment founded 1992; its membership numbered 750 by 1995, by which time "ecological parables" had spread far beyond the exotica of SF along very various academic food-chains.

Ecological Management and Control in Science Fiction

The heavy emphasis placed by modern ecological mystics on the injurious effects of the Industrial Revolution and the growth of "megacities" deflects attention away from the fact that the whole history and prehistory of humankind have been very largely a matter of ecological management and control. Even before the development of agriculture and animal husbandry, hunter/gatherer societies had a very considerable impact on their environments, although we have only recently become aware of the extent to which supposed "wildernesses" like the Amazon basin were shaped and altered by human activity over long periods of time.

The idea that future agriculture might—or must—ultimately "domesticate" the entire ecosphere was present in Utopian literature before the advent of scientific romance, and was therefore already commonplace before the emergence of genre SF. The instrumentality of that domestication is necessarily vague in such accounts of biotechnological empery as Princess Vera Zaronovich's *Mizora* (1880-81), and J. B. S. Haldane's propagandistic essay *Daedalus; or, Science and the Future* (1923) was similarly written in ignorance of the biochemical details of heredity; even so, Haldane rightly foresaw that when direct technological manipulation of genetic materials became possible, the management of the ecosphere would become a feasible goal. Haldane also pointed out in his essay, however, that the great biological inventions of the past were invariably seen in the first instance as horrific violations of the natural order, and had tended to be accepted only when they could be granted the status of reverent ritual.

Although the management and control of Earth's ecosphere rarely features as a foregrounded topic of pulp SF it is routinely assumed. The story series by Jack Williamson that introduced the notion of "terraforming" other planets in 1942-43—reprinted in the mosaic *Seetee Ship* (1951; originally bylined Will Stewart)—takes it for granted that the technologies used in terraforming have already been applied to Earth's ecosphere; Olaf Stapledon's *Last and First Men* (1930), in which Venus has to be carefully prepared for human habitation when the sun cools, had similarly skipped over that phase of the development of technologies of ecological control. Williamson was also the writer who introduced the term "genetic engineering" into pulp SF a few years after the Seetee stories in *Dragon's Island* (1951), although such technologies of ecospheric management had been foreshadowed in the "tectogenetics" featured in Norman L. Knight's "Crisis in Utopia" (1940).

As SF writers gradually came to terms with astronomical revelations about the utter inhospitability of the other planets in the solar system, the idea of effecting ecospheric metamorphoses inevitably became more important as a key element of the instrumentality of the Space Age. Because optimism was conserved in the case of Mars until the 1960s, the ecological management projects sited there in such works as Arthur C. Clarke's *The Sands of Mars* (1951) tended to be relatively modest, but terraforming Venus was seen as a more challenging prospect in such stories as Henry Kuttner's *Fury* (1950) and Poul Anderson's "The Big Rain" (1954). The notion that genetic engineering would be absolutely necessary to any colonization or "conquest" of the galaxy carried out by human beings was graphically developed by James Blish in the "pantropy" series assembled into the mosaic *The Seedling Stars* (1957). The final story in the series, "Watershed" (1957), proposes that there will come a time when human will have to be technologically readapted for life on Earth, whose physical environment will be so drastically altered by the developmental history of the human species as to make it uninhabitable by nature's design—a notion elaborately revisited by Williamson in his calculatedly elegiac *Terraforming Earth* (2001).

In the pantropy series James Blish, like Norman L. Knight, echoed Haldane's assumption that applications of genetic engineering to the human species, however necessary or desirable, would arouse fierce prejudices. Throughout the 1950s the dominance of genre SF by the myth of the Space Age—which insisted that the next phase of human history must involve the "conquest of space"—provided a counterweight to that kind of prejudice, accepting that some degree of biological modification might be useful in the colonization of other worlds. The myth of the Space Age was itself challenged, however, by increasing awareness of the difficulty of supplying spaceships with the "miniature ecospheres" necessary to sustain human passengers for any length of time. Although simple ecospheres can be isolated in glass globes or aquaria, human beings require much more elaborate support, as demonstrated by experiments carried out by the Moscow Institute for Biomedical Problems in the

1960s, by NASA in the 1970s and 1980s and—most ambitiously of all—by the "Synergians" who built and sustained the experimental Biosphere-2 in the 1990s. The notion that human beings might have to undergo genetic engineering even to travel in spaceships became increasingly common as the myth of the Space Age began to falter in the last decades of the twentieth century.

The resurgence of ecological mysticism in the 1960s complicated these practical questions with moral anxieties. The idea of terraforming other worlds—effectively destroying native ecospheres in order to substitute clones of Earth's—soon came to seem morally suspect, to the extent that Ernest Yanarella's study of science-fictional treatments of ecological themes, *The Cross, the Plow and the Skyline: Contemporary Science Fiction and the Ecological Imagination* (2001), looks back on the uses of that theme with outright horror, referring to it in the relevant chapter title as "the Specter of Terra (Terror)Forming." Observing that James Lovelock had attempted to apply the lessons of the Gaia hypothesis to the possibility of *The Greening of Mars* (1984, with Michael Allaby), Yanarella redefines the ideology of the Space Age as a kind of terrorism, echoing the views of historians who had become similarly skeptical of the morality of European colonization—including, and sometimes especially, the colonization of the Americas. Genre SF had evolved in parallel with the Western genre, sharing its ideology of frontiersmanship, routinely identifying alien species with Native Americans, as "savages" whose fate was to be contemptuously crushed and removed to reservations—John W. Campbell Jr. was notorious for his human chauvinism, and for his steadfast commitment to the notion that the Manifest Destiny of the human species was to defeat all competitors and rule the universe—but this view had come to seem horribly politically incorrect to many observers by the end of the century.

Although *The Greening of Mars* became a powerful influence on a glut of SF stories reconsidering the possibility of colonizing Mars in the light of information provided by the Viking landers, a distinct note of moral skepticism sounded in some such works—most notably, as might be expected, those produced by the self-declared "ecotopian" Kim Stanley Robinson in "Green Mars" (1985) and the trilogy subsequently developed from it, consisting of *Red Mars* (1992), *Green Mars* (1993) and *Blue Mars* (1996). Such anxieties were very much in tune with the rhetoric of conservation that had become very influential in discussions of the future management of Earth's ecosphere.

Qualms regarding the propriety of terraforming worlds that already harbored life could be set aside in accounts of terraforming worlds that had only the organic precursors of life, as in Pamela Sargent's trilogy begun with *Venus of Dreams* (1986), but the scale of such transformations made them difficult to contemplate. The implicit grandeur of the notion continued to override moral doubts in such lyrical celebrations of Martian terraformation as Frederick Turner's epic poem *Genesis* (1988) and Ian McDonald's picaresque *Desolation Road* (1988) but distant terraforming projects gone awkwardly or horribly awry became commonplace in such works as Dave Wolverton's *Serpent Catch* (1991), Kay Kenyon's *Rift* (1999) and Neal Asher's *Gridlinked* (2001), while would-be terraformers are featured as villains to be thwarted in such works as Monica Hughes' *The Golden Aquarians* (1994) and Joan Slonczewski's *The Children Star* (1998). Other kinds of large-scale ecological engineering—for which the emergent general term is ecopoesis—have yet to figure large in SF.

With regard to the ecological management of Earth itself, the last quarter of the twentieth century saw a dramatic decline in optimism. Any Utopian prospectus for the future, however tentative, had by then to take problems of ecological sustainability into account; the apparent difficulty of that achievement is clearly manifest in such future histories as those mapped out in Marge Piercy's *Woman on the Edge of Time* (1976), *The Third Millennium* (1985) by Brian Stableford and David Langford, and Kim Stanley Robinson's *Pacific Edge* (1988). The SF of the 1990s displayed a striking unanimity in assuming that our past and present mismanagement was now irredeemable in the short term, and that Utopian optimism must be displaced into a more distant future, dependent upon a wiser reconstitution of human society—and perhaps of human nature—in the wake of a global ecocatastrophe that is already under way.

Ecocatastrophes in Science Fiction

The precariousness of the human ecological situation must have been evident to almost all tribal societies, especially those which actually perished or were forced to migrate in search of new lands that might support them, sustained by unfulfillable dreams of free-flowing milk and honey. However, the first person to produce a clear statement of the fundamental problem and its applicability to a global stage, T. R. Malthus, soon retreated from the apocalyptic prophecies of his first extrapolation in his "second essay" of 1803, which incorporated the possibility that the future growth of the human population might be modified by "moral restraint." Many others following in his footsteps beat similar retreats from the uncomfortable conclusion, reassured by advances in agricultural technology that seemed to falsify Malthus's fundamental assumption that food production could only increase arithmetically.

In the early twentieth century literary images of worldwide disaster were commonplace, but they almost invariably laid the blame on agents external to human society. Tales of new deluges and great plagues abounded, while the world's vulnerability to manufactured ecocatastrophes was featured in such thrillers as *Nordenholt's Million* (1923) by J. J. Connington, but the idea that technologies of ecological management might be storing up trouble emerged more gradually. The possibility of an ecocatastrophe resultant from the "exhaustion" of the soil's crop-bearing capacities was explored in such scientific romances as A. G. Street's *Already Walks Tomorrow* (1938) and Edward Hyams' *The Astrologer* (1950) but it was not until Malthusian anxieties resurfaced in the 1950s, replete with a new urgency, that there was a sudden boom in ecocatastrophe stories.

In the spring of 1955 a number of interested parties formed the Population Council, whose eleven-strong committee became a significant disseminator of propaganda regarding the dangerous rapidity of world population growth. The March 1956 issue of *Scientific American* carried an alarmist article on "World Population" by Julian Huxley, which assisted the Council's efforts. Genre SF writers had already taken an interest in the issue—*Marvel Science Stories* featured a "symposium" in its November 1951 issue on the question of whether the world's population should be limited, and it had been addressed in Isaac Asimov's *The Caves of Steel* (1954) and Damon Knight's "Natural State" (1954)—but it was not until the Population Council began its work that the ecological problems of overpopulation began to feature in SF on a routine basis, foregrounded by such works as Robert Silverberg's *Master of Life and Death* (1957), J. G. Ballard's "Billennium" (1961) and Robert Sheckley's "The People Trap" (1968).

Although Malthus had focused narrowly on the problem of food supply, the Population Council and SF writers who took up the theme broadened the scope of their arguments to take in the exhaustibility of other resources—especially oil—and the dangers of environmental pollution. Early scientific romances dealing with catastrophes brought about by pollution—including W. D. Hay's *The*

Doom of the Great City (1880) and Robert Barr's "The Doom of London" (1892)—had concentrated on the perils of industrial smog, but the anxieties that grew in the 1950s, lavishly displayed in C. M. Kornbluth's black comedy "Shark Ship" (1958), were far more wide-ranging. Rachel Carson's alarmist best-seller *Silent Spring* (1962) made much of the particular problems caused by the use of the insecticide DDT, alerting its readers to more general problems caused by the use of synthetic organic compounds that were not "biodegradable"—which is to say that they could not re-enter the food chain in the way that almost all natural wastes could and routinely did.

Garrett Hardin, editor of *Population, Evolution, and Birth Control: A Collage of Controversial Ideas* (1964) produced a devastating summary of a new discipline of "ecological economics" in "The Tragedy of the Commons" (1968), which pointed out that the fundamental logic of capitalism, as exemplified by the workings of Adam Smith's "invisible hand," was bound to lead to ecological devastation unless some very powerful form of moral restraint could be imposed. The alarmist trend culminated in a best-selling account of *The Population Bomb* (1968) by Paul Ehrlich, who followed it up with a quasi-documentary account of his prophecies coming to fruition in "Ecocatastrophe," published in Ramparts 8 (1969). The environmental protection movement became briefly fashionable, its arguments and concerns summarized in such texts as Richard Lillard's *Eden in Jeopardy: Man's Prodigal Meddling with His Environment* (1966) and *The Environmental Handbook* (1970) edited by Garett de Bell. The possibility of ecocatastrophe became a significant topic of political discourse, reflected in such texts as J. Clarence Davies's, *The Politics of Pollution* (1970) and James Ridgeway's *The Politics of Ecology* (1970), in the founding of Green Parties in many European countries, and in the establishment of such pressure groups as Friends of the Earth (founded 1969) and Greenpeace (launched in 1971).

An organization calling for Zero Population Growth was quick to popularize its aims by producing an anthology of science fiction stories: *Voyages: Scenarios for a Ship Called Earth* (1971), edited by Rob Sauer and introduced by Paul and Anne Ehrlich. Sf stories describing the impending ecocatastrophe became exceedingly fashionable as this alarmism peaked, extreme examples including Harry Harrison's *Make Room! Make Room!* (1966), James Blish's "We All Die Naked" (1969), Norman Spinrad's "The Lost Continent" (1970), John Brunner's *The Sheep Look Up* (1972), Philip Wylie's

The End of the Dream (1972), Kurt Vonnegut's "The Big Space Fuck" (1972) and *Ecodeath* (1972) by William Jon Watkins and Gene Snyder. The British TV series *Doomwatch* (1970-72), originated by Kit Pedler and Gerry Davis, exported the anxiety to a much wider audience. Anthologies showcasing ecocatastrophe stories included *The Ruins of Earth* (1971) edited by Thomas M. Disch and *Saving Worlds* (1973; also known—more appropriately—as *The Wounded Planet*) edited by Roger Elwood and Virginia Kidd. When the political scientist W. J. M. Mackenzie summarized the politicization of ecological issues in *Biological Ideas in Politics* (1978) he paid considerable attention to the representations of science fiction, citing Samuel Butler and John Wyndham in his preface, beginning his introduction with a quote from Robert A. Heinlein's *Beyond This Horizon* (1942, initially bylined Anson MacDonald) and also making reference in his text to Brian Aldiss.

The debate about the scientific bases of ecocatastrophic alarmism became increasingly heated as opposition to environmentalism formed ranks; the environmentalists responded by elaborating and hardening their views. Although Barry Commoner objected to Paul Ehrlich's "neo-Malthusianism" and Garrett Hardin's "ecological Hobbesianism" in *The Closing Circle: Man, Nature and Technology* (1971) his own arguments about the "debt to nature" incurred by the false mythology of wealth-creation were no less apocalyptic. The argument was extended and further amplified by such works as Alvin Toffler's *The Eco-Spasm Report* (1975), Angus Martin's *The Last Generation: The End of Survival?* (1975) and Jonathan Schell's *The Fate of the Earth* (1982), which added the Greenhouse Effect and the depletion of the Earth's ozone layer to the ecocatastrophic mix. Inevitably, these new anxieties were reflected in such speculative fictions as Hal Clement's *The Nitrogen Fix* (1980), Trevor Hoyle's *The Last Gasp* (1983), Paul Theroux's *O-Zone* (1986), *Nature's End* (1986) by Whitley Strieber and James Kunetka, George Turner's *The Sea and Summer* (1987), David Brin's *Earth* (1990) and Michael Tobias's *Fatal Exposure* (1991).

Strident alarmism was only one facet of SF's response to the perception of impending ecocrisis; Brin's *Earth* attempted to carry forward the alternative response pioneered by such works as James Blish and Norman L. Knight's *A Torrent of Faces* (1968), John Brunner's *Stand on Zanzibar* (1968) and Robert Silverberg's *The World Inside* (1972), which had tried to imagine future societies designed to cope—more or less—with overpopulation and its attendant difficulties. Other works suggested that Malthusian checks would have to be artificially imposed in order to preserve social order, and tried to envisage means by which mass homicide might most conveniently be carried out in a relatively even-handed manner. Significantly, however, none of these works ever contrived to muster any conspicuous confidence in their artifice. While many genre SF writers collaborated eagerly in the alarmism of the apocalyptic ecocatastrophists, only a tiny minority took up the more optimistic note of such works as Murray Bookchin's *Towards an Ecological Society* (1980) or Fritjof Capra and Catherine Spretnak's *Green Politics: the Global Promise* (1984). Although a hopeful note was conscientiously maintained in much children's SF, "young adult" fiction dealing with ecological issues tended more to the apocalyptic as time went by, as evidenced by such fretful examples as Nancy Bond's *The Voyage Begun* (1989), Monica Hughes' *The Crystal Drop* (1992) and *A Handful of Seeds* (1993), and Karen Hesse's *Phoenix Rising* (1994).

To some extent, this imbalance reflects the parasitism of popular fiction on melodrama, which feeds far more avidly on bad news than hopeful constructivism, but it also reflects an authentic disenchantment within the genre. Even genre writers who were neither angry nor despairing accepted that an ongoing ecological crisis would be the most obvious feature of the history of the near future, and that its inflictions would constitute a kind of justice. As the twenty-first century began, the great majority of science-fictional images of the future were content to take it for granted that the ecocatastrophe was not only under way but already irreversible—and that the backlash against environmentalism in the US political arena was a manifestation of psychological denial.

From the 1960s onwards, almost all ecocatastrophe stories written by genre SF writers had been infected with a scathingly bitter irony; most genre writers who used the theme seemed to feel that human beings would get no more and no less than they deserve if they were to destroy their environment and poison their world. To some extent, this bleakness of outlook was a reaction to the declining fortunes of the myth of Space Age, which so many SF writers had long held dear. In the 1960s many SF writers still looked to the Space Age as an exit strategy from the evolving ecocatastrophe, but the likelihood of that exit strategy dwindled dramatically as time went by, reaching extreme improbability by the year 2000

The speculative relocation of the "conquest of space" to a much more distant future involved the acceptance that, if any such historical process were ever to happen, it would be the prerogative of "posthuman" or "transhuman" species: cyborgized and genetically engineered products of the kind of "technological singularity" first popularized by Vernor Vinge and such stories as Marc Stiegler's "The Gentle Seduction" (1989) but examined in far more detail in Charles Stross's Accelerando sequence (begun 2001) and Karl Schroeder's *Permanence* (2002). Unlike the conquest of space, the ecocatastrophe cannot be postponed; the near-universal assumption of early-twenty-first century SF is that if its problems are soluble—the price of failure being a drastic reversal of technological progress—the solution probably lies in some kind of managed evolution of posthumanity.

Whether this assumption is true or not—and SF's record as a medium of prophecy hardly inspires confidence—it is perhaps the most fascinating example available of SF's speculative extrapolation of questions and issues raised by the emergence of a new scientific discipline. Perhaps ironically, the promoters of the field of "ecocriticism"—which attempts to apply ecological principles to the study of literary phenomena—have tended either to ignore SF or to treat it as a Great Wen despoiling the landscape of "naturalistic" fiction, but that only demonstrates their failure to take aboard one of the most important principles of biological science: that no organism can reasonably be condemned as irrelevant or uninteresting on arbitrary aesthetic grounds.

PRIMARY BIBLIOGRAPHY

Aldiss, Brian W. *Helliconia Spring*. London: Jonathan Cape, 1982.
___. *Helliconia Summer*. London: Jonathan Cape, 1983
___. *Helliconia Winter*. London: Jonathan Cape, 1985
Allen, Grant, "A Child of the Phalanstery" *Belgravia* July 1884 (as J. Arbuthnot Wilson).
___. "Pausodyne" *Belgravia Christmas Annual*, 1881 (as by J. Arbuthnot Wilson).
Anderson, Poul. "The Big Rain". *Astounding Science Fiction* October 1954.
___. *Fire Time*. Garden City, NY: Doubleday, 1974.
___. "Question and Answer". *Astounding Science Fiction* June-July 1954; reprinted as *Planet of No Return*. New York: Ace, 1957.
___. "A Twelvemonth and a Day". *Fantastic Universe* January 1960; reprinted as *Let the Spacemen Beware!* New York: Ace, 1963.
___. *The Winter of the World*. Garden City, NY: Doubleday, 1975.
Andreae. Johann Valentin. *Reipublicae Christianopolitanae Descriptio*. Strasburg: Argentorati, 1619; tr. as *Christianopolis: An Ideal State of the Seventeenth Century translated from the Latin of Johann Valentin Andreae with an Historical Introduction* by Felix Emil Held, New York: Oxford University Press, 1916.
Anon. *Le Passage de pôle arctique au pôle antarctique*. [1780]. Reprinted in Garnier *op cit*.
Anon. [sometimes falsely attributed to Ludwig Tieck] "Wake not the Dead!" in *Popular Tales and Romances of the Northern Nations*, anon ed., London: Simpkin Marshall, 1823.
Anthony, Piers. *Omnivore*. New York: Ballantine, 1968.
Asher, Neal. *Gridlinked*. London: Macmillan, 2001.
___. *The Line of Polity*. London: Macmillan, 2003.
Asimov, Isaac. *The Caves of Steel*. Garden City, NY: Doubleday, 1954.
___. *Foundation's Edge*. Garden City, NY: Doubleday, 1982.
Bacon, Francis. *New Atlantis. A Worke Unfinished bound with Sylva Sylvarum, or a Naturall Historie*. London: J. H. for W. Lee, 1626 (actually 1627).
Ballard, J. G. "Billennium". *New Worlds* November 1961.

Barbey d'Aurevilly, Jules-Amadée. *Du dandyisme et de G. Brummel.* Paris: Poulet-Malassis, 1843.

Barr, Robert. "The Doom of London". *The Idler* November 1892.

Barrett, Neal. *Highwood.* New York: Ace, 1972.

Bateson Gregory. *Steps Towards an Ecology of Mind.* New York: Basic Books, 1972.

Baudelaire, Charles. *Les Fleurs du mal.* Paris: Poulet-Malassis, 1857.

Baudino, Gael. *Gossamer Ax.* New York: Roc, 1992.

Beauclerk, Helen. *The Love of the Foolish Angel.* London: Collins, 1929.

Bellamy, Edward. "The Blindman's World" *Atlantic Monthly* November 1886; reprinted in *The Blindman's World and Other Stories*, Boston: Houghton Mifflin, 1898.

___. *Dr Heidenhoff's Process*, New York: Appleton, 1880.

___. *Looking Backward, 2000-1887*, Boston: Ticknor, 1888.

Beresford. J. D., *Goslings*, London: Heinemann, 1913 (abridged version as A World of Women, London: Collins, 1920).

___. *The Hampdenshire Wonder*, London: Sidgwick & Jackson, 1912.

___. "The Man Who Hated Flies" in *The Meeting Place*. London: Faber & Faber, 1929.

___. *Signs and Wonders.* Waltham St Lawrence, Berks: Golden Cockerel Press, 1921.

Benson Stella. *Living Alone.* London: Macmillan, 1919.

Besant, Walter. *The Inner House.* Bristol: Arrowsmith, 1888.

Béthune, Chevalier de. *Relation du monde de Mercure.* Geneva: Barillot, 1750; reprinted in Garnier, *op. cit.*

Bester, Alfred. "Adam and No Eve". *Astounding Stories* September 1941.

Bierce, Ambrose. "Moxon's Master" in *The Collected Works of Ambrose Bierce, Volume Three: Can Such Things Be?* Washington: Walter Neale, 1909.

Bilderdijk, Willem. *Kort verhaal van eene aanmerklijke luctreis en nieuwe planeetokdekking.* The Hague: W. van Hoeve, 1813; tr. by Paul Vincent as *A Short Account of a Remarkable Aerial Boyage and Discovery of a New Planet by Willem Bilderrdijk.* Paisley: Wilfion Books, 1989.

Bixby, Jerome. "It's a *Good* Life" in *Star Science Fiction Stories* 2, ed. Frederik Pohl. New York: Ballantine, 1953.

Blair, Andrew. *Annals of the Twenty-Ninth Century; or, The Autobiography of the Tenth President of the World Republic.* London: Tinsley, 1874.

Blish, James. *The Seedling Stars.* New York: Gnome Press, 1956.

___. *Titan's Daughter.* New York: Berkley, 1961.

___. "We All Die Naked" in *Three for Tomorrow*, ed. Robert Silverberg, New York: Meredith, 1969.

Blish, James, and Norman L. Knight. *A Torrent of Faces.* Garden City, NY: Doubleday, 1968.

Bond, Nancy. *The Voyage Begun.* New York: Atheneum, 1981.

GOTHIC GROTESQUES, BY BRIAN STABLEFORD

Bookchin, Murray. *Towards an Ecological Society*. Montréal: Black Rose, 1980.

Borel, Pierre. *Discours nouveau prouvant la pluralité des mondes; que les astres sont des terres habités, at la terre un estoile, etc.* Geneva, 1657.

Boyd, John. *The Pollinators of Eden*. New York: Weybright and Talley, 1969.

Brin, David. *Earth*. New York: Bantam, 1990.

Brown, Fredric. "Knock". *Thrilling Wonder Stories* December 1948.

Brunner, John. *The Sheep Look Up*. New York: Harper, 1972.

___. *Stand on Zanzibar*. Garden City, NY: Doubleday, 1968.

___. *Total Eclipse*. Garden City, NY: Doubleday, 1974.

Brussof, Valery. "Respublika yuzhnavo kresta" [1905]; tr. as "The Republic of the Southern Cross" in *The Republic of the Southern Cross and Other Stories*. London: Constable, 1918.

Bulgakov, Mikhail. "Rokovy'e yaitsa" [1922]; tr. as "The Fatal Eggs" in *Diaboliad and Other Stories*. Bloomington: University of Indiana Press, 1972.

Bullett, Gerald. *Mr. Godly Beside Himself*. London: John Lane, 1924.

[Bulwer, Edward, later Bulwer-Lytton]. *The Coming Race*. Edinburgh & London: Blackwood, 1871

___. *A Strange Story*. Leipzig: Tauchnitz, 1862.

___. *Zanoni*. London: Saunders & Otley, 1842 (issued anonmously).

Burdekin, Key. *The Burning Ring*. London: Thornton Butterworth, 1927.

Burroughs, Edgar Rice. "Under the Moons of Mars" *All-Story* February-July 1912; reprinted as *A Princess of Mars*, Chicago: McClurg, 1917.

Butler, Samuel. *Erewhon; or, Over the Range*. London: Trübner, 1872.

Byron, Lord. *Manfred: A Dramatic Poem*. London: John Murray, 1817.

Caliban, Louisianax E. M., and Louis Ravensfield, eds. *In Blood We Lust: Depraved Sexual Fantasies for Vampires*. London: Dark Angel Press, 1999.

Callenbach, Ernest. *Ecotopia: A novel about ecology, people and politics in 1999*. Berkeley, CA: Banyan Tree, 1978.

Campbell, John W. Jr. (as Don A. Stuart) "Forgetfulness". *Astounding Stories* June 1937.

___. "Who Goes There?" *Astounding Stories*, August 1938.

Campbell, Thomas. *The Poetical Works of Thomas Campbell*. London: Walter Scott, 1886.

Campanella, Tommaso. *La Città del Sole; Dilaogo Poetico. The City of the Sun; A Poetical Dialogue*, Berkeley: University of California Press, 1981 [translation of manuscript version written in Italian in 1602]; the first publication (in Latin) of a revised version was *Civitas Solis* [1623].

Čapek, Karel. *The Makropoulos Secret*. Boston: Luce, 1925.

Capra, Fritjof, and Catherine Spretnak. *Green Politics: the Global Promise*. New York: Dutton, 1984.

Carson, Rachel. *Silent Spring*. Boston: Houghton Mifflin, 1962.

176

Cavendish, Margaret, Duchess of Newcastle. *The Description of A New World Called the Blazing World. Written by the thrice noble, illustrious and excellent Princess the Duchess of Newcastle.* Issued as an addendum to *Observations Upon Experimental Philosophy.* London: A. Maxwell, 1666.

Chadwick, Philip George. *The Death Guard.* London: Hutchinson, 1939.

Charnas, Suzy McKee. *The Vampire Tapestry.* New York: Simon and Schuster, 1980.

Chesney, George T. *The Battle of Dorking: Reminiscences of a Volunteer.* Blackwood's Magazine May 1871; reprinted as a pamphlet, Edinburgh & London: Blackwood, 1871.

Christopher, John. *The Death of Grass.* London: Michael Joseph, 1956,

Clarke, Arthur C. *The Sands of Mars.* London: Sidgwick & Jackson, 1951.

Clement, Hal. "Cold Front". *Astounding Science Fiction* July 1946.

___. *Cycle of Fire.* New York: Ballantine, 1957.

___. *Mission of Gravity.* Garden City, NY: Doubleday, 1953.

___. *The Nitrogen Fix.* New York: Ace, 1980.

Clifton, Mark. *Eight Keys to Eden.* Garden City, NY: Doubleday, 1960.

Collier, John. *Tom's A-Cold.* London: Macmillan, 1933.

Collins, Nancy. *Wild Blood.* New York: Roc, 1994.

Colomb, Rear-Admiral P. H., with Col. J. F. Maurice, Capt. F. N. Maude, Archibald Forbes, Charles Lowe, D. Christie Murray & F. Scudamore. "The Great War of 1892: A Forecast". *Black & White* January 1891-January 1892; reprinted as *The Great War of 189-.* London: Heinemann, 1893.

Commoner, Barry. *The Closing Circle: Man, Nature and Technology.* London: Jonathan Cape, 1972.

Conan Doyle, Arthur. *The Doings of Raffles Haw.* New York: J. W. Lovell, 1891)

___. *The Lost World.* London: Hodder & Stoughton, 1912.

___. *The Poison Belt: Being an Account of Another Amazing Adventure of Professor Challenger.* London: Hodder & Stoughton, 1913.

Coney, Michael G. *Hello Summer, Goodbye.* London: Gollancz, 1975.

___. *Syzygy.* New York: Ballantine, 1973.

Connington, J. J. *Nordenholt's Million.* London: Constable, 1923.

Constantine, Storm. *Stalking Tender Prey.* London: Signet, 1995.

Corelli, Marie. *The Sorrows of Satan.* London: Methuen, 1895.

Cousin de Grainville, Jean-Baptiste. *Le dernier homme.* Paris, 1805; tr. as *The Last Man; or, Omegarius and Syderia: A Romance in Futurity.* London: R. Dutton, 1806.

Cowper, Richard. *The Road to Corlay.* London: Gollancz, 1978.

Cromie, Robert. *The Crack of Doom.* London: Digby Long, 1895.

___. *A Plunge into Space.* London: Frederick Warne, 1890.

Crowley, John *Engine Summer.* Garden City, NY: Doubleday, 1979.

Cummings, Ray. "The Girl in the Golden Atom" All-Story 15 March 1919; incorporated into *The Girl in the Golden Atom*. London: Methuen, 1922.

Cyrano de Bergerac, Savinien. *Fragment d'histoire comique contenant les états et empires du soleil.* Paris: Charles de Sercy, 1662; tr. with following item by Richard Aldington in *Voyages to the Moon and Sun.* London: Routledge & New York: Dutton, 1923; tr. by Geoffrey Strachan in *Other Worlds: The Comic History of the States and Empires of the Moon and Sun.* London: Oxford University Press, 1963..

___. *Histoire comique contenant les états et empires de la lune.* Paris: Charles de Sercy, 1657.

Daniel, Gabriel. *Voyage au monde de Descartes.* Paris: S. Bernard, 1691; tr. as *A Voyage to the World of Cartesius.* London: T. Bennet, 1694.

Davies, J. Clarence. *The Politics of Pollution.* Indianapolis, Ind.: Bobbs-Merrill, 1970.

Davy, Humphry. *Consolations in Travel: The Last Days of a Philosopher*, London: John Murray, 1830.

de Bell, Garett, *The Environmental Handbook.* New York: Ballantine: 1970.

Derleth, August. *Watchers out of Time.* Sauk City, WI: Arkham House, 1974

Dick, Philip K. *Eye in the Sky.* New York: Ace, 1957.

Dickson, Gordon R. *Masters of Everon.* New York: Ace, 1979.

___. "Twig" in *Stellar* 1 ed. Judy-Lynn del Rey, New York: Ballantine, 1974.

Disch, Thomas M. *The Businessman: A Tale of Terror.* New York: Harper, 1984.

Disch, Thomas M., ed. *The Ruins of Earth.* New York: Putnam's, 1971.

Donnelly, Ignatius. *Caesar's Column: A Story of the Twentieth Century* (as Edmund Boisgilbert M.D.). Chicago: F. J. Schulte, 1890.

Duncan, Ronald. *The Last Adam.* London: Dennis Dobson, 1952.

Dunsany, Lord. *The Blessing of Pan.* London: Putnam 1927.

___. *The King of Elfland's Daughter.* London: Putnam, 1924.

Ehrlich, Paul. "Ecocatastrophe". Ramparts 8 (1969).

___. *The Population Bomb.* New York: Ballantine, 1968.

Ellis, Edward S. *The Steam Man of the Prairies.* New York: American Novels Publishing Co, 1868.

Elton, Charles. *Animal Ecology.* London: Sidgwick and Jackson, 1927,

Elwood, Roger, and Virginia Kidd, eds. *Saving Worlds.* Garden City, NY: Doubleday, 1973.

England, George Allan. *The Air Trust.* St. Louis: Phil Wagner, 1915.

___. *Darkness and Dawn.* New York: Small Maynard, 1914.

___. *The Golden Blight.* Cavalier 18 May-22 June 1912; reprinted, New York: H. K. Fly, 1916.

Farjeon, Eleanor. *Martin Pippin in the Apple-Orchard.* London: Collins, 1921.

Farley, Ralph Milne. *The Radio Man*. Argosy-All-Story 28 June-19 July 1924; reprinted, Los Angeles: Fantasy Publishing Co. Inc, 1948.

Farmer, Philip José. "Father". *The Magazine of Fantasy & Science Fiction* July 1955.

___. *The Lovers*. Startling Stories August 1952; expanded, New York: Ballantine, 1961.

Fawcett, Edgar. *The Ghost of Guy Thyrle*. Peter Fenelon Collier's Once-a-Week Semi-Monthly Library, 21 March 1895; reprinted, London: Ward Lock, 1895.

___. "Solarion. A Romance". *Lippincott's Monthly Magazine* September 1889.

Fawcett, E. Douglas. *Hartmann the Anarchist; or, The Doom of the Great City*. London: Richard Arnold, 1893.

Fearn, John Russell. *The Intelligence Gigantic. Amazing Stories* June-July 1933: Kingswood, Surrey: World's Work, 1943.

Fézandié, Clement, "Doctor Hackensaw's Secrets". 43-part series published irregularly between the May 1921 and September 1925 issues of *Science and Invention*

Flammarion, Camille. *La Fin du monde*. Paris: Flammarion, 1894; tr. by J. B. Walker as *Omega: The Last Days of the World*. New York: Cosmopolitan, 1894.

___. *Lumen*. Paris: Marpon et Flammarion, 1887; expanded edition, 1906.

___. *Les Mondes imaginaires et les mondes réels: voyage pittoresque dans le ciel et revue critique des théories humaines, scientifiques et romanesques, anciennes et modernes sur les habitants des astres*. Paris: Didier et cie, 1864; expanded ed. Paris: Marpon et Flammarion, 1892.

___. *Récits de l'infini: Lumen; Histoire d'une comète; Dans l'infini*. Paris: Didier et cie, 1872; tr. by S. R. Crocker as *Stories of Infinity: Lumen; The History of a Comet; In Infinity*. Boston: Roberts Bros, 1873; expanded ed. as *Récits de l'infini: Lumen, histoire d'une a[c]me; Histoire d'une comète; La Vie universelle et eternelle*. Paris: Marpon et Flammarion, 1892.

___. *Uranie*. Paris: Marpon et Flammarion, 1889; tr. by Mary J. Serrano as *Uranie*, New York: Cassell, 1890; tr. by Augusta Rice Stetson as *Urania*, Boston: Estes & Laurist, 1890 and London: Chatto & Windus, 1891; tr. by E. P. Robins as *Urania*, Chicago: Donohue, Henneberry & Co, 1892.

Foigny, Gabriel de. *La Terre australe connu: c'est à dire, la description de ce pays inconnu jusqu'ici*. Geneva: 1676; tr. as *A New Discovery of Terra Incognita Australis, or the Southern World, by James Sadeur, a French-man*. London: J. Dunton, 1693)

Fontenelle, Bernard le Bovier de. *Entretiens sur la pluralité des mondes*. Paris: C. Blageart, 1686; tr. by Sir W. D. Knight as *A Discourse of the Plurality of Worlds*. Dublin: William Norman, 1687; tr. by H. A. Hargreaves as *Conversations on the Plurality of Worlds*. Berkley, Los Angeles & Oxford: University of California Press, 1990.

Forward, Robert L. *Rocheworld*. *Analog* December 1982-February 1983; expanded as *The Flight of the Dragonfly*. New York: Pocket Books, 1984.

Fowler Wright, S. *The Amphibians: A Romance of 500,000 Years Hence*. London: Merton Press, 1925; subsequently incorporated into *The World Below*. London: Collins, 1929.

___. *Deluge*. London: Fowler Wright, 1928.

Fox, Warwick. *Towards a Transpersonal Ecology*. Boston: Shambhala, 1990.

France, Anatole. *La Révolte des anges*. Paris: Calmann-Lévy, 1914.

___. *Sur la pierre blanche*. Paris: Calmann-Lévy, 1905; tr. by Charles E. Roche as *The White Stone*, London: John Lane, 1910.

___. "La Tragédie humaine" in *Le Puits de Sainte Claire*, Paris: Calmann-Lévy, 1895.

Galland, Antoine. *Les Mille et une nuites: contes arabes*. Paris, 1704-17.

Gallun, Raymond Z. "Old Faithful". *Astounding Stories* December 1934.

Gardner, Thomas B., M.D. "The Last Woman". *Wonder Stories* April 1932.

Garnett, David. *Lady into Fox*. London: Chatto and Windus, 1923.

Garnier, Charles, ed. *Voyages imaginaires, songes, visions, et romans cabalistiques*. 36 vols. Amsterdam & Paris: Garnier, 1787-9.

Gaskell, Jane. *The Shiny Narrow Grin*. London: Hodder and Stoughton, 1964.

Gautier, Théophile. "Arria Marcella; souvenir de Pompeii". *Revue de Paris*, 1852.

___. "La Morte amoureuse". *Chronique de Paris* 23 & 26 Juin 1836.

Gernsback, Hugo, "Baron Munchhausen's Scientific Adventures". 13-part series published irregularly between the May 1915 and February 1917 issues of *Electrical Experimenter*.

Giesy, J. U. *Palos of the Dog Star Pack*. *All-Story* 13 July-10 August 1918; reprinted, New York: Avalon, 1965.

Godwin, Francis. *The Man in the Moone or a Discourse of a Voyage Thither by Domingo Gonsales, the Speedy Messenger*. London: Kirton & Warre, 1638.

Gourmont, Rémy de, "The Magnolia" in *Angels of Perversity*, tr. by Francis Amery. Sawtry: Dedalus, 1992.

Griffith, George. *The Angel of the Revolution*. *Pearson's Weekly* 21 January-14 October 1893; reprinted in abridged form, London: Tower, 1893.

___. *The Lord of Labour*. London: F. V. White, 1911.

___. "Stories of Other Worlds". *Pearson's Magazine* January-June 1901; expanded as *A Honeymoon in Space*. London: Pearson, 1901.

Haldane, J. B. S. *Daedalus; or, Science and the Future*. London: Kegan Paul, Trench & Trübner, 1923.

Haldeman, Joe W. *The Forever War*. New York: St Martin's Press, 1974.

Hale, Edward Everett, "The Brick Moon". *Atlantic Monthly* October-December 1869; reprinted, with sequel, in *His Level Best and Other Stories*, Boston: Roberts Brothers, 1872.

___. "Hands Off!" *Harper's New Monthly Magazine* March 1881.

Hamilton, Cicely. *Theodore Savage: A Story of the Past or the Future.* London: L. Parsons, 1922; revised as *Lest Ye Die: A Story from the Past or of the Future.* New York: Scribner's, 1928.

Hand, Elizabeth. *Waking the Moon.* London: HarperCollins, 1994.

Hardin, Garrett. "The Tragedy of the Commons". *Science* 162 (1968).

Hardin, Garrett, ed. *Population, Evolution, and Birth Control: A Collage of Controversial Ideas.* San Francisco: W. H. Freeman, 1964.

Harrison, Harry. *Make Room! Make Room!* Garden City, NY: Doubleday, 1966,

Hawthorne, Nathaniel. "The Birthmark". *The Pioneer* March 1843; reprinted in *Mosses from an Old Manse*, New York: Wiley & Putnam, 1846.

___. "Rappaccini's Daughter". *United States Magazine and Democratic Review*, December 1844; reprinted in *Mosses from an Old Manse*, New York: Wiley & Putnam, 1846.

Hay, George, Colin Wilson, and David Langford. *The Necronomicon: The Book of Dead Names.* Jersey: Spearman, 1978.

Hay, W. D. *The Doom of the Great City.* London: Newman 1880.

Heard, Gerald. "The Great Fog" in *The Great Fog and Other Weird Tales.* New York: Vanguard Pres, 1944.

Hecht, Ben. *Fantazius Mallare: A Mysterious Oath.* Chicago: Covici-McGee, 1922.

Heinlein, Robert A. *Beyond This Horizon. Astounding Science Fiction* April-May 1942 (as by Anson MacDonald); Reading, Penn.: Fantasy Press, 1948,

___. *The Puppet Masters.* Garden City, NY: Doubleday, 1951.

___. *Starship Troopers.* New York: Putnam, 1959.

___. *Stranger in a Strange Land.* New York: Putnam, 1961.

___. "They". Unknown April 1941.

___. "The Unpleasant Profession of Jonathan Hoag". Unknown October 1942 (as John Riverside).

Herbert, Frank. *Dune.* Philadelphia, PA: Chilton, 1965.

———. *The Green Brain.* New York: Ace, 1966.

Heron-Allen, Edward. *The Cheetah-Girl.* privately printed 1923; reprinted separately and in *The Collected Strange Papers of Christopher Blayre*, Leyburn, N. Yorks: Tartarus Press, 1998.

Hesse, Karen. *Phoenix Rising.* New York: Holt, 1994.

Hichens, Robert. "How Love Came to Professor Guildea" in *Tongues of Conscience.* London: Methuen, 1900.

Hinton, C. H. *Scientific Romances.* London: Swan Sonnenschein, 1884.

Hoban, Russell. *Riddley Walker.* London: Jonathan Cape, 1980.

Hodgson, William Hope. *The House on the Borderland*. London: Chapman & Hall, 1908.

___. *The Night Land*. London: Eveleigh Nash, 1912.

Holberg, Ludvig, *Nicolai Klimii iter subterraneum*. Leipzig: J. Preussii, 1741; tr. as *A Journey to the World Under-Ground by Nicholas Klimius*, London: Astley & Collins, 1742.

Hood, Thomas. *Poems of Wit and Humor*. London: E. Moxon, 1847.

Horne, Richard Henry. *The Poor Artist; or, seven eye-sights and one object*. London: John Van Voorst, 1850.

Hoyle, Trevor. *The Last Gasp*. New York: Crown, 1983.

Hudson, W. H. *A Crystal Age*. London: Fisher Unwin, 1887.

___. *Green Mansions*. London: Duckworth, 1902.

Hughes, Monica. *The Crystal Drop*. London: Methuen, 1992.

___. *The Golden Aquarians*. Toronto: HarperCollins, 1994.

___. *A Handful of Seeds*. Toronto: Lester, 1993.

Hunt, Robert. *Panthea, the Spirit of Nature*. London: Reeve, Bentham & Reeve, 1849.

___. *The Poetry of Science; or, Studies of the Physical Phenomena of Nature*. London: Reeve, Bentham & Reeve, 1848.

Huxley, Aldous. *After Many a Summer Dies the Swan*. London: Chatto and Windus, 1939.

___. *Brave New World*. London: Chatto & Windus, 1932.

Huxley, Julian. "The Tissue-Culture King" *Amazing Stories* October 1927.

Huygens, Christian. *Cosmotheoros, sive de Terris coelestibus earumque ornatu conjecturae*, The Hague: A. Moetjens, 1698; tr. as *The Celestial World discover'd, or Conjectures concerning the inhabitants, plants and products of the worlds in the planets*. London: T. Childe, 1698.

Huysmans, Joris-Karl. *À rebours*. Paris: Charpentier, 1884.

___. *Là-Bas*. Paris: Tresse et Stock, 1891.

Hyams, Edward. *The Astrologer*. London: Longmans Green, 1950.

Irwin, Margaret. *Still She Wished for Company*. London: Heinemann, 1924.

___. *These Mortals*. London: Heinemann, 1925.

Jackson, Shirley. *The Haunting of Hill House*. New York: Viking, 1959.

Jane, Fred T. *The Violet Flame. A Story of Armageddon and After*. London: Ward Lock, 1899.

Jefferies, Richard. *After London*. London: Cassell, 1885.

Jepson, Edgar. *The Horned Shepherd*. London: Sons of the Vine, 1904.

Joncquel, Octave & Varlet, Théo. *L'Agonie de la terre*. Amiens: E. Malfère, 1922.

___. *Les titans du ciel*. Amiens: E. Malfère, 1921.

Kast, Pierre. *Les Vampires de l'Alfama*. Paris: J'ai-lu, 1975.

Keats, John. "Lamia" in *Lamia, Isabella, The Eve of St Agnes, and Other Poems*, London: Taylor and Hessey, 1820.

Keller David H. "Life Everlasting". *Amazing Stories* July-August 1934.

___. "The Metal Doom". *Amazing Stories* May-July 1932.

Kenyon, Kay. *Rift*. New York: Bantam, 1999.

Kepler, John. *Joh. Keppler Mathematici Olim Imperatorii. Somnium se opus posthumus de astronomia lunare*. Frankfurt, 1634; tr. by Everett F. Bleiler as "Somnium: or the Astronomy of the Moon, An Allegory of Science by Johannes Kepler" in *Beyond Time and Space* ed. August Derleth, New York: Pellegrini & Cudahy, 1950; tr. & annotated by Edward Rosen, *Kepler's Somnium. The Dream, or Posthumous Work on Lunar Astronomy*, Madison, Wis.: University of Wisconsin Press, 1967.

King, Stephen. *'Salem's Lot*. Garden City, NY: Doubleday, 1975.

———. *The Shining*. Garden City, NY: Doubleday, 1977.

Kingsbury, Donald. *Courtship Rite*. New York: Timescape, 1982.

Kipling, Rudyard. "As Easy as A.B.C." *Weekly Magazine* 25 February & 12 March, 1912; reprinted in *A Diversity of Creatures*, London: Macmillan, 1917.

___. "With the Night Mail". *McClure's Magazine*, November 1905; expanded as *With the Night Mail. A Story of 2000 A.D. (Together with Extracts from the Contemporary Magazine in which it Appeared)*, New York: Doubleday Page, 1909.

Kircher, Athanasius. *Itinerarium Exstaticum quo mundi opificium, etc.* Rome: V. Mascardi, 1656.

Knight, Damon. "Natural State". Galaxy January 1954; expanded as *Masters of Evolution*, New York: Ace, 1959.

___. "Not with a Bang". *The Magazine of Fantasy & Science Fiction* Winter-Spring 1950.

Knight, Norman L. "Crisis in Utopia". *Astounding Science-Fiction* July-August 1940.

Kornbluth, C. M. "Shark Ship" in *A Mile Beyond the Moon*, Garden City, NY: Doubleday, 1958.

Krafft-Ebing, Richard. *Psychopathia Sexualis*. Stuttgart: F. Enke, 1886.

Kuttner, Henry. *Fury*. New York: Grosset & Dunlap, 1950.

Lang. Herrmann. *The Air Battle: A Vision of the Future*. London: William Penny, 1859.

Lasswitz, Kurd. *Auf Zwei Planeten*. Leipzig: B. Elischer Nachfolger, 1897; abridged tr. by Hans J. Rudnick, *Two Planets. Auf Zwei Planeten*, Carbondale: Southern Illinois University Press, 1971.

LaVey, Anton. *The Satanic Bible*. Secaucus, N.J.: University Books, 1969.

le Fanu, J. Sheridan. "Carmilla" in *In a Glass Darkly*. London: Bentley, 1872.

Le Guin, Ursula K. *Always Coming Home*. New York: Harper, 1986.

___. "Vaster than Empires and More Slow". 1971.

___. *The Word for World Is Forest* in *Again Dangerous Visions* ed. Harlan Ellison, Garden City, NY: Doubleday, 1972; reprinted New York: Berkley, 1976.

Leinster, Murray. "The Lonely Planet". *Thrilling Wonder Stories* December 1949.

Leland, Charles Godfrey. *Aradia: The Gospel of the Witches*. London: David Nutt, 1899.

Lem, Stanislaw. *Solaris*. New York: Walker, 1970 [original publication Warsaw, 1961].

le Queux, William. "The Invasion of 1910". *Daily Mail*, March-April 1906; reprinted as *The Invasion of 1910, with a Full Account of the Siege of London*. London: Eveleigh Nash, 1906.

Lewis, C. S. *Out of the Silent Planet*. London: John Lane, 1938.

Lillard, Richard. *Eden in Jeopardy: Man's Prodigal Meddling with His Environment*. New York: Knopf, 1966.

London, Jack, *Before Adam*. New York: Macmillan, 1906.

___. *The Iron Heel*. New York: Macmillan, 1907.

___. *The Scarlet Plague*. *London Magazine* May-June 1912; reprinted, New York: Macmillan, 1914.

___. "The Shadow and the Flash". *Bookman*, June 1903; reprinted in *Moon-Face and Other Stories*. New York: Macmillan, 1906.

___. "A Thousand Deaths". *The Black Cat* May 1899.

Long, Frank Belknap. "The Last Men". *Astounding Stories* August 1934.

Lorrain, Jean, "The Glass of Blood", tr. by Brian Stableford, in *The Dedalus Book of Decadence* ed. Brian Stableford, Sawtry: Dedalus, 1991.

Lovecraft, H. P. "The Shadow out of Time". *Astounding Stories* June 1936.

___. *The Shadow Over Innsmouth*. Everett, PA: Visionary Press, 1936.

Lovelock, James. *Gaia: A New Look at Life on Earth*. Oxford, UK: Oxford University Press, 1973.

Lovelock, James, and Michael Allaby. *The Greening of Mars*. London: André Deutsch, 1984.

Lowell, Percival. *Mars as the Abode of Life*. New York: Macmillan, 1908.

Machen Arthur. "The Bowmen". *Evening News* 29 September 1914.

___. *The Hill of Dreams*. London: Grant Richards, 1907.

Mackenzie, W. J. M. *Biological Ideas in Politics*. London: Penguin, 1978.

Maitland, Edward. *By and By*. London: Bentley, 1873.

Malthus, T. R. *Essay on the Principle of Population as it Affects the Future Improvement of Society*. 2nd ed. London: J. Johnson, 1803. {First ed. 1798]

Martin, Angus. *The Last Generation: The End of Survival?* London: Fontana, 1975.

Matheson, Richard. "Pattern for Survival". *The Magazine of Fantasy & Science Fiction* May 1955.

Mathews, Freya. *The Ecological Self*. Lanham, MD: Rowman and Littlefield, 1991.

Maupassant, Guy de. "La Chevelure". *Gil Blas* 13 Mai 1884.

———. "La Morte". *Gil Blas* 31 Mai 1887.

McAuley, Paul J. *Four Hundred Billion Stars*. London: Gollancz, 1988.

McAuley, Paul J., and Kim Newman, eds. *In Dreams*. London: Gollancz, 1992.

McDonald, Ian. *Desolation Road*. New York: Bantam, 1988.

McKenna, Richard. "The Night of Hoggy Darn". *If* December 1958; revised as "Hunter Come Home," *The Magazine of Fantasy & Science Fiction* March 1963.

Mercier, Louis-Sebastien. *L'An deux mille quatre cent quarante*. Paris, 1771; tr. by William Hooper as *Memoirs of the Year Two Thousand Five Hundred*, London: G. Robinson, 1772.

Merril, Judith. *Shadow on the Hearth*. Garden City, NY: Doubleday, 1950.

Merritt, A. "The Moon Pool" *All-Story* 22 June 1918; reprinted in abridged form, with a sequel, in *The Moon Pool*, New York: Putnam, 1919.

Michelet, Jules. *La Sorcière*. Paris: Dentu, 1862. Tr. by A. R. Allinson as *Satanism and Witchcraft*. New York: Citadel, 1939.

Miller, Walter M. *A Canticle for Leibowitz*. New York: Lippincott, 1960.

Mills, Robert P. "The Last Shall Be First". *Magazine of Fantasy & Science Fiction* August 1958.

Milton, John. *Paradise Lost*. London: S. Thomson, 1668.

Mirrlees, Hope. *Lud-in-the-Mist*. London: Collins, 1926.

Moffett, Judith. *Pennterra*. New York: Congdon and Weed, 1987.

Moore, Ward. "Lot". *The Magazine of Fantasy & Science Fiction* May 1953.

___. "Lot's Daughter". *The Magazine of Fantasy & Science Fiction* October 1954.

Morrow, Lowell Howard. "Omega, the Man". *Amazing Stories* January 1933.

Naess, Arne. *Ecology, Community, and Lifestyle: Outline of an Ecosophy*. Cambridge: Cambridge University Press, 1989.

———. "The Shallow and the Deep: Long Range Ecology Movements: A Summary". *Inquiry* 16 (1973).

Nau, John-Antoine. *Force ennemie*, Paris: Éditions de la Plume, 1903.

Niven, Larry. *Destiny's Road*. New York: Tor, 1997.

___. *The Integral Trees*. New York: Ballantine, 1984.

___. *The Smoke Ring*. New York: Ballantine, 1987.

Nodier, Charles. *Smarra, ou les démons de la nuit*. Paris: Ponthieu, 1821.

Noyes, Alfred. *The Last Man*. London: John Murray, 1940.

O'Brien, Fitz-James. "The Diamond Lens". *Atlantic Monthly* January 1858.

Odle, E. V. *The Clockwork Man*. London: Heinemann, 1923.

Oliver, Chad, and Charles Beaumont. "The Last Word". *The Magazine of Fantasy & Science Fiction* April 1955.

Onions, Oliver. "The Beckoning Fair One" in *Widdershins*. London: Martin Secker, 1911.

Orwell, George. *Nineteen Eighty-Four*. London: Secker and Warburg, 1949.

Packard, Vance. *The Hidden Persuaders*. London: Longmans Green, 1957.

___. *The People Shapers*. London: Macdonald and Jane's, 1978.

Piercy, Marge. *Woman on the Edge of Time*. New York: Knopf, 1976.

Piserchia, Doris. *Earthchild*. New York: DAW, 1977.

Poe, Edgar Allan. "The Colloquy of Monos and Una" *Graham's Lady's and Gentleman's Magazine* August 1841; reprinted in *Tales by Edgar Allan Poe*. New York: Wiley & Putnam, 1845.

___. "The Conversation of Eiros and Charmion". *Burton's Gentleman's Magazine* December 1839; reprinted in *Tales of the Grotesque and Arabesque*, Philadelphia: Lea & Blanchard, 1840.

___. *Eureka: A Prose Poem*. New York: G. P. Putnam, 1848

___. "The Facts in the Case of M. Valdemar". *American Review* December 1845.

___. "Hans Phaal", *Southern Literary Messenger* June 1835; revised as "The Unparalleled Adventure of One Hans Pfaal" in *The Works of the Late Edgar Allan Poe*, New York: J. S. Redfield, 1850-56.

___. "Mesmeric Revelation". *Columbian Lady's and Gentleman's Magazine*, August 1944; reprinted in *Tales by Edgar Allan Poe*, New York: Wiley & Putnam, 1845.

___. *The Narrative of Arthur Gordon Pym of Nantucket, Comprising the details of a Mutiny and Atrocious Butchery on Board the American Brig Grampus on her way to the South Seas*. New York: Harper, 1838.

___. "Sonnet—to Science" in *Al Aaraaf, Tamerlane and minor poems*. Baltimore: Hatch & Dunning, 1829.

___. "A Tale of the Ragged Mountains". *Godey's Lady's Book* April 1844.

Pohl, Frederik. *JEM*. New York: St Martin's Press, 1979.

Polidori, John. *The Vampyre: A Tale*. London: Sherwood, Neeley and Jones, 1819.

Ponson du Terrail, Pierre-Alexis. *La Baronne trépassée*. Verviers, Belgium: Marabout, 1975. [First published 1852].

Restif de la Bretonne, Nicolas-Edme. *La Decouverte Australe par un homme volant ou la Dédale français*. Paris: Veuve Duchesné, 1781.

Rice, Anne. *Interview with the Vampire*. New York: Knopf, 1976.

___. *Memnoch the Devil*. New York: Knopf, 1994.

___. *The Vampire Lestat*. New York: Knopf, 1985

Ridgeway, James. *The Politics of Ecology*. New York: Dutton, 1970.

Robida, Albert. *L'Horloge des siècles*. Paris: F. Juven, 1902.

Robinson, Kim Stanley. *Blue Mars*. London: HarperColllns, 1996.

___. "Green Mars". Isaac Asimov's Science Fiction Magazine September 1985.

___. *Green Mars*. London: HarperCollins, 1993.

___. *Pacific Edge*. New York: Tor, 1988.

___. *Red Mars* 1992. London: HarperCollins, 1992.

Robinson, Kim Stanley, ed. *Future Primitive: The New Ecotopias*. New York: Tor, 1994.

Roshwald, Mordecai. *Level Seven*. London: Heinemann, 1959.

Rosny, J. H. aîné, *La Mort de la terre*. Paris: Plon, 1910; tr. by George Edgar Slusser in *The Xipéhuz and The Death of the Earth*, New York: Arno Press, 1978.

___. *Les Navigateurs de l'infini*. Paris: Oeuvres Libres, 1925.

___. *Les Xipéhuz*. Paris: Savine, 1887; tr. by George Edgar Slusser in *The Xipéhuz and The Death of the Earth*, New York: Arno Press, 1978.

Roumier, Marie-Anne de (Mme Robert). *Voyages de Mylord Céton dans les sept planètes, ou le nouveau mentor*. Paris: La Haye, 1765-6; reprinted in Garnier, *op cit*.

Rousseau, Victor. *The Messiah of the Cylinder*. Chicago: McClurg, 1917.

Russell, Bertrand. *Icarus; or, Science and the Future*. London: Kegan Paul, Trench & Trübner, 1924.

Russell, Eric Frank. *Sinister Barrier*. *Unknown* March 1939; Kingswood, Surrey: World's Work, 1943.

___. "Symbiotica". *Astounding Science Fiction* October 1943.

Saberhagen, Fred *The Dracula Tape*. New York: Warner, 1975.

Sargent, Pamela. *Venus of Dreams*. New York: Bantam, 1986.

Sauer, Rob. *Voyages: Scenarios for a Ship Called Earth*. New York: Ballantine, 1971.

Scheerbart, Paul. *Astrale Noveletten*. Karlsruhe: Im Dreiliien Verlag, 1912.

Schell, Jonathan. *The Fate of the Earth*. New York: Knopf, 1982.

Schenck, Hilbert. *At the Eye of the Ocean*. New York: Timescape, 1980.

Schmitz, James H. "Grandpa". *Astounding Science Fiction* February 1955.

Schroeder, Karl. *Permanence*. New York: Tor, 2002.

Schumacher, Ernst. *Small is Beautiful: A Study of Economics as if People Mattered*. London: Blond and Briggs, 1973.

Serviss, Garrett P. *A Columbus of Space*. *All-Story* January-June 1909; revised ed. New York: Appleton, 1912.

___. *The Moon Metal*. New York: Harpers, 1900.

Shanks, Edward, *The People of the Ruins: A Story of the English Revolution and After*. London: Collins, 1920.

Sharkey, Jack. "Arcturus Times Three". *Galaxy* October 1961.

Sheckley, Robert. "The People Trap". *The Magazine of Fantasy & Science Fiction* June 1968.

Shelley, Mary, *Frankenstein; or, The Modern Prometheus*. London: Lackington, Hughes, Harding, Mayor & Jones, 1818.

___. *The Last Man*. London: Henry Colburn, 1826.

Shelley, Percy Bysshe. "A Defence of Poetry" in *Shelley's Poetry and Prose* ed. Mary Shelley. London: Edward Moxon, 1840.

___. *Prometheus Unbound, a Lyrical Drama in Four Acts, with Other Poems*. London: C. and J. Ollier, 1820.

Shiel, M. P. "The Empress of the Earth". *Short Stories* 5 February-18 June 1898; revised as *The Yellow Danger*, London: Grant Richards, 1898.

___. *The Purple Cloud*. *The Royal Magazine* January-June 1901; expanded version, London: Chatto & Windus, 1901.

Siddons, Anne Rivers. *The House Next Door*. New York: Simon and Schuster, 1978.

Silverberg, Robert. *Master of Life and Death*. New York: Ace, 1957.

___. *The World Inside*. New York: Garden City, NY: Doubleday, 1971.

Simak, Clifford D. "City". *Astounding Science Fiction* May 1944; integrated into *City*. New York: Gnome Press, 1952.

___. "Drop Dead". *Galaxy* June 1956.

___. "Tools". *Astounding Science Fiction* July 1942.

___. "You'll Never Go Home Again". *Fantastic Adventures* July 1951.

Simon. *The Necronomicon*. New York: Schlangekraft Inc/Barnes Graphics, 1977.

Sinclair, Alison. *Blueheart*. London: Orion, 1996.

Slonczewski, Joan. *The Children Star*. New York: Tor, 1998.

___. *Daughters of Elysium*. New York: Morrow, 1993.

___. *A Door into Ocean*. New York: Arbor House, 1987.

Somtow, S. P. *Valentine*. New York: Tor, 1992.

___. *Vampire Junction*. Norfolk, Va.: Donning, 1984.

Spinrad, Norman. "The Lost Continent" in *Science Against Man* ed. Anthony Cheetham, New York: Avon, 1970.

___. *Songs from the Stars*. New York: Simon and Schuster, 1980.

Springer, Nancy. *Apocalypse*. Novato, Cal.: Underwood Miller, 1989.

___. *Larque on the Wing*. New York: Morrow, 1994.

___. *Metal Angel*. New York: Roc, 1994.

Springer, Sherwood. "No Land of Nod". *Thrilling Wonder Stories* December 1952.

Stableford, Brian. "The Age of Innocence". *Asimov's Science Fiction* June 1995.

___. *The Angel of Pain*. London: Simon and Schuster, 1991.

___. "...And He Not Busy Being Born". *Interzone* 16 (Summer 1986).

___. *The Architects of Emortality*. New York: Tor, 1999 (expanded from "Les Fleurs du Mal" *Asimov's Science Fiction* October 1994).

___. "Ashes and Tombstones" in *Moon Shots* ed. Peter Crowther & Martin N. Greenberg, New York: DAW 1999.

___. *The Cassandra Complex*. New York: Tor, 2001.

___. "Cinderella's Sisters". *The Gate* 1 (May 1989).

___. "The Cure for Love". *Asimov's Science Fiction* mid-December 1993.

___. *The Empire of Fear*. London: Simon & Schuster, 1988.

___. *The Fountains of Youth*. New York: Tor, 2000 (expansion of "Mortimer Gray's *History of Death*", *Asimov's Science Fiction* April 1995).

___. "Hidden Agendas". *Asimov's Science Fiction* September 1999.

___. *Inherit the Earth*. New York: Tor, 1998 (expanded from "Inherit the Earth", *Analog* July 1995).

___. "The Invisible Worm". *The Magazine of Fantasy & Science Fiction* September 1991.

___. "The Man Who Loved the Vampire Lady". *The Magazine of Fantasy & Science Fiction* August 1988.

___. "The Pipes of Pan". *The Magazine of Fantasy & Science Fiction* June 1997.

___. "Sexual Chemistry". *Interzone* 20 (Summer 1987).

___. *Sexual Chemistry: Sardonic Tales of the Genetic Revolution*. London: Simon & Schuster, 1991.

___. "Skin Deep". *Amazing Stories*. October 1991.

___. *The Third Millennium: A History of the World, AD 2000-3000* (with David Langford). London: Sidgwick & Jackson, 1985.

___. "What Can Chloë Want?" *Asimov's Science Fiction* March 1994.

___. *The Werewolves of London*, London: Simon & Schuster, 1991

___. *Year Zero*. Mountain Ash: Sarob Press, 2000.

___. *Young Blood*, London: Simon & Schuster, 1992.

Stapledon, Olaf. *Last and First Men*. London: Methuen, 1930.

___. *Star-Maker*. London, Methuen, 1937.

Stenbock, Count Stanislaus Eric. *Studies in Death: Romantic Tales*. London: David Nutt, 1894.

Stevens, Francis. *The Heads of Cerberus. The Thrill Book* 15 August-15 September 1919; reprinted Reading, Penn.: Polaris Press, 1952.

Stiegler, Marc. "The Gentle Seduction". *Analog* April 1989.

Stockton, Frank, R. *The Great Stone of Sardis* New York: Harper, 1898.

___. *The Great War Syndicate*. New York: P. F. Collier, 1889.

___. "A Tale of Negative Gravity". *Century Magazine* November 1884.

___. "The Water-Devil". *Scribner's Magazine* October 1874.

Stoker, Bram. *Dracula*. London: Constable, 1897.

Street, A. G. *Already Walks Tomorrow*. London: Faber & Faber, 1938.

Strieber, Whitley, and James Kunetka. *Nature's End*. London: Grafton, 1986.

Stross, Charles. *Accelerando*. London: Orbit, 2005.

Strugatsky, Arkady and Boris. *The Snail on the Slope*. New York: Bantam, 1980 [original publication Moscow, 1966-68].

Sucharitkul, Somtow. *Starship and Haiku*. New York: Pocket Books, 1984.

Swedenborg, Emanuel, *Arcana coelestia quae in Scriptura sacra seu verbo Domini sunt detecta, etc.* [1749-56]; tr. as *Arcana Coelestia; or, Heavenly Mysteries contained in the Sacred Scriptures, etc.* vols 1-3 London: R, Hindmarsh, 1784-88; vols. 4-8, London: J. & E. Hodgson, 1802-3; vols. 9-12, London, 1807-34.

Swift, Jonathan. *Travels into Several Remote Nations of the World in Four Parts by Lemuel Gulliver, First a Surgeon, and Then a Captain of Several Ships*. London: Benjamin Motte, 1726. [Usually reprinted as *Gulliver's Travels*.]

Taine, John. *Seeds of Life. Amazing Stories Quarterly* Fall 1931; Reading, Penn.: Fantasy Press, 1951.

Taylor, Gordon Rattray. *The Biological Time-Bomb*. London: Thames and Hudson, 1968.

Tenn, William. "The Ionian Cycle". *Thrilling Wonder Stories* August 1948.

Tepper, Sheri S. *Grass*. Garden City, NY: Doubleday, 1989.

Theroux, Paul. *O-Zone*. London: Hamish Hamilton, 1986.

Tipler, Frank. *The Physics of Immortality*. New York: Doubleday, 1994.

Tobias, Michael. *Fatal Exposure*. New York: Pocket, 1991.

Toffler, Alvin. *The Eco-Spasm Report*. New York: Bantam, 1975.

Tolkien, J. R. R. *Lord of the Rings: The Fellowship of the Ring; The Two Towers; The Return of the King*. 3 vols. London: Allen and Unwin, 1954-55.

Tolstoi, Alexei. *Aëlita*. [1922]; tr. by Lucy Flaxman, Moscow: Foreign Languages Publishing House, 1957.

Tolstoy, Leo. *War and Peace*. New York: Gottsberger, 1886.

Tracy, Louis. *The Final War*. London: Pearson, 1896.

Trueman, Chrysostom, ed. *The History of a Voyage to the Moon: With an Account of the Adventurers' Subsequent Discoveries*. London: Lockwood, 1864.

Tsiolkovsky, Konstantin. *Vne zemli*. [1916]; tr. as "Outside the Earth" in *The Call of the Cosmos*, Moscow: Foreign Languages Publishing House, 1963.

Turner, Frederick. *Genesis: An Epic Poem*. Dallas, Tex.: Saybrook, 1988.

Turner, George. *The Sea and Summer*. London: Faber, 1987.

Vance, Jack. "Winner Loses All". *Galaxy* December 1951.

Van Vogt, A. E. *Slan*. *Astounding Science Fiction* September-December 1940; Sauk City, Wis.: Arkham House, 1946..

Varley, John. *Titan*. New York: Berkley, 1979.

Vernadsky, Vladimir. *The Biosphere*. Oracle, Ariz.: Synergistic Press, 1986. [Originally published in Russian, 1926].

Verne, Jules. *Autour de la lune*. Paris: Hetzel, 1870; tr. in an omnibus with *De la terre à la lune* as *From the Earth to the Moon Direct in 97 Hours and a Trip Around It*, London: Sampson Low, Marston, Searle and Rivington, 1873.

____. *De la terre à la lune*. Paris: Hetzel, 1865; tr. as *From the Earth to the Moon. Passage Direct in 97 Hours*, Newark NJ: Newark Printing & Publishing Co, 1869.

____. *Hector Servadac*. Paris: Hetzel, 1877; tr. as *Hector Servadac; or, The Career of a Comet*. London: Sampson Low, Marston, Searle and Rivington, 1878.

____. *Robur le conquérant*. Paris: Hetzel, 1886; tr. as *The Clipper of the Clouds*, London: Sampson Low, Marston, Searle and Rivington, 1887.

____. *Le Sphinx des glaces*. Paris: Hetzel, 1897; tr. as *An Antarctic Mystery*, London: Sampson Low, Marston, Searle and Rivington, 1898.

____. *Vingt mille lieues sous les mers*, Paris: Hetzel, 1870; tr. as *Twenty Thousand Leagues Under the Sea*, London: Sampson Low, Marston, Searle and Rivington, 1873 [actually 1872].

____. *Voyage au centre de la terre*. Paris: Hetzel, 1863; tr. as *A Journey to the Centre of the Earth*. London: Griffith and Farran, 1872.

____. [with Paschal Grousset] *Les Cinq cents millions de la begum*. Paris: Hetzel, 1879; tr. as *The Begum's Fortune*, London: Sampson Low, Marston, Searle and Rivington, 1880.

___. [with Michel Verne] "L'Eternel Adam" in *Hier et demain*. Paris: Hetzel, 1910; tr. as "The Eternal Adam" in *Saturn Science Fiction* March 1957, reprinted in *Yesterday and Tomorrow*, London: Arco, 1965.

Viereck, Georg S. *The House of the Vampire*. New York: Moffat Yard, 1907.

Voltaire, *Le Micromégas de mr. de Voltaire*. Londres (so advertised, but probably Berlin), 1752; tr. as *Micromegas, A Comic Romance. Being a Severe Satire upon the Philosophy, Ignorance, and Self-Conceit of Mankind*, London: Wilson & Durham, 1753.

Vonnegut, Kurt. "The Big Space Fuck" in *Again, Dangerous Visions*. Garden City, NY: Doubleday, 1972.

Wallis, George C. "The Last Days of Earth". *The Harmsworth Magazine* July 1901.

Walsby, Charnock. "The Last Man". *Comet* January 1941.

Warner, Sylvia Townsend. *The Kingdoms of Elfin*. London: Chatto and Windus, 1977.

___. *Lolly Willowes; or, The Loving Huntsman*. London: Chatto and Windus, 1926.

Watkins, William John, ad Gene Snyder. *Ecodeath*. Garden City, NY: Doubleday, 1972.

Webb, Jane (Mrs Loudon). *The Mummy! A Tale of the Twenty-Second Century*. London: Henry Colburn, 3 vols., 1827.

Weinbaum, Stanley G. "Flight on Titan". *Astounding Stories* January 1935.

___. "The Lotus Eaters". *Astounding Stories* April 1935.

___. "The Mad Moon". *Astounding Stories* December 1935.

Wells, H. G. "Aepyornis Island". *Pall Mall Budget*, December 1894; reprinted in *The Stolen Bacillus and Other Incidents*, London: Methuen, 1895.

___. "The Chronic Argonauts". *Science Schools Journal* 1888; revised and expanded as a series of seven separately-titled episodes, *National Observer* 17 March-23 June 1984; further revised as "The Time Machine", *New Review* January-May 1895; abridged as *The Time Machine: an Invention*, London: Heinemann, 1895.

___. "The Country of the Blind". *The Strand Magazine* April 1904; reprinted in *The Country of the Blind and Other Stories*, London: Thomas Nelson, 1911.

___. "The Crystal Egg". *New Review* May 1897; reprinted in *Tales of Space and Time*, London: Harper, 1899.

___. *The Dream*. London: Jonathan Cape, 1924.

___. "The Empire of the Ants". *The Strand* December 1905; reprinted in *The Country of the Blind and Other Stories*, London: Thomas Nelson, 1911.

___. *The First Men in the Moon*. London: Newnes, 1901.

___. *In the Days of the Comet*. London: Macmillan, 1906.

___. *The Invisible Man. A Grotesque Romance*. London: Pearsons, 1897.

____. *The Island of Doctor Moreau. A Possibility*. London: Heinemann, 1896.

____. "The Land Ironclads". *The Strand* December 1903; reprinted in *The Short Stories of H. G. Wells*. London: Ernest Benn, 1927.

____. "The Man of the Year Million". *Pall Mall Gazette* 6 November 1893.

____. "The Man Who Could Work Miracles". *The Illustrated London News* July 1898; reprinted in *Tales of Space and Time*, London: Harper, 1899.

____. "The Remarkable Case of Davidson's Eyes". Pall Mall Budget August 1894; reprinted in *The Stolen Bacillus and Other Incidents*, London: Methuen, 1895.

____. "The Star". *The Graphic* Christmas supplement 1897; reprinted in *Tales of Space and Time*, London: Harper, 1899.

____. "A Story of the Days to Come". *Pall Mall Magazine* June-October 1897; revised version in *Tales of Space and Time*, London: Harper, 1899.

____. "Under the Knife". *New Review* January 1896; reprinted in *The Plattner Story and Others*, London: Methuen, 1897.

____. *The War in the Air and Particularly How Mr. Bert Smallways Fared While it Lasted*. London: George Bell & Sons, 1908.

____. *The War of the Worlds*. London: Heinemann, 1898.

____. *When the Sleeper Wakes*. London: Harper, 1899; revised as *The Sleeper Awakes*, London: Thomas Nelson, 1910.

____. *The Wonderful Visit*. London: J. M. Dent, 1895.

____. *The World Set Free: A Story of Mankind*. London: Macmillan, 1914.

West, Wallace. "Eddie for Short". *Amazing Stories* December 1953/January 1954.

____. "The Last Man". *Amazing Stories* February 1929.

White, Ted. *By Furies Possessed*. New York: Signet, 1970.

Wilde, Oscar "The Canterville Ghost". *Court and Society Review* 23 February 1887.

____. "Pan" in *Poems*. Boston: Roberts Bros, 1881.

Wilhelm, Kate. *Juniper Time*. New York: Harper, 1979.

Wilkins, John. *The Discovery of a World in the Moone, or a Discourse Tending to Prove That 'tis Probable There May Be Another Habitable World in That Planet*. London: M. Sparks & E, Forrest, 1638; Book II as *A Discourse Concerning a New World and Another Planet*. London: John Maynard, 1640.

Williamson, Jack. *Darker Than You Think. Unknown* 1940; expanded Reading, Penn.: Fantasy Press, 1947.

____. *Dragon's Island*. New York: Simon and Schuster, 1951.

____. (as Will Stewart) *Seetee Ship*. New York: Gnome Press, 1951.

____. *Terraforming Earth*. New York: Tor, 2001.

Wilson, William. *A Little Earnest Book Upon a Great Old Subject*. London: Darton & Co, 1851.

Wolverton, Dave. *Serpent Catch*. New York: Bantam, 1991.

Wylie, Elinor. *The Venetian Glass Nephew*. New York: Doran, 1925.
Wylie, Philip. *The End of the Dream*. Garden City, NY: Doubleday, 1972.
Wyndham, John. *The Day of the Triffids*. London: Michael Joseph, 1951.
Yarbro, Chelsea Quinn. *Hôtel Transylvania: A Novel of Forbidden Love*. New York: St Martin's Press, 1978.
Young. Robert F. "To Fell a Tree". *The Magazine of Fantasy & Science Fiction* July 1959.
Zamyatin, Yegevny. *We*. New York: Dutton, 1924.
Zaronovitch, Princess Vera. *Mizora: A Prophecy*. New York: G. W, Dillingham, 1890; reprinted Boston: Gregg Press, 1975, attributed to Mary E. Bradley Lane (first appeared as a serial in the Cincinnati *Commercial* in 1880-81).

DISCOGRAPHY

Action Pact. "Gothic Party Time" on *People*, Fall Out, 1983.
Bauhaus. "Bela Lugosi is Dead" on *Press the Eject and Give Me the Tape*. Beggar's Banquet, 1982.
Christian Death. *All the Love, All the Hate*. Jungle, 1989.
___. *The Heretic's Alive*. Jungle, 1989.
Deicide. *Deicide*. Roadrunner, 1990.
Electric Hellfire Club, The. *Burn, Baby, Burn!* Cleopatra, 1993.
Endura. *Dreams of Dark Waters*. Endura, 1994.
___. *The Great God Pan*. Endura, 1996.
Fields of the Nephilim. *Elizium*. Bega, 1990.
___. *Moonchild*. Bega, 1988.
___. *The Nephilim*. Bega, 1988.
Garden of Delight, The. *Enki's Temple*. Dion Fortune, 1992.
___. *Epitaph*. Dion Fortune, 1992.
___. *Necromanteion IV*. Dion Fortune, 1994.
___. *Sargonid Seal*. Dion Fortune, 1993.
Incubus Succubus [later Inkubus Sukkubus]. *Belladonna and Aconite*. Pagan Fire, 1993.
___. *Beltaine*. Pagan Fire, 1992.
___. *Corn King*. Pagan Media, 1995.
___. *Wytches*. Pagan Media, 1994.
Pentagram. *Day of Reckoning*. Peaceville, 1993.
Rolling Stones, The. *Beggars Banquet*. Decca, 1968.
___. *Their Satanic Majesties Request*. Decca, 1967.
Venom. *At War with Satan*. Neat, 1983.
___. *Black Metal*. Neat, 1982.
___. *Welcome to Hell*. Neat, 1981.
Voice of Destruction. *Black are the Souls of the Damned*. Cleopatra, 1992.
Whores of Babylon, The. *Metropolis*. Candlelight, 1994.
[Various Artists] *Blackend*. Plastic Head, 1995.
___. *Dreams in the Witch House*. Grave News, 1995.

___. *"What Sweet Music They Make..."* Thee Vampire Guild, 1994.

FILMOGRAPHY

Browning, Tod. *Dracula*, 1931.
___. *London After Midnight*, 1927.
___. *Mark of the Vampire*, 1934.
Fisher, Terence. *Dracula*, 1958.
Wood, Edward W. Jr. *Plan 9 from Outer Space*, 1958,

SECONDARY BIBLIOGRAPHY

Ariès, Philippe. *L'Homme devant la mort*. Paris: Editions de Seuil, 1977; tr. as *The Hour of our Death*, London: Allen Lane, 1981.

Blish, James "The Biological Story". *Science Fiction Quarterly* May 1951.

Clute, John, and Peter Nicholls. *The Encyclopedia of Science Fiction*. London: Orbit, 1993.

Dubanski, Ryszard. "The Last Man Theme in Modern Fantasy and Science Fiction". *Foundation* 16 (May 1979).

Finucane, R. C. *Appearances of the Dead: A Cultural History of Ghosts*. London: Junction, 1982.

Frazer, James G. *The Golden Bough*. 2 vols. London: Macmillan, 1890. exp 3rd ed. 12 vols. London: Macmillan, 1911-15.

Glotfelty, Cheryll, and Harold Fromm, eds. *The Ecocriticism Reader: Landmarks in Literary Ecology*. Athens: University of Georgia Press, 1996.

Graves, Robert. *The White Goddess*. London: Faber and Faber, 1948.

Hargrove, Eugene, ed. *Beyond Spaceship Earth: Environmental Ethics and the Solar System*. San Francisco: Sierra Club, 1986.

Kadmon. "Oskorei". *Aorta* 20 (1995).

Latham, Robert. "Dark Historical Science Fantasy". *Necrofile* 2 (Fall 1991).

McCoy, Carl. Interview in *Melody Maker*, 15 September 1990.

Mercer, Mick. *Gothic Rock*. Los Angeles: Cleopatra, 1994.

Murray, Margaret. *The Witch-Cult in Western Europe* Oxford: Oxford University Press, 1921.

Penzoldt, Peter. *The Supernatural in Fiction*. London: Peter Nevill, 1952.

Reynolds, Simon. *Blissed Out: The Raptures of Rock*. London: Serpent's Tail, 1990.

Sargisson, Lucy. "Green Utopias of Self and Other." *The Philosophy of Utopia* ed. Barbara Goodwin. London: Frank Cass, 2001. 140-156.

Scholes, Robert. "The Orgastic Pattern in Fiction" in *Fabulation and Metafiction*. Chicago: University of Illinois Press, 1979.

Springer, Nancy. Interview in *Locus* 413 (June 1995).

Stableford, Brian, "The Biology and Sociology of Alien Worlds". *Social Biology and Human Affairs* 52, no. 1 (1988).

___. "Eroticism in Supernatural Literature". *The Survey of Modern Fantasy Literature* ed. F. Magill, Englewood Cliffs, N.J.: Salem Press, 1983.

___. "How Should a Science Fiction Story End?" *The New York Review of Science Fiction* 78 (February 1995).

___. "The Profession of Science Fiction, no. 42: A Long and Winding Road". *Foundation* 50 (Autumn 1990).

Stratton, Susan. "The Messiah and the Greens: The Shape of Environmental Action in Dune and Pacific Edge." *Extrapolation* 42, no. 4 (2001). 303-316.

Worley, Lloyd, "The Prenatal and Natal Foundations of the Vampire Myth", read at the International Conference for the Fantastic in the Arts, 1991.

Yanarella, Ernest J. *The Cross, the Plow, and the Skyline: Contemporary Science Fiction and the Ecological Imagination*. Parkland, FL: Brown Walker, 2001.

GOTHIC GROTESQUES, BY BRIAN STABLEFORD

INDEX

202

ABOUT THE AUTHOR

BRIAN STABLEFORD was born in Yorkshire in 1948. He taught at the University of Reading for several years, but is now a full-time writer. He has written many science fiction and fantasy novels, including: *The Empire of Fear, The Werewolves of London, Year Zero, The Curse of the Coral Bride*, and *The Stones of Camelot*. Collections of his short stories include: *Sexual Chemistry: Sardonic Tales of the Genetic Revolution, Designer Genes: Tales of the Biotech Revolution*, and *Sheena and Other Gothic Tales*. He has written numerous nonfiction books, including *Scientific Romance in Britain, 1890-1950, Glorious Perversity: The Decline and Fall of Literary Decadence*, and *Science Fact and Science Fiction: An Encyclopedia*. He has contributed hundreds of biographical and critical entries to reference books, including both editions of *The Encyclopedia of Science Fiction* and several editions of the library guide, *Anatomy of Wonder*. He has also translated numerous novels from the French language, including several by the feuilletonist Paul Féval.

Lightning Source UK Ltd.
Milton Keynes UK
05 August 2010

157977UK00001B/26/P